Pre-Classical Economic Thought

Recent Economic Thought Series

Warren J. Samuels, Editor
Michigan State University
East Lansing, Michigan, U.S.A.

Other titles in the series:
Feiwel, G. R., *Samuelson and Neoclassical Economics*
Wade, L. L., *Political Economy: Modern Views*
Zimbalist, A., *Comparative Economic Systems: Recent Views*
Darity, W., *Labor Economics: Modern Views*
Jarsulic, M., *Money and Macro Policy*
Samuelson, L., *Microeconomic Theory*
Bromley, D., *Natural Resource Economics: Policy Problems and Contemporary Analysis*
Mirowski, P., *The Reconstruction of Economic Theory*
Field, A. J., *The Future of Economic History*

This series is devoted to works that present divergent views on the development, prospects, and tensions within some important research areas of international economic thought. Among the fields covered are macromonetary policy, public finance, labor and political economy. The emphasis of the series is on providing a critical, constructive view of each of these fields, as well as a forum through which leading scholars of international reputation may voice their perspectives on important related issues. Each volume in the series will be self-contained; together these volumes will provide dramatic evidence of the variety of economic thought within the scholarly community.

Pre-Classical Economic Thought

From the Greeks to the Scottish Enlightenment

edited by
S. Todd Lowry
Professor of Economics and Administration
Washington and Lee University

Kluwer Academic Publishers
Boston/Dordrecht/Lancaster

Distributors

---

for the United States and Canada: Kluwer Academic Publishers, 101
Philip Drive, Assinippi Park, Norwell, MA, 02061, USA

for the UK and Ireland: Kluwer Academic Publishers, MTP Press Limited,
Falcon House, Queen Square, Lancaster, LA1 1RN, UK

for all other countries: Kluwer Academic Publishers Group, Distribution
Centre, P.O. Box 322, 3300 AH Dordrecht, The Netherlands

Library of Congress Cataloging-in-Publication Data

Pre-classical economic thought.

  (Recent economic thought series)
  Bibliography: p.
  Includes index.
  1. Economics — History. I. Lowry, S. Todd.
II. Series: Recent economic thought.
HB75.P72 1986   330′.09   86−20851
ISBN 0−89838−183−5

Printed in the United States of America

TP

Contents

v

Contributing Authors

William F. Campbell
Department of Economics
Louisiana State University
Baton Rouge, Louisiana 70803

M. Yassine Essid
9, Rue des Suffettes
Salammbo
Tunisie

Barry Gordon
Department of Economics
University of Newcastle
New South Wales, 2309
Australia

Peter D. Groenewegen
Department of Economics
University of Sydney
New South Wales, 2006
Australia

Robert Hébert
Department of Economics
Auburn University
Auburn, Alabama 36849−3501

Timur Kuran
Department of Economics
University of Southern California
Los Angeles, California 90089−0035

Odd Langholm
Norwegian School of Economics &
  Business Administration
Helleveien 30
N−5035 Bergen-Sandviken
Norway

S. Todd Lowry
Department of Economics
Washington and Lee University
Lexington, Virginia 24450

Lars Magnusson
Department of Economic History
Uppsala University
Box 513
751 20 Uppsala
Sweden

Roman A. Ohrenstein
Department of Economics
Nassau Community College
Stewart Avenue
Garden City, New York 11530

Salim Rashid
Department of Economics
University of Illinois at
  Urbana-Champaign Box 111
330 Commerce Building (West)
1206 South Sixth Street
Champaign, Illinois 61820

Herbert F. Thomson
Department of Economics
Muskingum College
New Concord, Ohio 43762

Stephen T. Worland
Department of Economics
University of Notre Dame
Notre Dame, Indiana 56556

Richard C. Wiles
Department of Economics
Bard College
Annandale-on-Hudson,
New York 12504

Preface

The scholars invited to contribute the primary essays for this collection were given three mandates. The first was to survey the contemporary research in their assigned fields and to provide a bibliography that would give any interested scholar an entree into the literature. The second was to develop their own interpretive perspective on the economic literature of their assigned period. The third, and perhaps the most difficult, was to be very brief and concise.

In a project of this type it would be difficult to extrapolate themes or evolutionary sequences that run through the literature over the two thousand years spanned by this survey. To some degree, the invited commentators provide a fund of suggestions that will stimulate interested readers to pursue this line of synthesis for themselves. The editor of this collection did not even entertain the idea of trying to coordinate the presentations and commentaries of this intellectually erudite and diverse group of scholars into agreed upon lines of interpretation. There is enough material, however, to provide a reference base for the interested scholar who desires to follow particular ideas from period to period.

The requirements of brevity placed frustrating limitations upon the authors of the principal papers. In most cases, it led the specialists invited to comment on each chapter to devote considerable attention to supplementing the essay they were criticizing. The commentators were free from the burden of systematic coverage and, therefore, were able to focus upon their primary interests and draw out their preferred lines of interpretation. One should read these pairs of essays with this unequal burden in mind.

The contributors and commentators were selected on the basis of their reputations and research in the particular areas in which they specialize and the result has been an international aggregation of cosmopolitan scholars. They have all been very prompt and cooperative in the course of preparing this collection for publication.

I am greatly indebted to my wife, Faye Cole Lowry, for her careful editorial scrutiny of all the contributions, and in particular for a heavy contribution to bibliographic research and the editing of my own chapter in this collection.

Finally, the advice and freedom of choice proffered by Warren Samuels, the general editor of this series created a pleasant academic incentive, as has the helpful cooperation of the staff at Kluwer Academic Publishers.

Pre-Classical Economic Thought

1 INTRODUCTION

S. Todd Lowry

Since modern economics is generally considered to have begun with the publication of Adam Smith's *An Inquiry into the Nature and Causes of the Wealth of Nations* in 1776, a survey of pre-Smithian economic thought requires some justification. Such an effort must offer both historical and methodological support for its contribution to the study of the history of modern economics.

This is the first book in a three-part series covering pre-classical, classical, and neo-classical economic thought. The general definition of "classical British political economy," Smith to Mill, would appear to set the boundaries that delineate the core of the series. This collection of essays on pre-classical or pre-Smithian economics, therefore, covers material that has been considered by some to represent fragments of political, commercial, and philosophical thought that preceded the development of systematic economics. Nevertheless, scholars are showing an increasing interest in the genesis of the key elements of their analyses and their methodological approaches. A broad view of the relevance of ideas that later acquired economic significance suggests that the beginnings of theories can be usefully traced back into the past before their separate idea patterns and premises were braided into a single strand. We also find earlier prototypes of coherent systems, albeit with different orientations. In addition, the elements and conceptual premises of our current theory are often found in strange associations, or appear to have been borrowed from other intellectual complexes [Lowry, 1974].

For our purposes, then, the fact that aggregations of ideas jelled into systems of thought that acquired acceptance as significant revelations at given times in history does not mean that they sprang forth as ideas, full grown, from Zeus' head, like Athena, goddess of crafts. An appreciation of the origins of our ideas, therefore, should offer a historical method for qualifying and re-examining their operational limits and empirical validity.

A social science such as political economy necessarily deals with the conscious effort of human beings to develop ideas that are considered relevant to economic decision-making. It is the beginning of such ideas that constitutes the beginning of economics. This raises many difficulties over the proper scope of economics as a discipline. We may find some cogency in the view of an institutionalist or economic anthropologist who suggests that ceremonial prescriptions followed by a neolithic shaman who leads his village in a ritual dance back and forth across the fields newly broadcast with seed, is reinforcing his leadership and authority to garner the surplus production and to control the distribution process. He is incidentally seeing to it that the seed is trodden into the ground and hoping for a good harvest. Many will suspect that the incantations and policies that are promulgated by some modern economic and political leaders are also "culturally embedded" and depend as much on hope for fortuitous events as on supportable theory.

We may follow others, oriented toward a broad cultural view of intellectual history, who will search for the earliest expressions of specific ideas or thought symbols. These ideas are frequently found to have been borrowed from different, often unrelated lines of analysis and appropriated bodily as empirical interpretations of data. For example, the analysis of exchange apparently began with Book V of Aristotle's *Nicomachean Ethics* which provided guidelines for the administration of justice in isolated exchange. It survived in Roman law and was worked over by the scholastic philosophers who strove to extend it from an appraisal of individual ethics and political policy to a policy approach to more general mercantile activity. Exchange analysis finally merged with a natural-order philosophy to become part of the theory of a self-regulating naturally equilibrating market process, the keystone of Smithian economic thought. When did exchange analysis become part of a formal economic theory? This is a different question from these: When does the study of the history of exchange theory help us understand how economic ideas have evolved in the past? How valid is our voluntaristic formulation of exchange in the present, and how or why may this analytic form evolve in the future?

Another idea or perspective that has a long history is the meticulous formulation of subjective individual measurement of the significance of things, the hedonic calculus. It was thoroughly detailized in ancient Greek literature in terms of pleasure and pain, perpetuated by Roman and Muslim scholars, and commonplace in scholastic and post-scholastic thought until enshrined by Jeremy Bentham as the basis of utilitarianism. It became the foundation for the classical emphasis on rational self-interest and the pivotal analytic element in Austrian and English marginal utility theory in the 1870s.

A third interesting economic premise is the scarcity tenet — the "curse of work" associated with the expulsion from the Garden of Eden — a conceptualization of nature as a hostile force against which humankind is doomed to struggle. This doctrine is deeply embedded in the Judeo-Christian tradition, and surfaces in its corollary, the labor theory of value. The thesis finds a congenial home in Malthusian population theory and Ricardian rent theory as well as in most contemporary textbook definitions of economics despite two centuries of conspicuous increases in population, productivity, and leisure. The premise obviously rejects cultural and political regulation of wants and the manipulation of desire through training or advertising. The mitigation of scarcity by technology is all too often the only acceptable variable in the equation of the greedy or needy individual confronting a resistant nature.

The most traditional approach to the history of economics follows J. A. Schumpeter's focus upon the development of systems of abstract analysis of commercial and productive activities. Carrying it to its ultimate, some contend that "truly modern" economics dates back to the comprehension of the total economy as a general equilibrium system subject to coherent mathematical analysis. This takes "truly modern" economics back only to Leon Walras in the latter part of the nineteenth century, and is dependent upon the emergence of a statistical base capable of supporting comprehensive national analyses. This approach, however, has roots that reach back into Parmenedean and Pythagorean mathematical presumptions of a totally rational world order, perpetuated in Platonic thought and drawn upon in the Enlightenment with Copernicus' and Kepler's analyses of planetary motion, and the post-Newtonian image of astronomy and physics as the ideals of scientific precision.

The problems that arise when defining the essence of modern political economy, and in finding a dividing line between its antecedents and its actual nascence, are intertwined with the term *classical* and our working designation in this collection of *pre-classical* political economy. In developing his general theory, John Maynard Keynes was prepared to designate his predecessors as "classical economists," including Alfred Marshall in that category. As pointed out in a recent review [Groenewegen, 1985], the author being discussed followed the analysis of the accumulation and disposition of a surplus in the economy, and traced classical thought from Quesnay to Marx. Groenewegen reminds us that the analytic interest in a disposable surplus can be found in Cantillion and Petty, before Quesnay. He adds that Marx considered classical economics to deal with a period ending with Ricardo, and that Marshall considered classical economics to refer to the writings of any economist whose work was of enduring value. In any event, the major tenets of nineteenth and twentieth century economics vary from school to school, and, although their more mature formulations may be properly designated as classical and neo-classical, they all had roots in the past that can be explored to advantage in different ways, emphasizing idea patterns, general concepts, and methodological or analytical approaches.

For simplicity's sake, we follow the pedagogic convention of dealing with thought before the publication of Adam Smith's *Wealth of Nations* as pre-classical, recognizing that any designation of a break in the continuum of human intellectual development is somewhat synthetic and arbitrary. Of course, true innovations do occur, but they are more incremental than people usually realize. They appear as prominent leaps from the historical perspective when people focus on their acceptance as respectable ideas. The qualitative transitions or scientific revolutions (as Thomas Kuhn would call them) are better understood as the culmination of a line of underground thought that has finally overturned the presumptive validity of the established view or paradigm.

The commitment to brevity in this collection has resulted in some conspicuous omissions in the coverage of the long history of relevant western European and Near Eastern thought. Most of the histories of economics that give attention to the pre-Smithian background ignore Judaic and early Christian thought, as well as Islamic economic ideas, although the Mediterranean crucible was the parent of the Renaissance while Muslim learning in the Spanish universities was a major source of light for non-Mediterranean Europe. While these two areas, the Judeo-Christian and the Islamic heritage, are given full places in this collection, Spanish thought which is receiving increasing attention [Grice-Hutchinson, 1978] is one of the omitted areas that deserves further study.

The same can be said of Italian economic thought. Most conspicuous of these omissions, however, is a thorough analysis of the economic premises and content of Roman law which evolved into the commercial law of the Middle Ages and matured into the Law Merchant adopted into the Common Law system of England on a case-by-case basis, primarily under the aegis of Lord Mansfield, Chief Justice of the Court of King's Bench, 1756–88 [Lowry, 1973]. Furthermore, there is a great deal of literature that falls outside the formal classifications of scholastic or mercantilist thought during the Renaissance and Enlightenment, the centuries in which commercial activity expanded across Europe. This literature gives us considerable insight into the level of understanding of the economy among merchants, statesmen, and ordinary citizens.

Despite these omissions, this collection offers a basic continuity. It is for the interested reader, however, to extrapolate from the material covered in these essays as well as other sources and to trace lines of intellectual development that shed light on how we have come to think as we do. Conversely, we may take current ideas, concepts, and analytic systems and look for their ancestors in order to evaluate the relative importance of their genealogies and appraise the empirical, operational, or ideological aspects of their geneses. It is always worth wondering to what extent the feedback from theory, through formal and informal education, finds concrete expression in patterns of conduct and eventually in commercial and political institutions. Put more broadly, to what extent do our experiences mold our theories, and to what extent do our theories mold our aggregate behavior, and consequently, our social experiences?

Every generation tends to believe that its outlook and conduct are based upon a valid and comprehensive theoretical foundation and that the perceptions and formulations of the real-world problems to which it addresses itself are based upon dispassionate appraisals of reality. Our methodology and our notions of what is important, our paradigms and our research programs, keep changing from generation to generation, both in evolutionary and revolutionary transitions. This would lead us to believe that the study of the history of thought is one of the best possible antidotes for intellectual ossification. Economic thought should be as dynamic and responsive to the challenges of the economy as are cultural and natural forces. The symbolic representation of *mutatis mutandis* in terms of billiard balls in a round-bottomed bowl, found in Appendix I of Alfred Marshall's *Principles*, is a useful image here. The economic ideas held by individuals have an influence on movements of thought in general, molding public policy and institutions, as well as the natural environment. This latter element is altered by the impact of agricultural practices on the land, acid rain, and the changing concentration of CO_2 in the atmosphere. The final image, therefore, should be one of dynamic interaction between individual thought, socio-economic processes, and the natural environment, mutually adjusting as both cause and effect. While the concept of an equilibrium denies secular change and may be a useful analytic device at any given instant, the presumption of the ultimate existence of an equilibrium is an offense against our historical understanding, a forfeiture of our dynamic intellectual birthright.

References

Grice-Hutchinson, Marjorie. *Early Economic Thought in Spain* 1177–1740. London: Allen and Unwin, 1978.

Groenewegen, P. D. "The Relevance of Classical Economics." *History of Economic Thought Newsletter*: Autumn 1985, 18–20.

Lowry, S. Todd. "Lord Mansfield and the Law Merchant: Law and Economics in the Eighteenth Century." *Journal of Economic Issues* 7, December 1973, 606–621.

————. "The Archaeology of the Circulation Concept in Economic Theory." *Journal of the History of Ideas* 35: July–Sept. 1974, 429–444.

2 THE GREEK HERITAGE IN ECONOMIC THOUGHT

S. Todd Lowry

0311

It is unfortunate that the demands for technical specialization in modern economics have led to a decrease in the attention given to the development of broad interdisciplinary and historical perspectives. To many, the study of the history of the discipline is merely a review of past error, an enterprise in which they see little utility. As a result, the history of economics, according to one economist [Blaug, 1978, p. 4], is "not so much the chronicle of a continuous accumulation of theoretical achievements as the story of exaggerated intellectual revolutions in which truths already known are neglected in favor of new revelations."

Most economists know that the name of their discipline is derived from an ancient Greek work, *oikonomia*. Few, however, are familiar with the art of estate management and public administration to which the Greeks applied the term, or with the use by the Greeks of such analytic formulations as the division of labor and the hedonic calculus. The intellectual debt of modern economic theory to the ancient Greeks has generally been ignored by those who assume that the use of such economic concepts dates only from the late eighteenth century when Adam Smith ingeniously framed self-interest and the division of labor as the keys to

7

the analysis of the explosion in productivity which characterized the emergence of the capitalist system.

In their writings, both Aristotle and Plato presented analyses of integrated economies in which specialization and the division of labor played significant roles. Self-interest, hedonism, and efficiency are all ideas utilized by the ancient Greeks. Only an ignorance of Greek literature and of its place in modern education makes plausible the claim that the use of such notions originated with eighteenth and nineteenth century economists.

In view of the general framing of methodological categories in ancient Greek literature that shaped subsequent scientific and philosophical thought in western Europe, our debt to the ancients is beyond question. What is surprising is that it could have been so quickly forgotten. Aristotelianism, brought to Europe by the Arabic scholars, dominated medieval thought, and although the vogue for Greek culture had periods of greater and lesser popularity in Europe, a knowledge of the classics was, until very recently, the universal mark of the educated man.

Of more significance for the history of economics was the resurgence of interest in the ancient Greeks in the British Isles in the eighteenth and nineteenth centuries, the period of emergence of classical political economy. Two recent studies [Jenkyns, 1980; Turner, 1981] have documented the pervading influence of this revival of the Greek heritage on a wide spectrum of Victorian scholarship, from philosophy, history, literature, and art, to comparative religion, archaeology, anthropology, and political science. "The rediscovery of the Greek heritage by British intellectuals in the late eighteenth and early nineteenth centuries," Frank M. Turner [1981, p. 450] writes, "coincided, and not accidentally so, with the vast transformations being wrought by those myriad forces designated by the terms liberal democracy, industrialism, and enlightenment."

Shackle [1972, p. 23] described economics as a discipline that "in its own right was late in the sequence of such disciplines to be constructed. . . . As a consequence," he added, "its inventors found ready to their hands all too many tools and schemes of thought which had been shaped for the purpose of systematizing other and very different fields of knowledge." If the world of the ancient Greeks was a very different one from the world of emergent capitalism which the classical economists sought to analyze, nevertheless some of the conceptual formulations bequeathed by the Greeks were convenient to the task of describing the new economic processes. Some of the ancient Greek economic writings were still studied and considered relevant to the times. For example, Xenophon's *Ways and Means*, a mid-fourth century B.C. proposal for developing the Athenian economy, was added as an appendix to the 1698 edition of Davenant's treatise on trade and to the 1751 edition of Petty's *Political Arithmetick*. The translator of the *Ways and Means* [Davenant, 1698, p. 8] described Xenophon as "the first Author that ever argu'd by Political Arithmetick, or the Art of Reasoning upon things by Figures" and commented on "the Exactness of his Calculations." There has never been a period when the works of Plato and Aristotle have not been studied in European universities, and a knowledge of Greek was a requirement for admission to both Oxford and Cambridge universities until after World War I [Turner, 1981, p. 5].

Turner [1981, p. 8] observed that "writing about Greece was in part a way for the Victorians to write about themselves." "Across the Western world," he added, "Victorian authors and readers were determined to find the Greeks as much as possible like themselves and to rationalize away fundamental differences." "We are all Greeks," Shelley had said, a statement which calls to mind the more recent claim that "We are all Keynesians now." The modes of thought which the classical economists applied to the economic phenomena of their day were molded by an educational system steeped in the study of Greek literature and philosophy.

Recent controversies about the ancient Greeks and their economy have revolved around three main issues. Starting with Karl Bucher's work in the 1890s, economic historians have argued about the primitiveness or modernity of the economy of ancient Greece. Although some economic historians have pictured ancient Greek commercial life as almost a small replica of a modern capitalist economy, few today would defend this view.[1]

Secondly, in recent years some economic anthropologists have emphasized that in pre-market societies economic activities are usually carried on in subservience to broader social considerations. From this perspective, economic life is "embedded" in the extended fabric of the community. These scholars, therefore, question whether the ancients could have had separate economic behavior patterns and perspectives that can be correlated with modern economic analysis. Others contend that the ubiquitous pressures of rational self-interest and utility maximization assert themselves at all times and in all places so that sound economic theory is universally applicable. This argument has been dubbed the "substantivist-formalist controversy."[2]

The third controversy, and the one of most interest to historians of economic thought, is over the question of whether the ancient Greeks ever actually formulated any relevant theories at all, and, if they did, whether these theories had any influence on modern economic ideas. Most historians of economic thought have implicitly denied the Greek contribution since most of the histories they have written begin only with Adam Smith or the scholastics.[3] Joseph A. Schumpeter's encyclopedic *History of Economic Analysis* gives some coverage of the Greeks. However, he dismisses Xenophon's writings as having little economic significance. Although he found the beginnings of economic analysis in Aristotle's writings, he characterized him generally as a dispenser of "pompous common sense" (p. 57).

Schumpeter's generally negative assessment of the economic writings of the ancient Greeks has been taken up by M. I. Finley, a prominent economic historian who has written extensively about the economic life of the Greeks. Commenting on Aristotle, Finley [1970, p. 15] goes even further than Schumpeter. "In the *Ethics*," he argues, "there is strictly speaking *no* economic analysis rather than poor or inadequate economic analysis." He bases his general approach to the study of ancient economic thought [1973, p. 22] on Eric Roll's [1956, p. 371] definition of an economic system as "an enormous conglomeration of interdependent markets," and the "central problem of economic enquiry" that of explaining the exchange process and the formation of price. Finding that the Greeks had neither such an economy nor any concern in their writings for the processes of price formation, Finley asserts that they wrote nothing of significance to economic theory. While he concedes [1973, p. 23] that precapitalist societies also had economies "with rules and regularities and even a measure of predictability," he denies that the ancient Greeks offered any analysis of whatever type of economy they did have.[4]

But if he is severe in judging Aristotle's contribution to economics, Finley is an even more unrelenting critic of Xenophon's writings. "In Xenophon," he writes [1973, p. 19], "there is not one sentence that expresses an economic principle or offers any economic analysis, nothing on efficiency of production, 'rational' choice, the marketing of crops."

On the question of whether Greek writings had any influence on modern economic theory, one can mention first Charles Fay's assertion [1956, p. 1] that both the *Theory of Moral Sentiments* and the *Wealth of Nations* "issued from the womb of the classics." William R. Scott [1949, pp. 79–80] argued that Greek sources "constituted an essential and fundamental element in the establishing of several of . . . [Smith's] central positions," and that they "in fact constitute, not alone the starting point in documentation, but the foundation of the whole." Smith's inaugural lecture [1795] for his chair in moral philosophy at the University of Glasgow, it will be recalled, contained an extensive elaboration of Plato's theory of the Ideas. Claims have been made for both Empedoclean [Foley, 1979] and Stoic [Waszek, 1984] influences on Smith, as well as Aristotelian influences on Edgeworth [Jaffé, 1974]. Evidence that Xenophon's writings may have influenced Smith's elaboration of the division of labor will be discussed later.

The burden of this essay is to show that the ancient Greeks developed many of the analytical formulations basic to modern economic theory and that the discipline of economics is heavily indebted to them. Forgetting a debt does not cancel it, and Theodor Gomperz [1955, pp. 528–29] was right when he spoke of the Greeks. "Even those who have no acquaintance with the doctrines and writings of the great masters of antiquity, and who have not even heard the names of Plato and Aristotle," he wrote, "are, nevertheless under the spell of their authority.... It is not only that their influence is often transmitted to us by their followers, ancient and modern: our whole mode of thinking, the categories in which our ideas move, the forms of language in which we express them, and which therefore govern our ideas — all these are to no small extent the products of art, in large measure the art of the great thinkers of antiquity.... A thorough comprehension of these origins," he warned, "is indispensable if we are to escape from the overpowering despotism of their influence." Perhaps we shall never be free of the Greeks but, at the very least, we should be aware of our debt.

Oikonomia: Efficiency as an Art

Protagoras, one of the most famous of the Sophist teachers, distinguished himself from other Sophists who, he said, when dealing with pupils who "have deliberately turned their backs on specialization," do not give them what they seek, but instead "plunge [them] into special studies again, teaching them arithmetic and astronomy and geometry and music." He claimed that he taught such a pupil only what he wished to learn: "the proper care of his personal affairs, so that he may best manage his own household, and also of the state's affairs, so as to become a real power in the city" (*Protag.* 318d–e). What Protagoras claimed to teach sounds very much like political economy.

In the *Oeconomicus*, Xenophon describes the art of the "good estate manager" (I.2.) An estate, he says, includes "the total of one's property." Property is defined as "that which is useful for supplying a livelihood" (VI.4). "Estate management" is "a branch of knowledge, like medicine, smithing and carpentry" (I.1). The job of an estate manager is to "manage his own estate well" (I.2). If he wishes, he may also "earn money by managing another man's estate" (I.4). His work will be considered satisfactory "if, after taking over an estate, he continues to pay all outgoings, and to increase the estate by showing a balance" (I.4). In the same dialogue, Socrates is pictured as having far less in material wealth than his friends, yet they look to him for help in managing their affairs. The reason is that he understands "one process by which wealth is created — how to create a balance." One of the characters in the dialogue muses, "So a man who saves on a small income can, I suppose, very easily show a large surplus with a large one" (II.10). That the Greek concept of *oikonomia*[5] included more than mere "estate management" or "household management" is evidenced by the definition of an estate in this dialogue. "Everything a man possesses," Xenophon insists, "even if the property is situated in different cities" (I.5) is part of the estate. Finley [1973, p. 17] traces the semantic origins of *oikonomia* to *oikos*, a "household," and to the root *nem-*, which connotes "regulate, administer, organize." Clearly *oikonomia* conveyed some sense of an administrative art.[6]

Elsewhere, in the *Memorabilia*, Xenophon refers to the art of the manager as the "kingly art" ((II.1.17) and expresses the opinion that "the management of private concerns differs only in point of number from that of public affairs." "They are much alike," he writes, in that "neither can be carried on without men" and "those who understand how to employ them are successful directors of public and private concerns, and those who do not, fail in both" (III.4.12). Plato was also of the opinion that "there is not much difference between a large household organization and a small-sized city" and that "one science covers all these several spheres," whether it is called "royal science, political science, or science of household management" (*Statesm.* 259c).

The Greek art of *oikonomia*, a formal, administrative art directed toward the minimization of costs and the maximization of returns, had as its prime aim the efficient management of resources for the achievement of desired objectives. It was an administrative, not a market approach, to economic phenomena.[7] Although there is no general discussion of supply and demand in response to impersonal market forces in ancient Greek writings,[8] there is no doubt that *oikonomia* was an early predecessor of political economy.

The ancient Greeks did not distinguish between agriculture, trade, and plunder as productive activities. Warfare was so common and so highly regarded as a source of material wealth that they may be said to have developed an "economy of warfare." Through it all, however, they emphasized the importance of the human variable, of one's personal effectiveness in achieving a successful outcome in any venture. From this anthropocentric point of view, improving human skill in the management of an enterprise meant nothing less than increasing the efficiency of production. In ancient Greece, the maximization of the human factor was considered as important as that of any other resource.[9]

In the *Oeconomicus* (XXI.3), Xenophon observes that a good leader can cause the crew of a boat to make a trip in half the time and that the crew will be high spirited when they finish their work, whereas a poorly led crew will not perform as efficiently and will be sullen and unhappy after the trip is over. A similar 2:1 quantitative ratio in the performance of properly led men is applied to farm work (XX.16–17). Diligent supervision that guarantees that men stay busy the full day, Xenophon asserts, will result in a twofold increase in the quantity of work accomplished. This is true, he says, "whether the one in charge is a steward or a supervisor, [for] those who can make the workers eager, energetic, and persevering in the work are the ones who accomplish the most good and produce a large surplus" (XXI.9).

Many examples can be cited of the Greeks' concern for the efficient management of both material and human resources. Xenophon's *Banquet* is an anecdotal account of the "good conversation" associated with the leisurely eating and drinking and subsequent entertainment that accompanied the formal dinner. But Socrates' remarks to the Syracusan impresario who provided the dancing girls and acrobats for the entertainment were not about their skill or grace, but about the "economics" of entertainment. "I am considering," he said, "how it might be possible for this lad of yours and this maid to exert as little effort as may be, and at the same time give us the greatest amount of pleasure in watching them — this being your purpose, I am sure" (VII.1–5).

In Xenophon's *Memorabilia*, a candidate for a generalship complains to Socrates that, even though he has had much military experience and has been wounded in action several times, his candidacy has been rejected in favor of another candidate without military experience, a businessman "who understands nothing but money-making" (III.4.1). Socrates justifies the appointment on the basis of the winning candidate's managerial skill. He points out that, although the man knows nothing about music or choir training, his choir has always won in competitions because "he showed himself capable of finding the best experts" (III.4.4). He predicts that the new general without military experience will be successful in leading a military force, for "whatever a man controls, if he knows what he wants and can get it he will be a good controller, whether he controls a chorus, an estate, a city or an army" (III.4.6).

Although the ancient Greeks viewed the natural environment as basically static or constant and, as a result, had a difficult time formulating theories of novation to account for the creation or production of new elements, they placed great emphasis upon the manipulation of *given* elements for increased returns.[10] For this reason, the concepts of order and combination in the management of human and material factors were important to them.

In the *Ways and Means*, Xenophon stressed the effectiveness of the efficient combination of human and material resources. "Every farmer," he writes, "can tell just how many yoke of oxen are enough for the farm and how many labourers. To put more on the land than the requisite number is counted loss" (IV.5). But this statement contains more than the idea of combining resources for an improved output. The notion that an excess of any resource "is counted loss" is an expression of a marginal element in productive combinations.[11]

In defining wealth, the Greeks emphasized use value rather than exchange value. In the *Oeconomicus* the point is made that a horse, to a man who keeps getting hurt by it, is not "wealth to him." Similarly, "land is not wealth...to a man who works it in such a way that his work results in loss" (I.8). The conclusion is that "what is profitable is wealth, what is harmful is not wealth" (I.9).

This utilitarian subjectivism in the measurement of the individual's microeconomic affairs is extended to the macro level in the *Hiero*. In this dialogue, the point is made that the aggregate wealth of the state can be enhanced by the use of prizes to stimulate higher general levels of agricultural production. The public returns stimulated by prizes are rated as a great bargain.

It is noteworthy that we find in Xenophon the development of many concepts that are part of modern economic analysis. They are, however, framed in terms of personal and public administrative perspectives rather than in terms of commercial market analyses.

Colonies and the Modelling of Political Economies

The ancient Greeks, D. F. Lawden [1968, p. 92] observed, "delighted in abstract thought to such an extent that they soon convinced themselves that their mental creations were no mere figments of the imagination but were glimpses of the aetherial reality which lay behind the mundane appearance of things." Plato's theory of the Ideas pictures the "real" world in terms of abstract models or prototypes and observable earthly phenomena as only pale reflections of the Ideas.

Describing ideal or utopian habitats for man seems to have had a special fascination for the Greeks. Even Hesiod's eighth-century B.C. *Works and Days* contains a description (pp. 230–35) of the nascent elements of an ideal economy. A farmer, Hesiod's self-sufficient utopian economy naturally has an agricultural setting:

> Neither famine nor inward disaster comes the way
> of those people
> who are straight and just; they do their work
> as if work were a holiday;
> the earth gives them great livelihood,
> on their mountains the oaks
> bear acorns for them in their crowns,
> and bees in their middles.
> The wool-bearing sheep are weighted down
> with fleecy burdens.
> Their women bear them children
> who resemble their parents.
> They prosper in good things throughout.
> They need have no traffic
> with ships, for their own grain-giving land
> yields them its harvest.

The inclination to think abstractly about the elements of the ideal community and, incidentally, about an economy may have been related to the colonization ventures of the Greeks. The founding of colonies seems to have been one solution to increasing population pressure upon the limited and eroding arable land upon which the Greeks depended. When contingents of citizens left the mother city for a new settlement, they took their particular customs and religious traditions with them, but in some cases they deliberately structured novel institutions to meet the demands of new situations. In 444 B.C., at the zenith of the cultural flowering of Periclean Athens, the intellectuals of Athens founded an ideal colony, Thurii, in southern Italy. Its constitution was drawn up by Protagoras, a leading Sophist and adviser to Pericles, and the physical layout of the city was designed by Hippodamus, the planner who had laid out the Piraeus, the Athenian port, in a grid pattern with square blocks.

Plato's account of the lost Atlantis in the *Critias* provided a prototype

for utopian models in subsequent Western literature, but the ideal
political economy described in his *Republic* is of more immediate interest
to economists. "The origin of the city," he declared, "is to be found in
the fact that we do not severally suffice for our own needs, but each of us
lacks many things...As a result of this...one man calling on another for
one service and another for another, we, being in need of many things,
gather many into one place of abode as associates and helpers, and to this
dwelling together we give the name city or state.... And between one
man and another there is an interchange of giving and taking, because
each supposes this to be better for himself.... Come, then, let us create
a city from the beginning, in our theory. Its real creator, as it appears,
will be our needs" (369b–c). In this brief statement of the economic
genesis of a state, Plato includes the concepts of economic interdependence,
subjective mutuality, the need for exchange, and even an indication of the advantages to be obtained from the division of labor.

Plato begins with the premise that, if each individual does only those
things for which he is best suited, by nature, maximum efficiency will be
achieved and the individual participants in the political economy will have
an appropriately larger share of an optimally large pie. Consequently, the
citizens of Plato's *Republic* are required to do what they do best *and that
only*. Those who insist on doing otherwise are to be banished from the
city (398a).

He illustrated the necessity of unquestioned rule by experts with the
analogy of a ship (the state), where chaos results when the crew tries to
do the job of the captain in piloting the ship rather than doing the
tasks assigned to them [*Republic*, 488–89]. In the *Statesman*, he draws a
gruesome picture of the fettering of experts in a law-ridden society where
not only are ship captains and doctors required to practice "by the code,"
but they are also restricted from investigating possible innovations or
variations in regimen. The arts, supervised by magistrates and citizens in
popular assemblies with no technical knowledge, are subjected to the
same indignities. This tension between regulation by a democratic
assembly and trust in the commitment to the public interest of self-
appointed experts has a distinctly modern ring. It avoids the question of
divergent values.

The Division of Labor

In the *Republic*, the division of labor is advanced as an authoritarian
concept required by the exigencies of efficient administration.[12] There are
other discussions of the division of labor in ancient Greek writings which

simply describe the procedure as an efficient economic process without any overtones of authoritarianism. The description in Xenophon's *Cyropaedia* (VIII.2.5–6) reveals clearly that he understood not only the efficiencies involved but also that specialization depends upon the "extent of the market," a formulation usually attributed to Adam Smith. "Just as all other arts are developed to superior excellence in large cities," he explains, "in that same way the food at the king's palace is also elaborately prepared with superior excellence. For in small towns the same workman makes chairs and doors and plows and tables, and often this same artisan builds houses, and even so he is thankful if he can only find employment enough to support him. And it is, of course, impossible for a man of many trades to be proficient in all of them. In large cities, on the other hand, inasmuch as many people have demands to make upon each branch of industry, one trade alone, and very often even less than a whole trade, is enough to support a man: one man, for instance, makes shoes for men, and another for women; and there are places even where one man earns a living by only stitching shoes, another by cutting them out, another by sewing the uppers together, while there is another who performs none of these operations but only assembles the parts."

In the recently discovered set of dated notes on Adam Smith's 1762–63 lectures on jurisprudence [Meek and Skinner, 1973] are found the same trades (door maker, cabinet or furniture maker, and the builder of houses) illustrating the division of labor. Moreover, Adam Smith's statement about the extent of the market is almost identical to Xenophon's. As noted elsewhere [Lowry, 1979], it is possible that Smith was indebted to Xenophon for what Meek and Skinner [1973, p. 1100] refer to as "the crucial principle that the division of labour is limited by the extent of the market," the analytical formulation that has been called [Wills, 1978, p. 41] "the methodological bridge between the first concept of labor's division and the larger scheme [of the *Wealth of Nations*]."

Citing Schumpeter's warning [1954, p. 54] that scholars "are prone to fall into the error of hailing as a discovery everything that suggests later developments, and of forgetting that, in economics as elsewhere, most statements of fundamental facts acquire importance only by the super-structures they are made to bear and are commonplace in the absence of such superstructures," Finley [1970, pp. 3–4] dismisses Xenophon's discussion of the division of labor, claiming it is only an elaboration of the sources of quality and craftsmanship. His insistence on the absence of quantitative analysis in Xenophon's writings and other Greek literature is hardly tenable. On the contrary, the Greeks are clearly the main source for our most conspicuous quantitative tradition, the hedonic calculus.[13] What both Schumpeter and Finley failed to grasp is that Xenophon elaborated an administrative process which served some of the functions of modern markets and that ancient writings, framed in administrative terms, *do* support an appropriate analytic superstructure, indeed the only one possible since capitalist markets did not exist in ancient Greece.[14]

Aristotle drew upon Plato's doctrine of natural specialization and the division of labor in his attempt in the *Politics* to delineate the characteristics of the city state or *polis*, and the elements he analyzes are primarily economic, with an emphasis on natural processes.[15] In Book I, he traces a series of "associations" — the family, the village, and the larger civic community, the *polis* — which culminate in a self-sufficient political economy.[16]

The extended family with its slaves was the basic social and economic "association" in Aristotle's day, and was the primary unit of agricultural production. It was made up of individuals with natural differences whose needs, he says, must be satisfied by beneficial combination with others having reciprocal needs: male and female, master and slave, and parent and child. The male and female are joined by their reciprocal biological needs; the master and slave, by the need for assistance and the need for supervision; and parents and children, by the need to leave offspring and the need for care and nurture. Emphasizing the specialization inherent in such interdependent combinations, Aristotle observes that nature "makes each separate thing for a separate end; and she does so because each instrument has the finest finish when it serves a single purpose and not a variety of purposes" (1252b). The family or household in Aristotle's *polis* provides "goods of the body," the basic necessities of life.

The next unit of Aristotle's political economy, the village, is an aggregation of households which, as a result of greater specialization and barter, can provide "something more than daily recurrent needs" (1252b). These are termed "external goods," products that contribute to a desirable standard of living above and beyond the requirements of survival (1323a).

The "final and perfect association" of Aristotle's political economy is the aggregation of villages into a *polis*, an association which permits not only self-sufficiency but also the production of psychic goods, or what Aristotle calls "goods of the soul." In this way, he introduced an ordinal theory of utility.

Homo Oikonomicus and *Homo Chrematisticus*

Aristotle's distinction between "necessary" and "unnecessary" exchange and his dictum in the *Politics* (1257a15–20) that "retail trade is not naturally a part of the art of acquisition" have been widely interpreted as a moralistic rejection of all commercial activity. Finley [1970, 18], for example, finds "not a trace" of economic analysis in the *Politics* and maintains that in this work Aristotle does not "ever consider the rules or mechanics of commercial exchange." On the contrary, he says, "his insistence on the unnaturalness of commercial gain rules out the possibility of such a discussion."

As we have seen, Aristotle's theory of association in the *Politics* is based upon mutual need satisfaction. Exchange, he says, also arises from a similar need, from the fact that "some men [have] more, and others less, than suffices for their needs" (1257a). Exchange, however, is not a natural use of goods produced for consumption. Where barter, the exchange of commodities for commodities (C-C') occurs, goods move directly from the producer to the consumer, and Aristotle considered this form of exchange a natural or "necessary" form of acquisition because, he says, it is "subject to definite bounds." The "bounds" are provided by the self-limiting, ordinal structure of needs and the diminishing utility of goods. "External goods," he explains, "like all other instruments, have a necessary limit of size.... Indeed," he adds, "all things of utility...are of this character; and any excessive amount of such things must either cause its possessor some injury, or, at any rate, bring him no benefit" (1323b).[17] Although not "natural," he viewed exchange with money used as an intermediary (C-M-C') as "necessary" when its ultimate purpose is to acquire items for consumption because the desire for goods is then still subject to the natural limit of diminishing utility.

He classified retail trade, where money is used to purchase commodities to sell in order to acquire more money (M-C-M) as an "unnecessary" form of exchange. Its objective, he says, is not the satisfaction of need but the acquisition of money which has no use in and of itself and is therefore not subject to a natural limit of desire, as he illustrates with the Midas legend. Further, this form of acquisition has "no limit to the end it seeks." It "turn[s] on the power of currency" and is thus unrelated to the satisfaction of needs. The "extreme example" of "unnecessary" or "lower" form of exchange, and a still greater perversion of the exchange process, Aristotle says, is usury, for it attempts to "breed" money — "currency, the son of currency." Usury "makes a profit from currency itself (M-M'-M'') instead of making it from the process which currency was meant to serve" (1258b).

Aristotle saw his *oikos*-oriented economy as stable precisely because of the natural limits placed on desire by the operation of diminishing utility, and this is why he opposed the "unlimited" or "unnecessary" form of exchange.[18] Chrematistics, made possible by monetary exchange, on the other hand, has no internal limiting factor, particularly when its practitioners, as was the case in his day, are *metics*, foreigners outside the pale.[19] Viewed in this light, his assertion that "retail trade is not naturally a part of the art of acquisition" is more understandable. Indeed, it reveals the fact that Aristotle was one of the first to realize the necessity of a theory of limit. To be self-regulating, any system with contending elements, economic or otherwise, requires an internal limit to prevent any one of the elements from overwhelming the others. Without an internal regulatory mechanism, it would logically be necessary for an external force to intervene to keep the system stable. This is why a theory of limit was crucial to Adam Smith's explanation of the operation of a self-regulating market and why, over the course of his lifetime, he tried repeatedly to solve this logical dilemma. In the *Moral Sentiments*, he fastened upon diminishing utility as the limiting factor. It would, he maintained, lead the rich, despite their "natural rapacity" to divide the produce of the earth equitably with the poor. In the same work, he developed the concept of "human sympathy," expressed through the "impartial spectator," as a socially induced self-restraint. Eventually, in the *Wealth of Nations*, Smith embraced an equilibrium of avarice, with the "invisible hand" of market competition counteracting the destructive tendencies of unrestrained greed by guiding self-interested individuals, almost against their wills, to work for the public good.

Aristotle's emphasis upon the necessity of a limit may also be viewed as a rational response to the scarcity of resources.[20] In the *Rhetoric* (1359b20–25), he commented that "men become richer not only by increasing their existing wealth but also by reducing their expenditures" and, in the *Politics* (1266b), he remarked that "it is more necessary to equalize men's desire than their properties."

Aristotle's Monetary Theory

Aristotle's monetary theory, according to Schumpeter [1954, p. 63], "is the basis of the bulk of all analytic work in the field of money" and "prevailed substantially to the end of the nineteenth century and even beyond."[21] All of the advances which have occurred in coinage since Aristotle's day have not changed the basic functions of money which he described over 2,000 years ago.

"Money," Aristotle points out in the *Ethics* (1133a15–30), "has become by convention a sort of representative of demand; and this is why it has the name *money* — because it exists not only by nature but by law and it is in our power to change it and make it useless." He continues, "Money...acting as a measure, makes goods commensurate and equates them" (1133b15). He described money as a store of value with the statement (1133b10) that "if we do not need a thing now we shall have it if ever we do need it — money is as it were our surety; for it must be possible for us to get what we want by bringing the money." Portability as an essential attribute of money was recognized with his statement in the *Politics* (1257a) that "men therefore agreed, for the purpose of their exchanges, to give and receive some commodity which itself belonged to the category of useful things and possessed the advantage of being easily handled for the purpose of getting the necessities of life."

These statements describe three of the four functions of money which modern economists recognize: as a medium of exchange, as a measure of value, and as a store of value. Schumpeter [1954, pp. 62–63] gave Aristotle credit for describing these functions, but claimed that he failed to cover a fourth function: to serve as a standard of deferred payment. It may be reasonably argued, however, that Aristotle's discussion of usury in the *Politics* (1258b) is ample evidence that he recognized money as a contractual standard of deferred payment.

Despite the widespread acceptance of subjective relativism in Aristotle's day and the many references to fiat money systems in ancient Greek literature,[22] Schumpeter [1954, p. 63] stoutly maintained that Aristotle was a metallist and that he held a bullionist or commodity theory of money,[23] a position which has been challenged by Barry Gordon [1961]. Nassau Senior [1826, pp. 30, 205] observed that "Aristotle's description of value as depending on demand approaches much more nearly perfect accuracy than Smith's." Senior went on to defend the bullionist position, at least on the origin of money, and criticized Aristotle for *not* taking a bullionist position. "The only point in which Aristotle seems to me to have been mistaken," he said, "is in supposing...that money may owe not only its currency, but also its value to convention."

Aristotle's Analysis of Exchange

Aristotle's discussion of justice in exchange in Book V of the *Nicomachean Ethics* has a tantalizingly modern ring about it. It even refers to a "figure of proportion" which may have been used in the original text to illustrate a mathematical basis for analyzing exchange.[24] And yet, just as the meaning of the passage on exchange seems to become clear, obscurities and ambiguities intrude, and one is left in doubt about exactly what Aristotle *really* meant. Schumpeter [1954, p. 61] thought Aristotle was "groping for some labor-cost theory of price which he was unable to state explicitly," but he cast doubt on his own interpretation by adding, "At least, I cannot get any other sense out of this passage."[25] Finley [1970, p. 13], too, confesses that he does not understand the meaning of the ratios used in Aristotle's discussion of exchange.

Book V of the *Ethics* begins with an analysis of the principles of public and private distributions of assets. The Athenian polity in Aristotle's day functioned in many ways as a distributive economy, allocating among its citizens public goods of various sorts: honors, rations of grain, public entertainment, and pay to citizens for attendance at assemblies and jury duty. Xenophon predicted that, by following his recommendations in the *Ways and Means*, the whole population of Athens could be maintained at public expense.

Aristotle (1133ab) extends his analysis of the just distribution of public assets to the problem of justice in a two-party transaction between a house builder and a shoemaker:

> Now proportionate return is secured by cross-conjunction. Let A be a builder, B a shoemaker, C a house, D a shoe. The builder, then, must get from the shoemaker the latter's work, and must himself give him in return his own. If, then, first there is proportionate equality of goods, and then reciprocal action takes place, the result we mention will be effected. If not, the bargain is not equal, and does not hold; for there is nothing to prevent the work of the one being better than that of the other; they must therefore be equated. . . . For it is not two doctors that associate for exchange, but a doctor and a farmer, or in general people who are different and unequal; but these must be equated. This is why all things that are exchanged must be somehow comparable. It is for this end that money has been introduced, and it becomes in a sense an intermediate; for it measures all things, and therefore the excess and the defect — how many shoes are equal to a house or to a given amount of food. The number of shoes exchanged for a house (or for a given amount of food) must therefore correspond to the ratio of builder and shoemaker. For if this be not so, there will be no exchange and no intercourse. And this proportion will not be effected unless the goods are somehow equal. All goods must therefore be measured by some one thing, as we said before. Now this unit is, in truth, demand [26] which holds all things together (for if men did not need one another's goods at all, or did not need them equally, there would be either no exchange or not the same exchange); but money has become by convention a sort of representative of demand; and this is why it has the name *money* — because it exists not by nature but by law and it is in our power to change it and make it useless. There will, then, be reciprocity when the terms have been equated so that as farmer

is to shoemaker, the amount of the shoemaker's work is to that of the farmer's work for which it exchanges. But we must not bring them into a figure of proportion when they have already exchanged (otherwise one extreme will have both excesses), but when they still have their own goods. Thus they are equals and associates just because this equality can be effected in their case.

Aristotle certainly *seems* to be analyzing an economic exchange here. His descriptions of barter and money are clear, but the references to proportion and reciprocity are obscure.[27] This is in large part the result of the sketchy nature and corruption of the surviving text. Because of the age-old reverence for Aristotle, however, nearly all reflections on price from Scholastic times to the eighteenth century have been influenced by his emphasis on voluntarism and mutuality in exchange. Although it seems clear that Aristotle's analysis was developed from the point of view of a judge trying to decide whether a particular sales transaction should be enforced, it served, in part because of its obscurity, as a provocative stimulus to all of the modern lines of price and value theory. Polanyi [1971] has even traced this influence into the nineteenth century in the work of Carl Menger.[28] Aristotle's influence on moral philosophy and ethics has also been traced [Worland, 1984] into neo-classical welfare theory.

Conclusion

When one compares ancient Greek economic ideas with those of modern political economy in the eighteenth and early nineteenth centuries, two conspicuous perceptual transitions stand out. The first of these is the emergence in the eighteenth century of the concept of natural order and natural justice which served as an effective counterpoise to the divine right which supported authoritarian sovereignty among the crowned heads of Great Britain and the continent. Natural right not only supported the emerging political democracy but also spilled over into the second emergent perception: that of the primary importance of the commercial and industrial process in society. There was, therefore, an image of a self-regulating mercantile process with political and class vindication of its growing dominance over the earlier feudal and manorial tradition and its agrarian ideology.

Despite the different political and economic orientation of the ancient Greeks, they developed many of the analytical building blocks used in the edifice of modern political economy. They laid out the hedonic calculus, and they formulated an abstract treatment of efficiency which they carried into an analysis of the division of labor. They also distinguished between use value and exchange value, and analyzed the mutual benefits which give exchange its broader social significance. Their frame of reference, however, was primarily administrative and legislative so that their ideas have clearer parallels with management and public policy studies than with conventional economic ones. Most conspicuously, however, and quite validly, they did not perceive commercial exchange as the dominant institution in their economy, nor did they entertain the premise that the resident aliens or *metics* and the foreign merchants with whom they dealt could be depended upon to serve their best interests in the absence of regulation and public intervention. The question remains as to whether the Greeks bequeathed us a political economy. It is clear that Aristotle left us a comprehensive description of a political-economic structure the small agricultural city-state with its limited reliance on foreign trade. The Greeks also left us a tradition of abstract idealism which they had extended to the perception of utopian and ideal types of political-economic organizations. This provided a basis for abstraction in social theory and associated mathematical patterns which suggested an ultimate truth. It is this theoretical bent, which has been perpetuated in philosophy and literature, that has characterized the most pervasive continuum between ancient and modern thought. Their cosmological theories also have contributed to a sense of macroeconomic process. The most conspicuous of these are the circulation concept,[29] which grew out of the Heraclitean theory of perpetual flux, and the organic simile comparing society to a great animal which provided the imagery from which money could be thought of as circulating like blood in the body.

The challenge, implicit in these investigations of past ideas, is to understand the differences between accumulated truths and more transient intellectual traditions.

Notes

1. An excellent discussion of this controversy may be found in Humphreys [1970]; reprinted in Humphreys [1978, pp. 136–58].

2. See Lowry [1979] for a summary of the literature and citations on the substantivist-formalist controversy.

3. Spiegel [1983] deals more comprehensively with Greek ideas than most textbook authors. Gordon [1975] provides supplementary coverage for this period, neglected in most histories of economic thought.

4. Commenting on Finley's *Past and Present* article cited above, Scott Meikle [1979, p. 57] notes that "the only conclusion . . . it would be proper to draw from such an exercise is

that Aristotle was not an orthodox economist of the twentieth century. The conclusion Finley draws, however, is that there is no analytical content at all in Aristotle, but only censoriousness." He adds, "It is ironical that Finley, such an unremitting opponent of anachronistic attempts to comprehend Antiquity in terms of the categories of modern capitalist economy, should himself fall victim to anachronism."

5. See the following: Singer [1958]; King [1948]; and Nitsch [1980].

6. Pericles' household management system exemplifies the administrative art. His household was supervised by one trained servant operating under a system structured to provide a method of internal control, to minimize waste, and to eliminate the need for Pericles' constant attention. See Campbell [1983].

7. Karl Pribram's [1983, p. 126] description of the administrative purpose of the *Wealth of Nations* makes clear that Adam Smith's approach was not far removed from that of the Greeks. "It was not meant," he writes, "to be a textbook on economics, but rather was intended to teach legislators and statesmen such measures as would enable the people to provide plentiful revenue for themselves and to supply the commonwealth with a revenue sufficient for the public service."

8. Claude Mossé [1975], however, calls attention to Xenophon's discussion in the *Ways and Means* of the negative response of coppersmiths to the limited demand for their products as a partial analysis of supply and demand.

9. A. A. Trever [1916, p. 9] evidently had this point in mind when he observed that "Aristotle struck the keynote in Greek economic thought in stating that the primary interest of economy is human beings rather than inanimate property."

10. For further analysis see Lowry [1965].

11. Emil Kauder [1953] discusses the value comparisons based on subjective marginal utility used by Aristotle in the *Topics*. The marginal analysis there, however, is applied only to an analysis of argument. See also Kauder [1965].

12. Vernard Foley [1974] analyzed the use of the concept in both ancient and modern writings. See also Paul J. McNulty [1975].

13. See Lowry [1981].

14. For a discussion of some parallels with modern market concepts, see Campbell [1985].

15. Spengler [1980, p. 95] calls attention to the fact that Aristotle believed that "the *polis* belongs to the class of things that exist by nature, and that man is by nature an animal intended to live in a *polis*."

16. John Gillies [1813, pp. vii–viii], a late eighteenth century translator of Aristotle, claimed that the writings of the economists of his day, "not excepting those of Hume and Smith," were based on Book V of the *Ethics* and the first book of the *Politics*. Schumpeter [1954, p. 60] seemed to agree with Gillies, at least as far as Adam Smith was concerned. In his *History of Economic Analysis* [p. 60], he stated that he would follow the fortunes of "the Greek bequest...right through A. Smith's *Wealth of Nations*, the first five chapters of which are but developments of the same line of reasoning."

17. On Aristotle's concept of a "natural limit," see Lowry [1974a]. The only goods which Aristotle exempts from diminishing utility are "goods of the soul," psychic goods. "The greater the amount of each of the goods of the soul," he says, "the greater is its utility" [1323b].

18. A. Anikin [1975, p. 29] commented that Aristotle might logically have used the term *homo chrematisticus* to connote a man with unlimited wants, while reserving the modern *homo economicus* for a man with wants that are naturally limited. Thomas J. Lewis [1978] interprets Aristotle's concern for a limit as a form of "anxiety" about transactions among friends.

19. Finley [1970, p. 24] criticized Sir John Hicks [1969, p. 48], who wonders about the ancient Greeks' toleration of competition from the *metics*. Finley points out that the primarily agricultural Greeks needed the *metics*.

20. William Kern [1983] discusses modern applications of the Aristotelian solution of limiting wants as a response to scarcity. See also Lowry [1974a].

21. Langholm [1984a, 1984b] has investigated Scholastic treatments of Aristotle's theory of money and analysis of usury. For nineteenth century expressions of Aristotelian monetary theory, see Palgrave [1910, p. 54]. Arnaud Berthoud's study [1981] contains a close textual analysis of Book V of the *Ethics* and Book I of the *Politics* with particular reference to economic matters and money, but he cites no secondary literature and his book has no index. Of special interest to modern economists are the fragments of a history of ancient currencies which Keynes never completed, recently published in his *Collected Writings* [1971–84, XXVIII, pp. 223–94].

22. The following are only a few. In Plato's *Laws* [742ab], a totally fiat system of money "of value at home but worthless abroad" was suggested for use in domestic exchange to insulate the citizens from trade with foreigners. The [Pseudo-] Aristotelian *Oeconomica* contains several anecdotal references to fiat money systems, including the minting of tin [II.2, 1349a30–35] and bronze [II.2, 1350a20–25]. In the [Pseudo-] Platonic *Eryxias* [399–400], a Carthaginian "money" is mentioned which apparently consisted of gravel sealed in a leather pouch.

23. In my opinion, Max Alter [1961, 1982] fails to successfully defend the Schumpeterian position. Andreades [1933, I, p. 143] maintained that the ancient Greeks "did not fall into the error of the bullionists" because of their distinction between "wealth in merchandise" and "wealth in money."

24. According to Langholm [1980], the Scholastics, from Grosseteste to Aquinas on, used illustrations with crossing diagonal lines in their commentaries on Aristotle's *Ethics*. One of these is featured on the dust jacket of Langholm's book. See also Lowry [1969].

25. Interpretations of Book V of Aristotle's *Ethics* have varied from Schumpeter's labor theory of value hypothesis to Karl Polanyi's [1957] status theory. Van Johnson [1939] argued against the labor theory of value interpretation. Meikle [1979, pp. 57, 71 ff.] questions the Weberian framework which, according to him, influenced the work of Polanyi and Finley.

26. Some specialists are of the opinion that *need* would be a better translation from the Greek than *demand*.

27. Josef Soudek's [1952] explanation of the significance of the reciprocal or harmonic proportion used in ancient Greek writings clarifies some of the confusion. Barry Gordon [1964] finds both labor and utility components in Aristotle's analysis, which he assumes to be focused on market exchange, and questions Soudek's denial of a labor theory of value in Aristotle. See also Gordon [1963]. Lowry [1969], following Soudek's thesis, explores the mathematical nuances of this material.

28. For a critical examination of Polanyi's work, see Humphreys [1969].

29. For a historical survey of an idea pattern that tended to precede its empirical verification in both physiology and economics, see Lowry [1974b].

Translations Used

Aristotle. *Politics*. Trans. by Ernest Barker. Oxford: Clarendon Press, 1946. All other translations of Aristotle's works cited are from *The Works of Aristotle*

Translated into English. Ed. by W. D. Ross. 12 vols. Oxford: Clarendon Press, 1908–1952.

Hesiod. *Works and Days.* Trans. by Richmond Lattimore. Ann Arbor: University of Michigan Press, 1959.

Plato. *Laws,* trans. by A. E. Taylor; *Republic,* trans. by Paul Shorey; *Statesman,* trans. by J. B. Skemp. In *The Collected Dialogues of Plato.* Ed. by Edith Hamilton and Huntington Cairns. Princeton: Princeton University Press, 1963.

Xenophon. Oeconomicus. Trans. by Leo Strauss. Ithaca, N.Y. and London: Cornell University Press, 1970. The Loeb Classical Library translations were used for the other cited works of Xenophon.

References

Alter, Max. "Aristotle, Schumpeter, and the Metallist Tradition." *Quarterly Journal of Economics* 75:1961, 608–14.

―――――. "Aristotle and the Metallist Tradition: A Note." *History of Political Economy* 14:1982, 559–63.

Andreades, A. M. *History of Greek Public Finance,* rev. ed. 2 vols. Cambridge, MA: Harvard University Press, 1933.

Anikin, A. *A Science in Its Youth: Pre-Marxian Political Economy.* Trans. by K. M. Cook. Moscow: Progress Publishers, 1975.

Berthoud, Arnaud. *Aristote et l'argent.* Paris: François Maspero, 1981.

Blaug, Mark. *Economic Theory in Retrospect,* 3rd ed. Cambridge: Cambridge University Press, 1978.

Bowley, Marian. *Nassau Senior and Classical Economics.* London: George Allen & Unwin, 1937.

Campbell, William F. "Pericles and the Sophistication of Economics." *History of Political Economy* 15:1983, 112–35.

―――――. "The Free Market for Goods and the Free Market for Ideas in the Platonic Dialogues." *History of Political Economy* 17:1985, 187–97.

Davenant, Charles. *Discourses on the Publick Revenues and the Trade of England.* London: Printed for James Knapton at the Crown in St. Paul's Churchyard, 1698.

Fay, Charles. *Adam Smith and the Scotland of His Day.* Cambridge: Cambridge University Press, 1956.

Finley, M. I. "Aristotle and Economic Analysis." *Past and Present* 47:1970, 4–25.

―――――. *The Ancient Economy.* Berkeley: University of California Press, 1973.

Foley, Vernard. "The Division of Labor in Plato and Smith." *History of Political Economy* 6:1974, 220–42.

―――――. *The Social Physics of Adam Smith.* West Lafayette, In: Purdue University Press, 1979.

Gillies, John. *Aristotle's "Ethics" and "Politics."* 3rd ed. London: Printed for T.

Cadell and W. Davies, 1813.

Gomperz, Theodor. *Greek Thinkers: A History of Ancient Philosophy*. Trans. by Laurie Magnus and George C. Berry from the German edition of 1896. New York: Humanities Press, 1955.

Gordon, Barry. "Aristotle, Schumpeter, and the Metallist Tradition." *Quarterly Journal of Economics* 75:1961, 608–14.

————. "Aristotle and Hesiod: The Economic Problem in Greek Thought." *Review of Social Economy* 21:1963, 147–56.

————. "Aristotle and the Development of Value Theory." *Quarterly Journal of Economics* 78:1964, 115–28.

————. *Economic Analysis Before Adam Smith: Hesiod to Lessius*. New York: Barnes & Noble, 1975.

Hicks, Sir John. *A Theory of Economic History*. Oxford: Clarendon Press, 1969.

Humphreys, S. C. "History, Economics and Anthropology: The Work of Karl Polanyi." *History & Theory* 8:1969, 165–212.

————. "Economy and Society in Classical Athens." *Annali della Normale Superiore di Pisa* 39:1970, 1–26.

————. *Anthropology and the Greeks*. London: Routledge & Kegan Paul, 1978, pp. 136–58.

Jaffé, William. "Edgeworth's Contract Curve: Part 2. Two Figures in Its Proto-history: Aristotle and Gossen." *History of Political Economy* 6:1974, 381–404.

Jenkyns, Richard. *The Victorians and Ancient Greece*. Cambridge: Harvard University Press. 1980.

Johnson, Van. "Aristotle's Theory of Value." *American Journal of Philology* 60:1939, 445–51.

Kauder, Emil. "Genesis of the Marginal Utility Theory." *Economic Journal* 63:1953, 638–50.

————. *A History of Marginal Utility Theory*. Princeton: Princeton University Press, 1965.

Kern, William. "Returning to the Aristotelian Paradigm: Daly and Schumacher." *History of Political Economy* 15:1983, 501–12.

Keynes, John Maynard. *The Collected Writings of John Maynard Keynes*, 29 vols. Ed. by Elizabeth Johnson and Donald Moggridge. Cambridge: Cambridge University Press [for the Royal Economic Society], 1971–84.

King, James E. "The Origin of the Term 'Political Economy.'" *Journal of Modern History* 20:1948, 230–31.

Langholm, Odd. *Price and Value in the Aristotelian Tradition: A Study in Scholastic Sources*. Bergen, Oslo, and Tromsø: Universitetsforlaget, 1979.

————. Personal letter, November 13, 1980.

————. *Wealth and Money in the Aristotelian Tradition: A Study in Scholastic Economic Sources*. Bergen, Oslo, Stavanger, Tromsø: Universitetsforlaget, 1984a.

————. *The Aristotelian Analysis of Usury*. Bergen, Oslo, Stavanger, Tromsø: Universitetsforlaget, 1984b.

Lawden, D. F. "Modelling Physical Reality." *Philosophical Journal* 5:1968, 87–104.

Lewis, Thomas J. "Acquisition and Anxiety: Aristotle's Case Against the Market." *Canadian Journal of Economics* 11:1978, 69–90.

Lowry, S. Todd. "The Classical Greek Theory of Natural Resource Economics." *Land Economics* 41:1965, 204–8.

—————. "Aristotle's Mathematical Analysis of Exchange." *History of Political Economy* 1:1969, 44–66.

—————. "Aristotle's 'Natural Limit' and the Economics of Price Regulation." *Greek, Roman and Byzantine Studies* 15:1974a, 57–63.

—————. "The Archaeology of the Circulation Concept in Economic Theory." *Journal of the History of Ideas* 35:1974b, 429–44.

—————. "Recent Literature on Ancient Greek Economic Thought." *Journal of Economic Literature* 17:1979, 65–86.

—————. "The Roots of Hedonism: An Ancient Analysis of Quantity and Time." *History of Political Economy* 13:1981, 812–23.

McNulty, Paul J. "A Note on the Division of Labor in Plato and Smith." *History of Political Economy* 7: 1975, 372–78.

Meek, Ronald L., and Andrew S. Skinner. "The Development of Adam Smith's Ideas on the Division of Labour." *Economic Journal* 83:1973, 1094–1116.

Meikle, Scott. "Aristotle and the Political Economy of the Polis." *Journal of Hellenic Studies* 99:1979, 57–73.

Mossé, Claude. "Xenophon économiste." In *Hommages à Claire Préau.* Ed. by J. Bingen, G. Gambier, and G. Nachtergael. Brussels: Univ. libre de Bruxelles Fac. de Philos. & Lettres 62 (1975), pp. 169–76.

Nitsch, Thomas O. "On the Origin, Renaissance, and Recrudescence of *Politikē Oikonomia*: A Progress Report." *Midsouth Journal of Economics* 4:1980, 83–94.

Palgrave, Sir R. E. I. *Dictionary of Political Economy*, 3 vols. 1910. Reprint, Detroit: Gale Research Company, 1976.

Polanyi, Karl. "Aristotle Discovers the Economy." In *Trade and Market in the Early Empires: Economies in History and Theory.* Ed. by Karl Polanyi, Conrad M. Arensberg, and Harry W. Pearson. New York: Free Press, 1957.

—————. "Carl Menger's Two Meanings of 'Economic.'" In *Studies in Economic Anthropology.* Ed. by George Dalton. Washington, DC: American Anthropological Assn., 1971.

Pribram, Karl. *A History of Economic Reasoning.* Baltimore and London: John Hopkins University Press, 1983.

Roll, Eric. *A History of Economic Thought*, 3rd ed. Englewood Cliffs, NJ: Prentice-Hall, 1956.

Schumpeter, Joseph A. *History of Economic Analysis*, Ed. by Elizabeth B. Schumpeter. New York: Oxford University Press, 1954.

Scott, William R. "Greek Influence on Adam Smith." In *Études dédiées à la Mémoire D'André M. Andréadès*, publiées...sous la presidence de K. Karvaressos. Athens: Prysos, 1949, pp. 79–99.

Senior, Nassau. Unpublished lectures, 1826–30, Course 1, Lecture 4, "On the Nature of Exchange and Money." In *Nassau Senior and Classical Economics.* Ed. by Marian Bowley, London: George Allen & Unwin, 1937.

Shackle, G. L. S. *Epistemics & Economics, A Critique of Economic Doctrines.* Cambridge: Cambridge University Press, 1972.

Singer, Kurt. "*Oikonomia*: An Inquiry into the Beginnings of Economic Thought and Language." *Kyklos* 11:1958, 29–54.

Smith, Adam. "The History of the Ancient Logic and Metaphysics." In *Essays on Philosophical Subjects.* London: T. Cadell and W. Davies, 1795.

Soudek, Josef. "Aristotle's Theory of Exchange, An Enquiry into the Origin of Economic Analysis." *Proc. of the American Philosophical Society* 96:1952, 45–75.

Spengler, J. J. *Origins of Economic Thought and Justice.* Carbondale and Edwardsville, IL: Southern Illinois University Press; London and Amsterdam: Feffer & Simon, 1980.

Spiegel, H. W. *The Growth of Economic Thought*, rev. ed. Durham, NC: Duke University Press, 1983.

Trever, A. A. *A History of Greek Economic Thought*, 1916, reprint ed. Philadelphia: Porcupine Press, 1978.

Turner, Frank M. *The Greek Heritage in Victorian Britain.* New Haven: Yale University Press, 1981.

Waszek, Norbert. "Two Concepts of Morality: A Distinction of Adam Smith's Ethics and Its Stoic Origin." *Journal of the History of Ideas* 45:1984, 591–606.

Wills, Garry. "Benevolent Adam Smith." *New York Review of Books* 25:Feb. 9, 1978, pp. 40–43.

Worland, Stephen T. "Aristotle and the Neoclassical Tradition: The Shifting Ground of Complementarity." *History of Political Economy* 16:1984, 107–34.

Commentary by William F. Campbell

The Old Art of Political Economy [p. 7] ,

The purpose of this comment is to take a different tack than Todd Lowry has chosen. He has primarily focused on the positive aspects of Greek economic thought in order to emphasize the continuities between the present and the past. I wish to emphasize the normative aspects of ancient economic thought with only occasional glances at modern "positive" economics. The concerns of classical political philosophy are distinctively different and challenging to the more mechanical models of modern economics or the alleged value-free individualism of modern welfare economics. Not only is it different but I believe the approach of classical political philosophy is also correct. It provides a more adequate understanding of human nature and the social arrangements appropriate to such a nature.

In contrast to the ideological or utopian modes of thought which establish an unworkable ideal or norm precisely because it is permanently unachievable and therefore serves as a base for a permanent critique of whatever exists, the great tradition is fundamentally realistic. It does not blind itself to the human reality that people are often selfish, weak, stupid, and perverse; but it is not "realistic" in the more modern sense that men are only motivated by narrow self-interest or the love for power.[1]

The chief merit of the classics is that they refuse to be reductionist. Man cannot be conceived simply as a utilitarian pig who has a slightly more advanced understanding of cause and effect than the animals. Plato's city of pigs is close to an economist's paradise — men peacefully pursuing their material wants through labor and exchange. But unfortunately, the honor-loving part of the soul asserts itself. There must be distinction, variety, relishes. The desire for more, what the Greeks called *pleonexia*, lies behind avarice and ambition. Unlike physical appetites, this desire is not easily satiable. In fact, the Greeks were confronted with the identical problem that faces modern economics — infinite wants confronting finite resources.[2] But their response to the basic problem is totally different.

Modern neo-classical economics conceives the problem to be an engineering one of converting inputs to outputs. Everything is constrained maximization to alleviate the problem of scarcity. Satisfy as

31

many of those self-chosen infinite wants as you can at the least cost is the meaning of efficiency. Consumer sovereignty maintains the amoral, subjective utility, and individualistic nature of the modern endeavor. The political economy appropriate to this definition is either a constitution of liberty defined in terms of the absence of coercion, or a series of mechanical constructs ingeniously articulated by the public choice and law and economics movements to get around certain technical impediments caused by public goods and externalities. The left wing and the right wing in modern economics only differ in the side constraints they impose upon the pursuit of liberty or the maximization procedure. The left wing might add constraints which achieve equality or security, but these are still treated as subjective preferences.

Classical political philosophy is the exact opposite of the modern formulation. There is no generic problem of scarcity defined in an engineering sense. The man of infinite wants is the problem, and it is a moral problem, not an amoral engineering problem. Consumer sovereignty is flattering the people in a democracy; the man of infinite wants is a tyrant. To try to solve the problem of scarcity defined in modern terms is simply to appease the tyrant. Modern economics would be rejected as the science of indulgence.

For the ancients the end of activity and all human institutions is human happiness. Economics is not conceived as an autonomous abstract inquiry but as a subordinate, concrete, and morally oriented discipline. Politics is the master discipline, the art of arts, in terms of which the Greek understanding of economics, acquisition of material possessions of the household, is subordinated. The art of arts, for the Greeks as well as the later Christian tradition, is the cure of souls. Physical health requires the treatment, and occasionally harsh treatment, of the body. The health of the soul also requires training, education, and culture.

The cure of souls requires a radical individualism or personalism that goes far beyond the abstractions of methodological individualism and the problem of scarcity. It is precisely the bewildering variety of men in their circumstances which makes economics and politics into an art rather than a science in the modern sense. Socrates does not start from some abstract problem of scarcity. He starts by confronting individual persons of all sorts and conditions. He starts from opinions and feeling which must be the raw material for all rational process. Reason is the sifting out of this opinion, the examination of the wants and desires that men express, and thus by its nature *ad hominem*. This radical personalism helps to explain the elusive form of discourse and dialectic which the Greeks used to express their teachings.

On the basis of what has been said so far, it can be seen that the term "political economy" must be used with some care. Their politics is much broader than ours in that it includes the health of souls which entails consideration of philosophy and theology; their economics, as we shall see, is both broader and narrower than ours. It is narrower in that their economics is not the science of rational choice, but the art of household management; it is broader in that much of what the ancients meant by "economics" would be found in a marriage and the family course, or in the college of agriculture rather than the department of economics. If we were to focus solely on their "economics" narrowly construed we would miss the larger context of their "welfare economics" as we might call it today.

Let us set the stage for the entire discussion by focusing on the problem of justice. Certainly no one would deny the centrality of justice for the concerns of political economy and welfare economics.

Cicero, one of the great Roman synthesizers of the Greeks, provided a summary definition of *justice* which captures the manifold nature of the realities which the ancients tried to preserve. He states that justice teaches one "to consider the interests of the human race, to render to each his own, and not to tamper with that which is sacred, that which is public, and that which belongs to another."[3] By refusing to reduce reality to one of its simple elements, Cicero properly instructs us in the art of combining ingredients to make a constitution.

His constitutionalism is not a construction gerrymandered out of private utility or private interests as is done in so much modern political economy. A proper constitution obviously has a healthy respect for private property and private property rights, but it is not defined or constructed solely in terms of that private good.

The Art of Acquisition

The treatment of private property in classical political philosophy is significant. We come the closest to modern economic concerns in the ancient treatises on household management and agriculture. So close do we come, in fact, that Hans Baron has described Xenophon's work as "probably of all classical works the most kindly disposed towards economic acquisition, and the closest to the capitalistic spirit."[4] So near, but yet so far.

Xenophon's treatment of economics seems much closer to the old Marshallian concept which defines economics as concerned with the everyday business of life. Economics, or household management, as a practical art has to concern itself with the everyday administration of the things of the household. The order and arrangement of the physical implements and material possesions of the household is about as pedestrian a thing as can be imagined. Economists would relegate such matters to the home economics department as being too trivial for them to notice. But it should be noted that the theory of the firm and the theory of production functions were considered too trivial to notice by the early nineteenth-century classical economists. Only insofar as the "law of diminishing returns" had macro implications when combined with the "principle of population" did the theorists pay any attention to it.

In the agricultural literature can be found similar examples of concerns with production functions. Pliny, for example, in his *Natural History* relates the story of C. Furius Cresinus who was accused of sorcery before a Roman court. The charge was based on his "reaping much larger crops from his very small spot of ground than his neighbours did from their extensive fields." Cresinus defends himself by producing "his strong implements of Husbandry, his well-fed oxen and a hale young woman his daughter, and pointing to them, says, 'These, Romans! are my instruments of witchcraft: — But I cannot here show you my labours, sweats and anxious cares.'"[5] One can almost see the numbers popping out for a numerical example of a production function.

It is interesting to note as Lowry pointed out in his essay, that Xenophon was described in the seventeenth century as "the first Author that ever argued by Political Arithmetick, or the Art of Reasoning upon things by Figures" and commended for "the Exactness of his Calculations." Xenophon attributes to Socrates a similar but more complicated argument in the *Memorabilia*: "He also thought it a kind of impiety to importune the gods with our inquiries concerning things of which we may gain the knowledge by number, weight, or measure; it being, as it seemed to him, incumbent on man to make himself acquainted with whatever the gods had placed within his power: as for such things as were beyond his comprehension, for these he ought always to apply to the oracle; the gods being ever ready to communicate knowledge to those whose care had been to render them propitious."[6]

The important observation here is that the ancient politics is certainly open to modern positive economic theory and even econometrics when they are appropriately applied to the realms of the commensurables. But it is equally certain that the ancients would not try to methodologically proscribe knowledge to what can be forced on the Procrustean bed of number, weight, and measure. In fact, Xenophon attributes to Socrates a view that stresses the "science of divination" in the free choice of occupations:

> He likewise asserted, that the science of divination was necessary for all such as would govern successfully either cities or private families: for, although he thought every one might choose his own way of life, and afterwards, by his industry, excell therein; whether architecture, mechanics, agriculture, superintending the labourer, managing the finances, or practising the art of war; yet even here, the gods, he would say, thought proper to reserve to themselves, in all these things, the knowledge of that part of them which was of the most importance; since he, who was the most careful to cultivate his field, could not know, of a certainty, who should reap the fruit of it. He who built his house the most elegantly, was not sure who would inhabit it.... Socrates therefore, esteemed all those as no other than madmen, who, excluding the Deity, referred the success of their designs to nothing higher than human prudence.[7]

Although this has a possible libertarian interpretation to it all, it probably more closely resembles the doctrine of "lawful callings" that we meet in the Common Law and Sir Edward Coke. According to Xenophon, Socrates' accuser said that Socrates "often cited that line of Hesiod's, 'Employ thyself in any thing, rather than stand idle,' it was pretended he meant to insinuate it as the poet's opinion, 'that no employment whatever could be unjust or dishonourable from whence profit might arise: 'whereas, in truth, nothing could be farther from the design of Socrates; for although he constantly maintained that labour and employment were not only useful, but honourable, and idleness no less reproachful than pernicious to man; yet he never concluded without saying,' that he alone could be considered as not idle who was employed in procuring some good to mankind; but that the gamester, the debaucher, and every other whose only end was evil, were emphatically to be called so...."[8]

Another example of production theory which would seem to emphasize the importance of property rights and incentives can be found in the (Pseudo-) Aristotelian *Economics* which draws on Xenophon and Aristotle: "No one, indeed, takes the same care of another's property as of his own; so that, as far as is possible, each man ought to attend to his own affairs in person. We may commend also a pair of sayings, one asked what best conditions a horse, replied, 'His master's eye.' The Libyan, when asked what kind of manure is best, answered, 'The master's footprints.' The master and mistress should, therefore, give personal supervision, each to his or her special department of the household work. In small households, an occasional inspection will suffice; in estates managed through stewards, inspections must be frequent. For in stewardship as in other matters there can be no good copy without a good example; and if the master and mistress do not attend diligently to their estates, their deputies will certainly not do so."[9]

Schumpeter described Aristotle's work as "decorous, pedestrian, slightly mediocre, and more than slightly pompous common sense." The economical observations cited above share all of these characteristics, except for being "slightly pompous." In comparison with modern abstract theories of economics, Schumpeter's description might even be considered as an endorsement. Granted that these germs of supply side economics, X-efficiency theory, monitoring costs, entrepreneurship, and the importance of trust, emulation, and envy did not flower into a research program of model building in the modern sense, they did flower into a research program of model building in the older sense of character formation.

The emphasis on leadership and moral qualities which must be grounded ultimately in self-governance is by its nature concrete knowledge or skill, an art, rather than an abstract science founded on number, weight, and measure. If the personal attention to detail is warranted in understanding physical production functions, it is even more important in dealing with the human beings involved in the household.

The marriage and family tone of the so-called third book of the (Pseudo-) Aristotelian *Economics* has been described by one of its editors as a "graceful homily on married life, worthy of Aristotle himself. Indeed the chaste and tender spirit which it breathes is almost Christian. As a favourable example of enlightened Greek thought about marriage and the family, it is well worth presenting in an English dress."[10] He also points out the similarities to Xenophon's *Oikonomikos* and the discourse of Ischomachus in that dialogue.

Aristotle, when he treats of the subject of wealth, also deals with husband and wife, master and servant, parent and child. In Book I of the *Politics* he discusses these matters in the context of the art of acquisition. To see the difference between the treatment of wealth in classical political philosophy and modern economics, one must focus for a minute on that perennially knotty problem of economics — utility. Both Xenophon and Aristotle, for example, could be called utilitarians, but only if the objective utility were included. A good must not only be subjectively pleasing, i.e., productive of subjective utility, but must be combined with the wisdom of the user to really produce good. The focus of both theorists is on human need, with all the overtones of objectivity which make that word an unacceptable substitute for want in modern economic theory.

The key term is *chrematistics*. Polanyi argues that the term is "deliberately employed by Aristotle in the literal sense of providing for the necessaries of life, instead of its usual meaning of 'money-making.'"[11] In other words, Aristotle transformed the term which originally meant an "unlimited pursuit of wealth" into the "limited pursuit of provisions for the satisfaction of man's needs."

The word *chrema* and *chreia* which are at the roots of *chrematistics* have wreaked havoc in the history of thought. They are involved in the knotty questions of the proper translation and transmission of Aristotle's thought by the medieval translators to which Odd Langholm has devoted so much care and attention.

Whatever the consensus is about the meaning intended by the scholastics, I believe that Aristotle's understanding is much closer to the understanding of the word "needful" when Jesus tells Martha, "Martha, Martha, you are anxious and troubled about many things; one thing is needful. Mary has chosen the good portion, which shall not be taken away from her."[12]

If Aristotle meant by *chreia* the word *demand* based in the modern sense on subjective utility, then he should be judged on the basis of modern positive analytical standards, and be found confused or wanting. But if he really means *need* or *deficiency* defined in terms of man's nature and the conditions for human happiness, then it is a normative framework which must be judged in terms of Aristotle's adequacy in describing the nature of man's happiness.

The art of acquisition is subject to being corrupted by the vice of avarice, the unlimited desire for wealth. This vice can either take the expansive form of increasing money without limit or the niggardly form of fearing to lose it. The art of living well which is more than the mere continuance of life should temper these unlimited desires but Aristotle recognizes that "as their desires are unlimited, they also desire that the means of gratifying them should be without limit. Those who do aim at a good life seek the means of obtaining bodily pleasures; and, since the enjoyment of these appears to depend on property, they are absorbed in getting wealth...."[13]

What provides the limits for the wealth acquisition process? The limits for all subordinate arts are provided by the end they are meant to accomplish. Aristotle argues that both the family and the state are association of living beings who have a sense of good and evil, just and unjust, as well as sharing with the animals in pains and pleasures. Other animals have voices which allow the expression of pain and pleasure, but only humans have the gift of speech. (It is important whether, for example, the First Amendment to the American Constitution guarantees the freedom of speech, or the freedom of expression, as it has been expressed by the recent decisions.)

As Aristotle claims, "Thus it is clear that household management attends more to men than to the acquisition of inanimate things, and to human excellence more than to the excellence of property which we call wealth, and to the virtue of freemen more than to the virtue of slaves."[14]

It is in light of the fact that the household is ultimately oriented to wealth only as a means of being able to foster excellence in human beings that we find limits being imposed upon the means of acquisition and the consequent censuring of some of the methods such as retail trade (*kapelike*) and usury.

Aristotle also discusses debased forms of the art of acquisition in his later treatment of the art of liberality. He argues that "others again exceed in respect of taking by taking anything and from any source, e.g., those who ply sordid trades, pimps and all such people, and those who lend small sums and at high rates. For all of these take more than they ought and from wrong sources. What is common to them is evidently sordid love of gain, and little gain at that."[15]

Where money becomes an end in itself rather than a means to acquiring objects of true use value, i.e., those objects which satisfy real human needs, it is perverted. Both in the earliest forms of association (the household) and in the highest forms of association (philosophic friendship), money was thought to be inappropriate because all things are held in common.

Barter exchange, villages, and the city-state or *polis* all require exchange, and the latter two require money because of the increasing complexity of arrangements. The importance of trust and friendship still impose limits at these higher levels of social complexity. The moral purposes of the *polis* are not forgotten.

Aristotle recognizes that man is not only a household being (essentially private) and a political being (essentially public) but there are the intermediate forms of association, *koinonia*, whose meaning ranges from community to association. The importance of the range of institutions which Aristotle deals with and the conditions necessary for their excellence is an important part of his constitutionalism. The constitutionalism of classical political philosophy would thus include what has come to be called in American jurisprudence, the "police powers," which are the responsibilities of state and local government jurisdictions. These are the powers located in the "small republican" portion of American federalism which are concerned with public health, education, and morals.

In the light of this tradition, we can see why Cato, Solon, Lycurgus, and Xenophon were considered to be the great "economists" before the rise of the physiocrats and Adam Smith who changed the focus of economics.

The Art of Liberality

The art of wealth is involved not only in the acquisition of wealth but the uses of wealth once it is accumulated. The main economic virtue is that of liberality. In Aristotle's words, "With regard to giving and taking of money the mean is liberality, the excess and the defect prodigality and meanness. In these actions people exceed and fall short in contrary ways; the prodigal exceeds in spending and falls short in taking, while the mean exceeds in taking and falls short in spending."[16]

The concrete nature of the virtue, the reason that it is an art, is made clear by Aristotle. In defense of the idea that it is no easy task to be good, he argues that "any one can get angry — that is easy — or give or spend money; but to do this to the right person, to the right extent, at the right time, with the right motive, and in the right way, *that* is not for everyone, nor is it easy; wherefore goodness is both rare and laudable and noble."[17] Aristotle's full development of liberality occurs in Book IV of the *Nicomachean Ethics*.

The art of giving and spending requires that attention be paid to the views of justice held by the classical political philosophers. Much of the scholarship devoted to Aristotle's economic thought, for example, has revolved around the knotty and crabbed significance of Book V of the *Nicomachean Ethics*. Many modern views of justice are simply a remnant or portion of Aristotle's complex and overlapping views.

Central to the concept of justice is the idea of distribution of good things (including punishment!) to men in accordance with their natures. The oldest versions go back to the shepherd or the herdsman who treats the herd equally because they are equal in the relevant characteristic of being led, i.e., devoid of reason. In fact, the concept of a whole as distinguished from a compound depends on a prior distinction between ruling and subject elements. The herdsman can help us in both cases, but he treats his sheep in one fashion and his household in another.

The very term *nomos* in the compound *economics* goes back to the verb *nemo*. Kurt Singer has emphasized the older connection with liberality and generous giving associated with the word. The modern idea of the *homo oeconomicus* is almost the exact opposite of the generous

man who was the original economist: "The herdsman. . . is never regarded
as a close-fisted calculator or model of petty thriftiness but everywhere
admired for his large-hearted hospitality, even in dire circumstances. It is
time to remember that, at least in Homer, the verb *nemo* is mostly used
of generous hosts dispensing meat and drink, not in order to allocate
scarce resources according to marginal utilities. But in order to do honour
to guests and justice to their own great-mindedness."[18]

Let me conclude by suggesting that there are untold riches still to be
discovered by economists in the thought of the ancients. Plutarch is
virtually untouched by political and economic commentators. The comparisons between Numa, Lycurgus, Solon, and Poplicola ("Publius" for
those Americans familiar with their *Federalist Papers*) contain models of
just distribution and the limits of largesse which still have relevance for
understanding the contemporary welfare state, land reform, and the
nature of political economy. As is better known, Lycurgus by himself is a
wonderful model of the totalitarian temptation, but he is also a superb
positive economist in that he understands all the conditions necessary for
a flourishing economy. Unfortunately, his goal was different.

We could also learn from the ancients, historians as well as the philosophers, that comparative economic systems should not be taught in the
light of an assumed agreement about ends. The ancients recognized that
what is at stake are ways of life, the nature of the *politeia*, and the
constitution. But they would not be paralyzed by calling these "value
judgments." They would say, Let's get on with the work at hand and start
sifting the evidence. The point is to make reasonable judgments about
these claims to be the good life. Precision or certainty is not to be
expected for these are not the types of questions resolvable by number,
weight, and measure.

The riddle of Aristotle's reciprocal justice may be resolved when it is
stressed that it deals with the problem of the incommensurables. There is
a disproportion between gods and men, parent and child, philosopher and
student which no money payment can equate. Men normally want to
return evil for evil and good for good. The first may be simply revenge
and the second the false pride of independence and autonomy. The
temple of the Graces is necessary to teach us the political economy of
gratitude and friendship. We must accept the grace of ruling elements and
serve them in return as best we can with the honor that is their due.

Although there are many suggestions in both Plato and Xenophon
which would help elucidate Aristotle's meaning, Plato's *Apology* formu-
lates the issues most clearly. The startling claim by Socrates that he is a
gift of god *and* a gadfly should make us wonder as to how societies can

justly compensate such men. The positive economics of honoraria and modest competences has still to be worked out, but Socrates' demand to be set up in the Prytaneum, provided with a modest material competence and leisure, provokes us to think about the fact that societies *need* gadflies, but don't usually *want* gadflies. Political economy today avoids the realm of the incommensurables by commensurating them in terms of money, ability and willingness to pay, or voluntary consent. The Temple of the Graces is still needed to keep economists from indulging in the reductionist fallacy.

Notes

1. Irving Kristol, "Utopianism, Ancient and Modern." In *Two Cheers for Capitalism*. New York: Basic Books, 1978, pp. 153–170, is a healthy antidote to the usual blueprint utopian interpretation of Plato. The similarities between modern "realism" and the ancient Sophists needs to be further developed. The attack on Convention (*nomos*), and the laws made by the weak, in the name of Nature (*physis*), the right of the strong to have more, characterizes the teachings of the Sophists, and Athenian statesmen in the age of Pericles. On the appearance of the "common good unjustly understood," see Leo Strauss' account of the Melian dialogue in Thucydides and its relationship to Callicles, Thrasymachus, and Pericles, *The City and Man*. Chicago: Rand McNally & Company, 1964, p. 193.

2. For a more extended treatment of these themes, cf. William F. Campbell, "Towards a Conservative Economics." *Modern Age* 26(1): Winter 1982, 27–38; and "Political Economy: New, Old, and Ancient." *Intercollegiate Review* 12(2): Winter 1976–77, 67–79.

3. Quoted in Joseph J. Spengler, *Origins of Economic Thought and Justice*. Carbondale: Southern Illinois University Press, 1980, p. 110.

4. Hans Baron, "Franciscan Poverty and Civic Wealth as Factors in the Rise of Humanistic Thought." *Speculum* 13(1): January, 1938, 25. Sombart expressed the same view and claimed that Xenophon was "more widely read and more highly esteemed than Aristotle." Werner Sombart, *The Quintessence of Capitalism*. London: T. Fisher Unwin, 1915, p. 226.

5. Pliny, *Natural History*, Book XVIII, chapter 7.

6. Xenophon, *The Whole Works*. London: Henry G. Bohn, 1849, p. 520.

7. *Ibid.*

8. *Ibid.*, p. 528.

9. (Pseudo-) Aristotle, *Oeconomica*. Cambridge: Harvard University Press, 1962, I:6:3–4, p. 341. Leonardo Bruni translated Book I and Book III of the (Pseudo-) Aristotelian *Economics* into Latin from the Greek. This work, thought to be by Aristotle, is probably by an early Peripatetic student of Aristotle, possibly Theophrastus. Book I and Book III drew heavily from Xenophon and Aristotle. Although a great deal of scholarly work has gone into the tracing of translations, not much attention has been given to the substance of the economic thought. There is a movement in economics from the paradigm of virtue to the pardigm of control which parallels the similar "profanation of politics" described so well by Irving Kristol in his examination of the movement from the (Pseudo-) Aristotlian *Secretum*

Secretorum to Machiavelli. Irving Kristol, "Machiavelli and the Profanation of Politics." In *Reflections of a Neoconservative.* New York: Basic Books, 1983, pp. 123–135.

10. *Ibid*, p. 325.

11. Karl Polanyi, *Primitive, Archaic, and Modern Economies.* Ed. George Dalton. New York: Doubleday and Company, 1968, p. 113. In addition to the sources cited in Lowry, the most extensive recent treatment of Aristotle's "art of acquisition" is in Warren R. Brown's "Aristotle's Art of Acquisition and the Conquest of Nature." *Interpretation* 10 (2–3): 1982, 159–195.

12. Luke 10:41–41. Also cf. Thomas J. Lewis, "Acquisition and Anxiety: Aristotle's Case Against the Market." *Canadian Journal of Economics* 11(1):1978.

13. Aristotle, *Politics* (1258a). All quotations from Aristotle's *Nicomachean Ethics and Politics* are the Ross and Jowett translations, respectively, in *The Basic Works of Aristotle.* Ed. Richard McKeon. New York: Random House, 1941.

14. Aristotle, *Politics* (1259b).

15. Aristotle, *Nicomachean Ethics* (1121b–11221).

16. *Ibid*, 1107b.

17. *Ibid.*, 1109a.

18. Kurt Singer, "*Oikonomia*: An Inquiry into the Beginnings of Economic Thought and Language." *Kyklos* 11:1958.

3 BIBLICAL AND EARLY JUDEO-CHRISTIAN THOUGHT: GENESIS TO AUGUSTINE

Barry Gordon

0311

We have been turned out of Paradise. We have neither eternal life nor unlimited means of gratification. Everywhere we turn, if we choose one thing we must relinquish others which, in different circumstances, we would wish not to have relinquished. Scarcity of means to satisfy ends of varying importance is an almost ubiquitous condition of human behaviour.

— Lionel Robbins, *An Essay on the Nature and Significance of Economic Science*

Biblical literature (c. 900 B.C.–A.D. 100) reflects a chain reaction of major developments in the history of ideas. At root, the Bible is a study of the fortunes of an extended family. The family is that of Abraham and his descendants, and its predicaments are subject to recurring, searching analyses. In addition, there is advice on how to deal with those predicaments, plus observations on the guidelines that should regulate relationships between family members.

The author is indebted to Professor Roman A. Ohrenstein, Nassau College, New York, for his helpful suggestions regarding this chapter.

Analysis, advice, and guidelines change as the concept of the family — the people of God — alters. They change also with the perceived relationship of the people to the Land (i.e., Canaan). Successively, the people are: sojourners, guest workers, wanderers, possessors, sharers, dispossessed, and out-journeying pilgrims. The first six of these categories relate to the Old Testament. The seventh is applicable only in the context of the New Testament. Each mode of relationship to the Land is associated with a particular understanding of how the economic problem is to be confronted. The sequence of understandings is prefaced by an examination of the origin and implications of the phenomenon of scarcity.

Scarcity and Work

At the very outset of biblical literature stands the Yahwistic account of the nature and origin of the problem of scarcity. The Yahwist wrote in the era of enlightenment identified with "the enthroned merchant," Solomon. He collected the old traditions which had circulated orally, analyzed their content, and gave them context. Most of the primeval history in *Genesis* is his (Gen. 2–11), and in it, he considers the phenomenon of scarcity at length.

The niggardliness of nature and the toil and trouble of acquisition are more awesome facts of existence for Adam than they are for even the economic men of Thomas Malthus or Adam Smith (see, e.g., Gen. 3:17–19). The predicament of man subject to the pressures of scarcity is underlined by the contention that he was not designed to be obliged to cope with the problem. According to Yahweh's plan, man was to live in the Garden of Eden where his consumption needs are met directly by the Creator's providence (Gen. 2:9, 16). However, man *was* designed to be a worker (Gen. 2:5, 15). Work, then, is not, in itself, the result of the presence of scarcity.[1] Its basic rationale is not the satisfaction of the worker's consumption requirements. Rather, its chief significance is in its fulfilling an ordinance of God which relates to man's very being.

The problem of work involves choices that evoke opportunity costs, i.e., a foregoing of the benefits of the outcomes of the possibilities discarded. In the Garden, man is to shoulder the burden or problem of choice in a manner analogous to that of the Creator when he set about his work. "Real" costs — toil, trouble, sweat — enter with the Fall when Adam and Eve choose to try to capitalize on the distinctive gift given them by Yahweh, i.e., the gift of the ability to disobey him. Man takes on the responsibility of catering himself for his consumption requirements.

He takes on the problem of scarcity in addition to the problem of work. In his work now, he is doing "double duty," and is incurring real as well as opportunity costs.

Innovation and Mercy

In accord with his initial responsibilities, man is given the power to innovate (Gen. 2:19–20). After the Fall this power is retained, but it is not used wisely or well, in the main. God must step in from time to time to save man from himself. This theme is illustrated in a variety of episodes. In sequence, these episodes include: the provision of clothing (Gen. 3:7–21); the introduction of the division of labor (Gen. 4:2–22); conduct of agriculture (Gen. 3:17; 5:29; 8:21–22); and the attempt at large-scale, joint enterprise (Gen. 11:1–9).

With each of these stories — the fig leaves and the skins, Cain and Abel, the Covenant with Noah, the Tower of Babel — there is emphasis on the inability of mankind to cope independently, despite its endowments. Among the stories, that of Cain and Abel is of particular note in that the descendants of Cain (who are unable to farm successfully) are obliged to innovate to survive. They build towns, take up pastoral pursuits, become musicians, or invent metalworking crafts (Gen. 4:17–22). Economic development is born of the merciful response of Yahweh (in this case, the "mark" of Cain) to man's mistakes and misdeeds.

The Solution by Faith: Abraham

The Yahwist's reflections on primeval history prepare the way for demonstrations of how his readership can cope successfully with the problem of scarcity. The first demonstration is associated with patriarchal history, when Abraham is called and elected.

God tells Abraham to leave one of the main, regional centers of civilization and economic activity (Haran, or perhaps, Ur) for an unspecified destination, and Abraham accepts the command (Gen. 12:1–4). In the new life that his act of faith has opened up, Abraham and his dependents prosper (Gen. 13:2). Then, God commands Abraham to give up the chance of posterity by killing his only son (Gen. 22:2), a deprivation of even greater magnitude than that of giving up the ownership of land by embracing the life of a sojourner. The patriarch responds positively. Even greater prosperity follows this act of faith (Gen. 24:35).

The Solution by Wisdom: Jacob and Joseph

In the case of the Abraham-Faith solution, the people of God are sojourning. The general strategy for dealing with the problem of scarcity alters, however, when the people of God are guest workers. This latter alteration is first encountered with Jacob. Because of his own machinations and those of his mother, Jacob is obliged to go into exile with his mother's relatives. There, he becomes rich through the exercise of unusual managerial skill as a herdsman and breeder (Gen. 30:32–43).

As a wisdom figure, however, the wily Jacob comes to be far outshone by "the son of his old age," Joseph. The latter, sold into slavery, rises to become grand vizier of Egypt. In the "court story" which details his agrarian policy, Joseph emerges as the consultant administrator without peer (Gen. 47:13–26). He manipulates the tools of macroeconomic policy to deal with the onset of scarcity on a grand scale, and much to the profit of his ruler.

Apart from its celebration of economic policymaking as an exercise in Wisdom, this story is striking in its schematic presentation, attention to the detail of policy, and attempt to show the functional relationships of the steps involved (see, especially, Gen. 41:33–36, 53–57; 47:13–25). There is nothing elsewhere in the Old Testament to match the story's regard for technical economics. Both its character and setting raise the question of whether something approaching economic analysis was taught in the wisdom schools of Egypt long before the Greeks took their first steps along such a path with the Sophists.

The Solution by Faith: Moses

As the fortunes of the people of God as guest workers in Egypt begin to deteriorate, Moses is called to rescue his people. He is no wisdom figure. For example, he is so lacking in eloquence that he needs Aaron as his spokesman. Rather, like Abraham, he is a man of faith, and it is through his faith that his people are rescued and sustained. As such, he can be identified with a radical extension of the solution by faith.

This radical extension is evoked by the contrast between the circumstances of Abraham and those of Moses. The former is the head of a sojourning family, but the latter heads a polyglot band of wanderers. With Moses in the desert, it is the question of sheer survival of the people of God which is often at issue.

In these circumstances, the Solution by Faith is expressed in forthright terms that the related emphases of patriarchal history only foreshadow. The wanderers are sustained by water from the rock (Ex. 17:1–7), they are fed with manna from the heavens (Ex. 16:4–5, 14–15), and "a wind from Yahweh" brings quails (Num. 11:31–35). From these quite unexpected quarters, their extremity is relieved when Moses, in his faith, listens to God. In the desert, there is no "soil" and no city, but the Israelites survive without the aid of either.

The Solution by Observance of the Law: Deuteronomy and Leviticus

The strategy concerning scarcity alters appreciably when the people of God cease to be sojourners, guest workers, or wanderers. Having gained possession of the Land, faith and wisdom give way to the Law. This change of emphasis is most strongly depicted in the Book of Deuteronomy. Writers in the deuteronomic tradition tend to treat the Solution by Faith rather as a relic of a bygone era (see, for example, Jos. 5:10–12). It was Faith in the desert and in the time of sojourning. It is Law in the Land. The way to prosperity, like the way to God, is now through the Law of Moses rather than through his Faith (or Abraham's). Further, Wisdom, so seemingly beneficent, resulted in slavery in Egypt. The Book of Leviticus takes much the same stand as that of Deuteronomy.

The authors of these books feel obliged to reiterate the Solution proposed. With repeated emphasis they attach to their codes of law the promise that the community or the individual adhering to the codes will not know deprivation. For example, in "The First Discourse of Moses," the law-giver proclaims:

> Listen to these ordinances, be true to them and observe them, and in return Yahweh your God will be true to the covenant and the kindness he promised your fathers solemnly. He will love you and bless you and increase your numbers; he will bless the fruit of your body and the produce of your soil, your corn, your wine, your oil, the issue of your cattle, the young of your flock, in the land he swore to your fathers he would give you. You will be more blessed than all peoples (Dt. 7:12–14).

There are many passages with the same import, including those of chapter 28 which detail prospective blessings and curses (Dt. 28:1–46). For the same emphasis in Leviticus, see, for example, Lv. 26:3–5. The significance of such passages for subsequent thinking proved to be profound. The agonized wrestling with the problem of the prosperity of the wicked in later Old Testament literature is just one manifestation of their impact.

Economic Welfare and Regulation

Explicit discussion of welfare provisions and regulation of economic relationships is mainly associated with the literature in the tradition of the Solution by Observance of the Law. The earliest writings are those collections of law found in the Pentateuch. The main collections are: the Decalogue (Ex. 20:1–17); the Code of the Covenant (Ex. 20:22–23; 33); the Code of the Renewal of the Covenant (Ex. 34:10–26); the restatement of the Decalogue (Dt. 5:6–21); the Deuteronomic Code (Dt. 12:1–26:15); the Holiness Code (Lv. 17–26); and the appendix concerning dedicatory gifts (Lv. 27:1–34). Also in this tradition is the *Mishnah*, a collection of oral law coming down from the Scribes and Pharisees (see below).

The law codes of the Pentateuch pay considerable attention to the detail of the day-to-day conduct of economic matters. The law-givers seek to "contain" the economy in the sense that its workings are at all times compatible with Israel's fulfilment of its obligations under its covenant with God.

Provisions of the codes treat the use of free labor. Work is affirmed as a divine ordinance for man (Ex. 20:9; Dt. 5:13), although it does not exhaust the meaning of life. A general and quite fundamental restriction on the application of labor is the command to rest on the sabbath day (Ex. 20:10–11; 23:12). The codes also concern themselves with the use of arable land. The soil must be allowed to lie fallow for one year in every seven (Ex. 23:10–11; Lv. 25:1–7). Further, the soil must be allowed to rest in the "fiftieth year," the Year of Jubilee (Lv. 25:11–12). An additional provision of jubilee is the return of possession of agricultural land to the descendants of the family which had been allocated that land in the original expropriation of Canaan (Lv. 25:23–28). A member of another family who has purchased the right to the use of that land is obliged to give it up. Leviticus 25 also provides for the redemption of land outside jubilee.

The use of slaves and other forms of real capital is also subject to regulation. The Book of the Covenant contains a number of specific provisions to protect both male and female slaves (see especially, Ex. 21:1–27). The Deuteronomic Code provides for the release of slaves after six years of service (Dt. 15:12–18). Leviticus provides for a general release of Hebrew debt-slaves and their families every 50 years, although this does not apply to non-Hebrew human capital (Lv. 25:39–46). Conditions of use are placed on the sowing of seed and the employment of work animals (Dt. 22:9–10; 25:4; Lv. 19:19). Even trees are of concern to the law-givers. Newly planted fruit trees must be allowed to mature for five years before their produce is systematically harvested (Lv. 19:23–25). One of the laws of warfare forbids the destruction of fruit trees in aid of the siege of a town (Dt. 20:19–20).

The existence of a monetized economy is a fact which the earliest codes are quite ready to accept. At certain points they actually stipulate payment in money, excluding the alternative of payment in kind (Ex. 21:33–34; 22:16–17). Deuteronomy goes further than the earlier legislation, in that it positively encourages monetization as a vital aid to the promotion of centralization of cultic observance (Dt. 14:24–26). The Holiness Code requires the priests of the sanctuary to be extraordinarily adept at handling the intricacies of a money economy if they are to ensure fulfillment by Israel of its covenant obligations (see, especially, Lv. 27).

There is no doubt, then, that the law-givers view money as a useful social institution which can be employed to enhance the service of God. Nevertheless, there is one use of money for which they entertain the strongest reservations. That use is deriving income by virtue of its loan. Interest-taking on money loans, as on loans in kind, is subject to severe restrictions which might be interpreted as amounting to outright prohibition.

The opposition to interest-taking does not appear to be associated with any particular theory of the nature and functions of money. Rather, it seems to be bound up with the desire to minimize the incidence of slavery for debt. The status of slave is not regarded as one befitting an Israelite. Leviticus declares: "It is I, Yahweh your God, who have brought you out of the land of Egypt so that you should be their servants no longer. I have broken the yoke that bound you and have made you walk with head held high." (Lv. 26:13). Yet what is to be done, in justice, when a member of the covenant community borrows from, but does not repay the principal to, his fellow? By not repaying he has "damaged" the other, and the *Lex Talionis* requires: "Life for life, eye for eye, tooth for tooth, hand for hand, foot for foot", (Dt. 19:21).[2] Given this latter principle, compensation is due, and there may be circumstances in which the only available source of compensation is the use of the labor services of the debtor and/or members of his family.

To satisfy justice and to uphold the rule of law it may be necessary to tolerate debt-slavery as a temporary status for a son of Israel. However, it is too much to compromise the convenant ideal any further by allowing practices which are not obviously required by justice and which enhance the chances of reduction to slavery in particular instances. Interest-taking is one such practice. To the ancients it was by no means obvious that justice required the debtor to pay back more than the principal of a loan, provided the latter was forthcoming at the time and in the manner specified by the contract. Further, the obligation to find a larger sum increased the probability of default and, hence, servitude.

It is a contentious issue as to whether the law codes of the Pentateuch place a total ban on one Israelite's lending to another at interest. The Code of the Covenant, for example, is not entirely free from the charge of ambiguity on the matter. It states:

> If you lend money to any of my people, to any poor man among you, you must not play the usurer with him: you must not demand interest from him. If you take another's cloak as a pledge, you must give it back to him before sunset (Ex. 22:25–26).

This seems to rule out interest-taking on any loans to the poor, and it could well be interpreted even more broadly. It has been observed, however, that this edict refers only to *neshek* (a discount taken initially from the sum lent) and not to *tarbit* (a premium paid above the amount of the loan when the loan is repaid).[3]

Problems are encountered also with the relevant section of Deuteronomy. This introduces a demarcation between "brother" and "foreigner," the latter in the sense of an alien who is not a resident of Israel. The section reads:

> You must not lend on interest to your brother, whether the loan be of money or food, or anything else that may earn interest. You may demand interest on a loan of a foreigner, but you must not demand interest from your brother; so that Yahweh your God may bless you in all your giving in the land you are to enter and make your own (Dt. 23:20–21).

Here, some commentators find a distinction between classes of loans rather than between persons.[4] It is argued that when this statute was formulated, Israel was still an agricultural society, and commercial activity was the almost exclusive preserve of foreign traders and merchants. Hence, lending to a foreigner is co-extensive with the idea of "commercial loan." The law does not necessarily preclude taking interest from a fellow Israelite should he have borrowed for commercial purposes. The only clear ban is on a demand for a surplus over and above the principal in the case of a consumption loan.

The Law of Holiness throws no direct, additional light on the foreigner-versus-brother issue. Leviticus instructs:

> If your brother who is living with you falls on evil days and is unable to support himself with you, you must support him as you would a stranger or a guest, and he must continue to live with you. Do not make him work for you, do not take interest from him; fear your God, and let your brother live with you. You are not to lend him money at interest, or give him food to make a profit out of it (Lv. 25:35–37).

It might be inferred from this that, given the silence on "foreigners" and given the emphasis on the brother who has "fallen on evil days," the priests do not forbid interest-taking from merchants or prosperous Israelites. Yet this remains conjectural.

Somewhat more substantial is the view that the priests made a conscious attempt to clear up the ambiguity that might be associated with Exodus on interest (Ex. 22:25–26). They seem to ban both lending money at a discount (*neshek*) and lending with the proviso of future additional repayment (*tarbit*). This point is obscured in the Jerusalem Bible translation, given above, but it is brought out by the Revised Standard Version. This reads: "Take no interest from him *or increase* [emphasis added], but fear your God, that your brother may live beside you" (Lv. 25:36).

Although there are doubts concerning an absolutely total prohibition of interest in lending among Israelites, it is clear that each of the major codes put substantial restrictions on the use of money as a source of income by virtue of its loan. It should be noted, too, that these restrictions were allied with others relating to pledges given as security for loans. Deuteronomy, for example, forbids the taking of certain items of fixed capital as security, and it regulates the manner in which possession of securities is to change hands (Dt. 24:6, 10–13).

Such is the degree of restriction that, it might be claimed, there must have been virtually no economic incentive for lending in early Israel if the law had been strictly observed. This claim appears to overlook the possibility of the widespread practice of *antichresis* in the economy. The practice has been noted by Robert North who, following Max Weber, Abram Menes, and others, finds it offers a ready economic basis for lending. In addition, it helps explain certain of the economic aspects of the Sabbatical Year and of Jubilee. North writes that *antichresis* is:

> ...a form of mortgage in which the creditor has the usufruct as well as the custody and hypothetical ownership of the pledge, until the debt is paid. The

usufruct not merely supplies the place of interest-payments, but constitutes also a gradual amortization of the principal.... During six years, a canny creditor could get enough profit out of a slave or a piece of farmland to equal or surpass his original outlay, so that he loses nothing by releasing his holding. This supposition also adequately solves the problem of interest on loans. The Levitical legislator tried to force this particular (sabbath-year) shemitta into line with another prevailing practice, the universal fifty-year land redistribution.[5]

Even with strict observance of the law regarding interest, it was possible to profit from a money loan to a brother. The key element in this was the productivity of the asset taken as a pledge, and there may have been an increasing tendency to require means of production as pledges from fellow Israelites. This seems to be borne out by the complaints of the Book of Job concerning those who take as security "the orphan's donkey," "a widow's ox," or "stones for pressing oil" (Jb. 24:2–11). Strive as they might to contain economic practice within the bounds of the covenant ideal, the law-givers could not entirely eliminate exploitation of the weak.

The classic, underprivileged groups of the law codes are the widows, the orphans, and the strangers. Associated with these from the time of Deuteronomy are the Levites. Centralization of the cult left very many of the latter deprived of their customary sources of income.[6] There is absolutely no suggestion that such disadvantaged people should find their poverty a state to be welcomed. The codes express, "the negative and quite unascetic estimate of poverty characteristic of the earlier Israel. It is an evil out of which nothing of value can be extracted."[7]

In accord with this general outlook, the Code of the Covenant is concerned for the protection of widows and orphans. It warns that harsh treatment of these will be requited with harsh treatment of their oppressors by Yahweh (Ex. 22:21–24). If strangers are in difficulties, Israelites are instructed to reflect on their own national experience: "You know how a stranger feels, for you lived as strangers in the land of Egypt" (Ex. 23:9).

Deuteronomy goes much further than the earlier code. It specifies occasions on which the needy are to be cared for, and in a definite manner. At the end of every three years, the needy are to have open access to a tithe of the produce of that year's harvests (Dt. 14:28–29; 26:12–13).[8] Each year, they are to be included in the feasting during the feast of Weeks and the feast of Tabernacles (Dt. 16:10–14). Beyond these, the underpriviledged have continuous gleaning rights. These rights are specified with a fine eye to detail (Dt. 24:19–21).

The sabbatical year provisions of the Deuteronomic Code require creditors to grant remission of all the debts of all the "brothers" who have bound themselves to work for their creditors in the event of their defaulting. The law commands: "You must remit whatever claim you have on your brother. Let there be no poor among you then" (Dt. 15:3–4). Creditors are urged to continue to lend freely to the poor even when the year of remission is drawing near (Dt. 15:7–9). In addition, special regard is given the position of the poor day-laborer. That position may be worse, in material terms, than the circumstances of a slave. Hence, there is a strict command that the wage of the day-laborer is to be paid each day before sundown (Dt. 24:14–15).

The Code of Holiness repeats the principle of daily wage payment (Lv. 19:13). It also reiterates the gleaning rights of the poor (Lv. 19:19–20; 23:22). Further, in the priest's code there is a heightened emphasis on care for the stranger. According to Leviticus: "You must count him as one of your own countrymen and love him as yourself" (Lv. 19:34). Such is the status of the stranger, that the manner in which he is to be treated is put forward as a model for dealing with the Hebrew poor (Lv. 25:35).

The Solution by Mediation: Isaiah, Ruth, Job

The people of God were to experience many bitter and traumatic decades before an alternate to the Solution by Observation began to emerge. The Third Isaiah, writing near the end of the sixth (or sometime during the fifth) century, B.C., could look back on political disintegration, military defeat, exile in Babylon for the leading elements of Jewish society, and a kind of shared possession of part of the Land which was a far cry from the era of consolidation following the initial penetration and conquest of Canaan.

Despite the reversals of the past, this Isaiah is very optimistic concerning the possibilities of the future. He looks forward to the emergence of a new and glorious Jerusalem, a city adorned with the finest products of any level of economic development conceivable at that time and place (Is. 60:1–7). The affluence will be achieved if the sabbath is observed (Is. 56:2; 58:13–14; 66:23), and if there is social justice in the Land (Is. 58:3–12; 61:1–2). These are not new preconditions in terms of earlier thought. However, a third type of precondition is new, namely, that it is necessary that Israel accepts the role of mediator between Yahweh and the peoples of the surrounding nations.

In Isaiah's conception, Israel will prosper if it becomes a priestly nation, and realizes that Yahweh is not its exclusive possession. The wealth of other nations will be bestowed on the people of Israel in return for the ministry it exercises (Is. 61:5–6). The people will be freed from the pressures of scarcity if they act in terms of a much broader conception of the people of God than most earlier writings suggest (Is. 66:18–21).

The third Isaiah is not alone in promoting the Solution by Mediation. In fact, he is anticipated by another prophet, Jeremiah, who claims that one of the preconditions for Israel's restoration is that the captives in Babylon pray for the welfare of the Babylonian economy (Jr. 29). The same Solution is proffered in the epilogue of the Book of Job. A perfect observer of the Law, Job has become destitute. Yet, when he mediates between Yahweh and his visiting accusers (who are probably men outside the Covenant), Job's wealth and well-being are restored. Mediation, rather than Observance of the Law, proves to be the key (see Jb. 42:10).

The Solution stated briefly in the epilogue of Job is at the core of the Book of Ruth. The central character of the book is the Job-like figure of Naomi, who is Ruth's mother-in-law. Over the course of the narrative, the Israelite Naomi is translated from extreme deprivation to joyful fulfillment by virtue of God's response to her mediatory efforts on behalf of a foreigner, the Moabitess, Ruth.

The Apocalyptic Solution: Joel, Daniel

As Israel continued to languish as a national entity, and the empirical validity of the Solution by Observance of the Law became even more questionable, yet another response to the problem of scarcity emerged. That response is reflected in apocalyptic literature, and is anticipated in the prophecies of Joel. These latter were probably written down in the first half of the fourth century B.C., and they direct attention to the promise of an Ultimate Solution for the people of God. Joel's solution turns on a massive and decisive intervention by God in world history. It is through this intervention that the righteous can hope for enduring relief from the pressures of economic necessity.

Joel employs an old concept, the Day of Yahweh, to shake the complacency of his contemporaries at a point where the Judean economy has been devastated by a combination of locust, plague, and drought (Jl. 1:7, 10). The prophet calls for national repentance — a quite orthodox reaction — but he is prepared to go further in the face of current events. The advent of the plague, according to Joel, marks the beginning of the coming of an ultimate intervention by God who will make his home in Zion. On that Day, the reign of scarcity in Judah will be ended. The lands of enemies will become deserts, but the Land itself will be filled with abundance (Jl. 4:18).

This line of thought is taken up and developed subsequently in the apocalyptic genre, which genre includes *The Book of Daniel* (c. 165 B.C.). In such writings, the Land is not currently possessed (as with Deuteronomy), nor is it even shared (as with Isaiah). Rather, it has been lost. Apocalyptic literature:

> ...is essentially a literature of the oppressed who saw no hope for the nation simply in terms of politics or on the plane of human history. The battle they were fighting was on a spiritual level; it was to be understood not in terms of politics and economics, but rather in terms of "spiritual powers in high places." And so they were compelled to look beyond history to the dramatic and miraculous intervention of God who would set to rights the injustices done to his people Israel.[9]

National recovery, on this view, will be effected suddenly and at a preordained time. Its occurrence will be quite independent of prior efforts concerning economic, political, or social policy.

The Solution by Seeking the Kingdom: Jesus

For Jesus of Nazareth (c. 6 B.C.–A.D. 30), the people of God are a pilgrim people. They are moving out of the Land. Jerusalem is a beginning rather than an end (see, for example, Lk. 24:47). In accord with this conception, the people solve the economic problem as a byproduct of adherence to their pilgrim goal, i.e., "the Kingdom." In the Gospels, this Solution is presented in its most explicit form in the Sermon on the Mount.

From a variety of New Testament passages (most notably, sections of the Pauline epistles and *The Acts of the Apostles*) it seems that the early Jewish-Christian community at Jerusalem did not organize its economic behavior in terms of the new Solution. Rather, its model was that proposed by Isaiah, i.e., the Solution by Mediation. Community members sold off their capital, drew on donations from non-Jerusalem Christians, and concentrated on a priestly function. The Isaiah model was not seen as relevant to Christians in general, however, and it ceased to have even particular relevance when the Second Temple was destroyed (A.D. 70). Pilgrimage was obligatory for all from that point.

In the gospel of Matthew, as in that of Luke, Jesus is confronted by the devil on the issue of what he (Jesus) is going to do about the phenomenon of scarcity. The devil challenges Jesus to turn stones into loaves of bread. Jesus' reply indicates that his mission is oriented to life through God's word, and that he does not intend to deny mankind its primeval choice of coping itself with its consumption needs (Mt. 4:3–4). After this, in the Matthean sequence, Jesus hears that John the Baptist has been arrested; he begins preaching and recruits the first four disciples. As well as proclaiming "the Good News of the Kingdom," he heals the sick. These activities set the scene for the Sermon on the Mount.

The opening chapter of the Sermon (Mt. 5) is about the character of the Father, and about living in terms of the kingdom. Then Jesus moves on to teach his listeners how to pray (Mt. 6:9–13; see also Lk. 11:2–4). They are encouraged to address the Father in intimate, filial terms and to petition him, as dependent children, for their "daily bread." These passages lead to an extensive section on how to approach the scarcity issue (Mt. 6:25–34; see also Lk. 12:22–31).

Jesus advises that the rational course is to avoid anxiety about consumption requirements. A number of reasons are given for the adoption of this course (Mt. 6:25–27). The appearance of Solomon in his kingly robes is compared unfavorably with that of the flowers of the field (Mt. 6:28–29). This section of the Sermon reaches its climax with the following:

> Therefore do not be anxious saying, "What shall we eat"? or "What shall we drink"? or "What shall we wear"? For the Gentiles seek all these things; and your heavenly Father knows that you need them all. But seek first his kingdom and his righteousness, and all these things shall be yours as well. Therefore do not be anxious about tomorrow, for tomorrow will be anxious for itself. Let the day's own trouble be sufficient for the day (Mt. 6:31–34; see also, Lk. 12:29–31).

From this it appears that the Solution by Seeking the Kingdom involves trust in the Father, recognition of personal dependence, low present valuation of future needs, and rejection of one's own material welfare as the focal point of activity. Satisfaction of material needs comes as a byproduct. It is notable, too, that the term "seek" is used, rather than "find." This suggests that there ought to be a willingness to live with uncertainty and to take risks, just as Abraham and Moses were obliged to do in the courses of their respective journeys.

The Pauline Epistles

The former Pharisee, Paul of Tarsus, addressed himself to questions of social life in the bustling trading centers of the eastern Mediterranean.

His economic thought, then, has a quite categorical urban orientation which is set against a background of possibilities for regional economic growth in areas which accepted the *Pax Romana*. His readers were drawn from a wide variety of walks of life, included both pagans and Jews, and a significant proportion of them were well-to-do citizens. The traditional body of Pauline writing includes 14·letters, and it seems most probable that 10 of these stem directly from Paul. The 10 were written during an interval which can be estimated as ranging from 8 years (A.D. 50–58) to 13 years (A.D. 49–62).

Paul's letters are characterized by the expression of a very strong work ethic, and he is absolutely opposed to the idea of the right to a share in the output of the community for the voluntarily unemployed (2 Th. 3:6,10). He endeavors to lead by example in that he allocates much of his own time and energy to the mundane business of earning a living (1 Th. 2:9). On numerous occasions, he urges members of his church communities to apply themselves steadily to their usual productive avocations (e.g., 1 Th. 4:10–12; 2 Th. 3:11–12; Ep. 4:28).

The approach to the problem of scarcity is a matter-of-fact one, and Paul is no advocate of an individual's embracing poverty for its own sake. Rather, he emphasizes self-sufficiency as a primary goal. A Christian aims at not imposing himself as a drain on the output of others. Should a Christian possess a surplus in terms of his needs, he should be ready to use that surplus to come to the aid of those in want. However, such charity should not be taken to the extent that the giver impoverishes himself (2 Co. 8:12–14). Further, there is no suggestion that persons with capital who have come to Christianity should engage in disinvestment. Rather, each person "should stay as he was before God at the time of his call" (1 Co. 7:24). Those with capital in the form of slaves, for example, are under no obligation to divest themselves of such assets (see, for example, Col. 3:18–4:1).

There are points of contact between Paul's approach to economic activity and that of the Sermon on the Mount, although these points are obscured by Paul's reliance on the concept of "the household" rather than that of "the kingdom." For Paul, each Christian is a member of a special household in addition to the one to which he is attached in a purely temporal sense. The head of that special household is God the Father, and the administrator, or steward, entrusted with ensuring that the household runs according to the wishes of its head, is the Son, Jesus. Membership of this household is the ultimate social reality in the life of a Christian. Hence, all of his social activities (including the economic) are to be referred back to it for any assessment of their ultimate worth. Jesus the Steward is the final arbiter of the manner in which these activities have served the Father's intentions.

All economic activity, for Paul, should be undertaken as an exercise on behalf of an obligation to Jesus the Steward (Ep. 6:7; Col. 3:17–24). Such activity is depicted by Jesus, eschewing demagoguery, as part of the seeking of the Kingdom. In both expositions, the individual's economic problem is solved as a byproduct. There is a difference, however; Jesus looks to the beneficence of his Father to provide the by-product, while Paul looks to the cohesion of the Christian community, "the body of Christ." The difference is explicable, given the events between the teaching of Jesus and the preaching of Paul. Jesus' teaching may also be contrasted with that of Paul in that it involves the dynamic of "seeking" something to come as against the much more static "household" idea. Nevertheless, it must be appreciated that Paul could assume a background of ongoing growth and development in the areas with which he was concerned, whereas Jesus was addressing a stagnant economy on the brink of extinction as an entity.

Mishnaic Refinements

The historical bases for this particular post-Biblical development are given by the establishment of the Solution by Observance of the Law, and by the humanizing codes for community welfare and economic regulation which were elaborated in the deuteronomic tradition (see above). In addition, the development draws on oral law coming down from the Scribes and Pharisees.

The *Mishnah* is a collection compiled by Rabbi Judah the Patriarch (c. A.D. 135–200). It is a very important document in terms of the history of economic thought, and in Jewish religious literature only the Scriptures take precedent over it. This document formed the basis of both the Babylonian and Palestinian Talmuds. Its legalistic approach looks back to the era when the people of God possessed the Land, and the approach is in marked contrast with much of the later Old Testament literature, the New Testament, and early post-Biblical Christian writings.

Various sections of the Mishnah refine and clarify earlier economic legislation. In "Zeraim," for example, there is an extensive treatment of the welfare provisions set out in Deuteronomy and Leviticus. In "Baba Metzia" (see especially 5:1–11), there is further probing of the problem of interest payments. Here, *neshek* and *tarbit* are carefully distinguished, and legitimate rental charges on fixed property are differentiated from usury. Various ways in which a lender may attempt to take usury are detailed. The rabbis are also concerned to identify the bases for profit-taking and the payment of wages. They go on to consider the questions of hours of work, working conditions, and nonwage benefits for wage earners. Rabban Simeon b. Gamaliel's dictum is cited: "Everything should follow local use" (Baba Metzia, 7:1). The clear emphasis is that the appropriate minimum return to hired labor is governed by local custom and will vary accordingly. Modes of wage payment are distinguished (Baba Metzia, 9:11).

In many respects, the *Mishnah* goes well beyond the economic thought of the early law codes in that it attempts to be specific where the Biblical literature is general or silent. For example, neither Deuteronomy nor Leviticus attempts to list or rank legitimate occupations. Yet in "Shabbath" (7:2), productive activity is classified into 39 main types of tasks. Much more significant are the greatly extended treatments of acts of exchange and price determination.

The Holiness Code took up issues relating to the sale and purchase of the use of land (Lv. 25:14–23). It also discusses the price of slave capital (Lv. 25:49–50). However, except where the Temple is involved directly (see, for example, Lv. 27:9–16), little attention is given to the exchange of goods and services in everyday trade. By contrast, the *Mishnah* is very careful in defining acts of exchange (see Baba Metzia, 4:12; Shebiith, 10:9), and a variety of refinements are added to the basic analysis (see Kiddushin, 1:5; Baba Bathra, 5:7–8, 10:3; Gittin, 3:2; Shebuoth, 7:6).

On price, the earlier and later literatures are at one in that they assume the existence of competitive markets in which prices fluctuate freely. However, whereas the Biblical codes are content merely to enjoin the use of just weights, measures, and balances in such markets (Dt. 25:13–16; Lv. 19:35–36), the *Mishnah* proceeds to establish full knowledge and a perfect market as conditions bearing on exchange justice in individual transactions (Baba Metzia, 5:7). These conditions apply especially in retail trade. Exemptions are made for wholesale dealing in agricultural products held in stock, and for purchases of products intended to serve toward further production.

Other areas in which the *Mishnah* displays very considerable analytical sophistication with respect to economic activity include the treatments of deposits, loans, and guardianship (in "Baba Metzia"). In the face of such sophistication, one might readily conclude with Werner Sombart that "Some of the Rabbis speak as though they had mastered Ricardo and Marx, or to say the least, had been brokers on the Stock Exchange for several years."[10] Yet, reflecting on these and the other analytical achievements of the rabbis, it seems necessary to correct Sombart in one respect. It is not classical or Marxian economics which ought to be cited as modern analogies for the rabbis' command of economics. The more appropriate analogy, it can be claimed, is what has come to be termed "neo-classical" economics. Despite the very different points of departure involved, the rabbis and the neo-classical economists address much the same range of microeconomic phenomena.

The Christian Fathers

The economic thought of the Christian Fathers lacks the unity of that of the post-Biblical rabbis. The Fathers were part of a pilgrim people moving out into uncharted territory, whereas the rabbis were able to reason *as if* the people of God still possessed the Land. As the Fathers explored the new territory they experienced problems in understanding the contemporary economic implications of what Jesus and Paul had said to their respective contemporaries. When in doubt, they generally had recourse to the pagan (i.e., "classical") wisdoms they had acquired in the schools of higher education of which some of them were distinguished graduates. Cynic and stoic attitudes to economic life abound in the patristic thought. Those attitudes recommend that serious attention to the question of economic well-being is individually demeaning and socially useless. Only "Christian Charity" cuts across the pagan despair and indifference. Meaningful economic activity is reduced to the question of distribution at the micro level. As the late Jacob Viner remarked: "No Father seems to have recognised the possibility that income or property in excess of current need might help the poor more if used productively to provide them with cheap necessaries or with remunerative employment than if distributed as alms."[11]

Conventionally, the first major figure in patristic thought is Justin Martyr (A.D. 110–165). The last is Augustine of Hippo (A.D. 354–430). Of all the Fathers, Augustine is by far the most important in terms of the history of economic thought, especially in that he begins to work out the implications of Christians being a pilgrim people. Both the Jewish "dweller in the Land" and the Classical *persona* entrapped in a repetitive historical cycle are rejected as models for an individual's understanding of himself. Augustine admits both conflict and approximation as features of both individual and communal life in any particular short run. Such admissions open up the possibility of movement toward more rational conduct of economic relationships at any stage in any particular society.

In fact, with Augustine, there is even the possibility of economic growth which does not depend on either a community's experiencing benefits resulting from events outside its borders or undertaking conquest which expropriates the surpluses of others.

Before Augustine, the assessments of the role of economic activity in the life of a member of the new people of God vary widely. Lactantius (A.D. 250–325), who wrote after Christianity was made a licensed cult of the Roman Empire (A.D. 313), is the most willing to see the possibilities for accommodation between Christian living and day-to-day practice in the Empire. Among the particular features of his thought of special interest are the rejection of common ownership and use of property as an ideal, and the thorough-going condemnation of public price-control as introduced by the emperor Diocletian in A.D. 301. A somewhat later Father to adopt a general approach similar to that of Lactantius was Theodoret, bishop of Cyrus (A.D. 393–457).

At the other extreme is Tertullian (A.D. 160–223), a lawyer strongly influenced by stoicism and who eventually allied himself with the heretical puritan Montanist sect. Tertullian sees little or no chance of accommodation. Business activities, for example, imply acquisitive behavior based on the sin of covetousness, and covetousness is a type of idolatry. He is also very pessimistic concerning the future of society. In his *De Anima* he raises the bogey of the problem of overpopulation in terms of resources as a pressing contemporary problem. Like the Reverend Thomas Malthus (some 1600 years later) Tertullian views "epidemics, famines, wars, and the earth's opening to swallow whole cities" as types of events which tend to check the imagined imbalance.

Saint Jerome (A.D. 342–420) is another of the Fathers to affirm the Malthusian analysis of the human condition. Often branded a fanatic ascetic, there are passages in his writings touching on economic life which support such an assessment. Jerome, for example, seems completely innocent of the idea that there might be mutual gains from trade and exchange. He affirms that all wealth is the result of iniquity, and if one person gains, it means another has lost. All riches are the result of exploitation. The obvious inference from such statements is that Christians should keep their market engagements to an absolute minimum if they hope for salvation. Against the foregoing, however, there are statements which allow that those persons with assets may be able to use them wisely and well without abandoning all ownership of capital in alms to the poor. Again, Jerome admits that the biblical case of Abraham indicates that it is not impossible for the rich to be righteous.

Much less grudging than Jerome concerning economic activity as part of Christian living is Clement of Alexandria (A.D. 150–215). Clement, who was born in Athens, attempts the first extensive synthesis of Christianity and Hellenism, and he is able to admit the relevance of temporal pursuits without compromising the premier role of spiritual goals. Clement writes:

> The possession of the necessities of life keep the soul free and independent if it knows how to use earthly goods wisely.... We must be busy with material concerns not for themselves, but for the body, the care of which is required by the very care of the soul, to which all things must tend (*Stromata*, IV, 5).

Elsewhere, he argues that, "it is not at all forbidden to busy oneself with an unworldly mind with worldly things according to the will of God" (*The Pedagogue*, III, ii). Further, to rid oneself of capital can be a most irrational type of behavior. Persons with assets have the obligation of making sure that those assets are employed to maximum social benefit (*Quis dives salvetur?* XIV; see also XI).

With the advent of Saint Augustine, sometime professor of rhetoric and later (c. 396) Bishop of Hippo in North Africa, the groundwork is laid for a fresh assessment of economic activity in Christian terms. Augustine revolutionizes the classical conception of human personality, breaks with traditional pagan understandings of the shape of human history, and suggests a new and more socially responsible role for the Christian church. Among his surviving works, the *City of God* is the most significant with respect to economic implications, but other writings are also relevant.

Augustine's economic thought has strong affiliations with that of the Socratic philosophers, but unlike these latter he does not envisage the possibility, or even the desirability, of "final" social solutions in terms of ideal city-states. Rather, Augustine looks to a progressive search for better solutions. True justice (*vera justitia*) is an attribute of "the Kingdom," and the justice of any particular historical *res publica* can only be an imperfect approximation of the truth.

With Augustine there is something of a return to the dynamics of Jesus of the New Testament Gospels. The "people of God" are not only untrammelled by the Land, but they are also pilgrim in terms of current social frameworks. Augustine advises:

> Use the world, let not the world hold you captive. You are passing on the journey you have begun; you have come, again to depart, not to abide. You are passing on your journey, and this life is but a wayside inn. Use money as the traveller at an inn uses table, cup, pitcher, and couch, with the purpose not of remaining, but of leaving them behind (*In Joann. Evangel.*, XL, 10).

Augustine rejects the ideas that it is impossible for a rich man to gain salvation, and that disinvestment is a necessary condition of Christian living. In addition, he is prepared (in contrast with some of the earlier Fathers) to sanction the activities of merchants, and he relates the profits of merchants to compensation for expenditure of labor. Even further, he links market evaluation of goods to subjective estimates of individual need (*The City of God*, XI, 16). Such particular observations were to prove most influential in the deliberations of the medieval theologians during the decades of economic development in certain parts of Europe before the coming of the Black Death (i.e., before A.D. 1348). Most of those theologians, however, failed to perceive the nonpagan dynamic underlying Augustine's approach to social issues.

The Understanding of Work

Reviewing the foregoing changes in thought from Genesis to Augustine, it can be remarked that they are often related to differing assessments of the role of "work" (in an everyday sense) in the life of an individual person. These differing assessments offer one of the best single sequences of perspectives from which alterations in the understanding of economic activity can be gauged.

In the Old Testament, work is a Divine Ordinance, and in obeying that ordinance, mankind is acting in accord with its having been fashioned in the image of the Creator. Further, work takes on a special and specific meaning for "the people of God" once they are in possession of the Land. These types of understanding continue through to the *Mishnah* and beyond in Jewish thought.

In the gospels of the New Testament, work has no necessary relationship to the Land, but rather it can be associated with the seeking of the Kingdom. This association is often remarked in modern biblical exegesis. For example, John Paul II writes:

> Earthly progress must be carefully distinguished from the growth of Christ's kingdom. Nevertheless, to the extent that the former can contribute to the better ordering of human society, it is of vital concern to the Kingdom of God.... Let the Christian who listens to the word of the living God, uniting work with prayer, know the place that his work has not only in earthly progress but also in the development of the Kingdom of God....[12]

Saint Paul, as we have seen, did not employ "the Kingdom" concept, but rather situates work in the context of the household of which the

Father is head and Jesus is steward. "The household" setting for work
lacks the explicit growth dimension of Jesus' exposition, but it has many
of the same implications.

With many of the Christian Fathers, these biblical understandings of
work are modified greatly by what they had been taught in the course of
their formal educations. The Greek tradition of work is very different
from the biblical and, in the former, work is, "the most oppressive
misfortune that Zeus imposes upon men from their very birth" (Homer,
Iliad, 10, 71). In the face of the Greek understanding, some of the
leading Fathers (including Jerome, Basil, and John Chrysostom, among
others) rationalized the phenomenon of work as essentially an institution
by a beneficent Creator to help protect mankind from occasions of sin.
Saint John Chrysostom, for example, is willing to apply the rationalization even to Adam in his state of innocence before the Fall. "God
commanded man to till and keep it [the Garden of Eden]," writes
Chrysostom, "in order to prevent him from becoming haughty through
having everything too much to his liking — for it is through idleness that
man learned all evil." With such sentiments abroad in patristic thought, it
is little wonder that some of the general assessments of economic activity
by Christians bore scant resemblance to the teachings of Jesus and his
Jewish predecessors.

Notes

1. According to Genesis, God created the world "unfinished" and man-the-worker as
His co-worker (see Gen. 2:3). The Hebrew word *Laasot*, if literally translated, means
"which God created to make." This indicates that the world is still unfinished, and it is
man's privilege to help finish it. Such a view of work, it should be remarked, is in marked
contrast with that of the early Greek writer Hesiod in his *Works and Days* (c. 750 B.C.) and
with those of most subsequent writers in the Greek tradition.

2. This prescription occurs elsewhere in the Pentateuch; see Ex. 21:23–25, and Lv. 24:
17–22.

3. *Neshekh* may be termed "advanced interest," and *Tarbit*, "accrued interest." On this
distinction see Roland de Vaux, *Ancient Israel* (London: Darton, Longman and Todd,
1978), p. 170, and B. J. Meislin and M. L. Cohen, "Backgrounds of the Biblical Law against
Usury," *Comparative Studies in Society and History* 6:1963–64, 260.

4. See, for example, R. A. Ohrenstein, "Economic Aspects of Organized Religion in
Perspective: the Early Phase," *Nassau Review*: Spring, 1970, 34. If Dt. 23:20–21 is pointing
to a distinction between classes of loans, then it can be accounted a rare passage in terms of
ancient literature. In the ancient world the household was not merely an economic unit for
purposes of consumption. It was also an economic unit for purposes of production. Hence,
the difference between a consumption loan and a commercial loan, which may seem obvious
in modern societies where the household is distinct from the "firm" or business undertaking,
was anything but obvious to the ancients.

5. Robert North, *Sociology of the Biblical Jubilee*. Rome: Pontifical Biblical Institute, 1954, p. 180. See also Boaz Cohen, *Antichresis in Jewish and Roman Law*. New York, 1950, p. 80. At a later stage in the development of Jewish law, the Babylonian Rabbis legalized antichretic sales (Ket. 86a, Kidd. 47a).

6. Levites who had previously tended shrines in rural areas must have faced particular difficulties in an economy dominated by agriculture. Possession of land was the key to self-sufficiency, yet the Levites had "no share of inheritance with Israel; they shall live on the foods offered to Yahweh and on his dues" (Dt. 18:1). On the status of the Levites, their duties and their dues, consult the Book of Numbers (Nb. 3; 4; 8:5–26; 18:1–32; and 35:1–8).

7. G. von Rad, *Deuteronomy, A Commentary*. London: S.C.M., 1976, p. 107. In later Jewish literature the concept of "the poor of Yahweh" enters.

8. The tithe was a levy in support of the maintenance of the sanctuary and to provide for participation in sacrificial meals there. Now, in every third year, this is to be retained for distribution in the area in which it was collected. On the relationship of the triennial tithe and the Temple tithe, see Y. Zakovitch, "Some Remnants of Ancient Laws in the Deuteronomic Code," *Israel Law Review* 9:1974, 346–349.

9. D. S. Russell, *The Method and Message of Jewish Apocalyptic*. London: S.C.M., 1971, pp. 17–18. The Apocalyptic Solution, it should be observed, has some links with the Solution by Faith which was considered earlier in this chapter. In fact, each of the Solutions represents a different emphasis rather than a totally new departure. For example, with Abraham, the man of Faith, the element of Wisdom is also present. This latter is illustrated by his success as a military strategist (Gen. 14:14–16). Law and Wisdom also are by no means mutually exclusive. Moses tells the people: "See, as Yahweh my God has commanded me, I teach you the laws and customs that you are to observe in the land you are to enter and make your own. Keep them, observe them, and they will demonstrate to the peoples your wisdom and understanding. When they come to know all these laws they will exclaim, 'No other people is as wise and prudent as this great nation'" (Dt. 4:5–6). The figure of Moses itself portrays the association of Faith and Law. Essentially a man of faith, he is also the great law-giver.

10. W. Sombart, *The Jews and Modern Capitalism*. New York: Collier, 1962, p. 291.

11. J. Viner, "The economic Doctrines of the Christian Fathers," *History of Political Economy* 10:1978, 23. Clement of Alexandria might be accounted an exception in terms of this generalization (see below).

12. John Paul II, *Laborem Exercens: On Human Work*, Australian edition. Sydney: 1981, p. 107. Other passages of the encyclical are relevant to this theme.

Related Studies

Barker, E. *From Alexander to Constantine*. Oxford: Clarendon Press, 1956.

Barraclough, R. *Economic Structures in the Bible*. Canberra: Zadok Centre, 1980.

Bingham, T. J., and A. T. Mollegen. "The Christian Ethic." In R. W. Battenhouse (ed.), *A Companion to the Study of St Augustine*. New York: Oxford University Press, 1955.

Breuggemann, Walter. *The Land: Place as Gift, Promise and Challenge in Biblical Faith*. Philadelphia: Fortress, 1977.

Cochrane, Charles N. *Christianity and Classical Culture.* London: Oxford University Press, 1957.

Davies, W. D. *Paul and Rabbinic Judaism.* London: S.P.C.K., 1962.

————. *The Setting of the Sermon on the Mount.* Cambridge: Cambridge University Press, 1966.

————. *The Sermon on the Mount.* Cambridge: Cambridge University Press, 1969.

————. *The Gospel and the Land.* Berkeley: University of California Press, 1974.

Dawson, Christopher. *The Dynamics of World History.* 1956: New York: New American Library, 1962.

Derrett, J. D. M. *Law in the New Testament.* London: Darton, Longman and Todd, 1970.

————. *Jesus's Audience.* London: Darton, Longman and Todd, 1973.

de Vaux, Roland. *Ancient Israel.* London: Darton, Longman and Todd, 1978.

Engnell, I. "The Biblical Attitude to Work: Work in the Old Testament." *Svensk Exegetisk Arsbok* 26:1961, 5–12.

Giordani, I. *The Social Message of the Early Church Fathers.* Paterson, NJ: St Anthony Press, 1944.

Gordis, Robert. *The Book of God and Man: A Study of Job.* Chicago and London: Chicago University Press, 1973.

Gordon, Barry. *Economic Analysis Before Adam Smith: Hesiod to Lessius.* London: Macmillan, 1975.

————. "Lending at Interest: Some Jewish, Greek and Christian Approaches, 800 B.C.–A.D. 100". *History of Political Economy* 14:1982, 406–26.

Grant, Frederick C. *The Economic Background of the Gospels* (1926). New York: Russell and Russell, 1973.

————. "The Economic Background of the New Testament." In W. D. Davies and D. Daube (eds.), *The Background of the New Testament and its Eschatology.* Cambridge: Cambridge University Press, 1964, pp. 96–114.

Heaton, E. W. *Solomon's New Men.* London: Thames and Hudson, 1974.

Hengel, M. *Judaism and Hellenism*, 2 volumes. London: S.C.M., 1974.

————. *Property and Riches in the Early Church.* London: S.C.M., 1974.

John Paul II. *Laborem Exercens: On Human Work*, Australian edition. Sydney, 1981.

Judge, E. A. *The Social Pattern of Christian Groups in the First Century.* London: Tyndale Press, 1960.

Karris, R. J. "Poor and Rich: the Lukan Sitz im Leben." In C. H. Talbert (ed.), *Perspectives on Luke — Acts.* Edinburgh: Clark, 1978.

Lipinski, E. (ed.). *State and Temple Economy in the Ancient Near East,* vol. 2. Leuven: Department Orientalistiek, 1979.

Meislin, B. J., and M. L. Cohen. "Backgrounds of the Biblical Law Against Usury." *Comparative Studies in Society and History,* 6:1963–64.

Nelson, B. *The Idea of Usury.* Chicago and London: University of Chicago Press, 1969.

Neufeld, E. "Socio-Economic Background of Yobel and Semitta." *Rivista Degli Studi Orientali* 33:1958, 53–124.

Niebuhr, H. Richard. *Christ and Culture*. New York: Harper, 1951.

North, Robert *Sociology of the Biblical Jubilee*. Rome: Pontifical Biblical Institute, 1954.

Ohrenstein, Roman A. "Economic Thought in Talmudic Literature in the Light of Modern Economics." *American Journal of Economics and Sociology* 27:1968, 185–96.

——————. "Economic Self-Interest and Social Progress in Talmudic Literature." *American Journal of Economics and Sociology* 29:1970, 59–70.

——————. "Economic Aspects of Organized Religion in Perspective: The Early Phase." *The Nassau Review*: Spring, 1970, 27–43.

——————. "Economic Analysis in Talmudic Literature: Some Ancient Studies of Value." *American Journal of Economics and Sociology* 38:1979.

——————. "Some Studies of Value in Talmudic Literature in the Light of Modern Economics." *The Nassau Review* 4:1981, 48–70.

Reumann, J. "Oikonomia — Terms in Paul in Comparison with Lucan 'Heilsgeschichte.'" *New Testament Studies* 13:1966–67, 147–67.

——————. "Jesus the Steward: An Overlooked Theme in Christology." In F. L. Cross (ed.), *Studia Evangelica, V*. Berlin: Akademie-Verlag, 1968, pp. 21–29.

Richardson, A. *The Biblical Doctrine of Work*. London: S.C.M., 1958.

Silver, Morris. *Prophets and Markets: The Political Economy of Ancient Israel*. Boston: Kluwer-Nijhoff, 1983.

Soss, N. M. "Old Testament Law and Economic Society." *Journal of the History of Ideas* 34:1973, 323–44.

Viner, J. "The Economic Doctrines of the Christian Fathers." *History of Political Economy* 10:1978, 9–45.

von Waldow, H. E. "Social Responsibility and Social Structure in Early Israel." *Catholic Biblical Quarterly* 32:1970, 182–204.

Wansbrough, H. "St Luke and Christian Ideals in an Affluent Society." *New Blackfriars* 49:1968, 582–87.

Weinfeld, M. *Deuteronomy and the Deuteronomic School*. Oxford: Clarendon Press, 1972.

Westbrook, Raymond. "Jubilee Laws." *Israel Law Review* 6:1971, 209–26.

——————. "Redemption of Land." *Israel Law Review* 6:1971, 367–75.

Zakovitch, Y. "Some Remnants of Ancient Laws in the Deuteronomic Code." *Israel Law Review* 9:1974, 346–51.

Commentary by Roman A. Ohrenstein
Some Socioeconomic Aspects of Judaic Thought [p.43]

It is by now inevitable that every generation rewrites the history of economic thought to take account of newly acquired knowledge and experience. If this is common with regard to economic thought in general, how much more compelling would it be to write a history of economic thought in Biblical literature, a source permeated with economic ideas and practices of modern significance. To be sure, some valuable investigations in this area have been made in the recent past, but these are mostly fragmented studies and a far cry from a comprehensive history of this subject.

It is, therefore, refreshing to see that an attempt, albeit a modest one, is being made by Professor Barry Gordon in writing a chapter on "Biblical and Judeo-Christian Thought: Genesis to Augustine." While reading its content it becomes evident that this is a valiant, perhaps pioneering, undertaking, since he is tackling a period that encompasses the longest span in recorded history, (2500 B.C.E. – 150 C.E.) and beyond, and that, from the point of view of a historian of economic thought.

Generally, all that is required of a historian is a descriptive interpretive approach to economic phenomena. But Gordon does much more than that, for he presents us in a masterly fashion with the entire Biblical panorama concisely, lucidly, and analytically. One can discern that his familiarity with the subject is formidable; his thoughts are compact, his argument is tight, and his evidence is wide ranging.

Challenge and Response

To begin with, according to Genesis, God created the world "unfinished" and man the worker as His co-worker.[1] Primordial man was initially content to bask in the opulence of "God's garden." But in the process of evolution, man tasted of the "fruit of knowledge." As he expanded his mental horizon he realized that the world is not confined to "paradise island." He lifted up his eyes and saw what amounts to a "Malthusian

---

I am indebted to Dr. Tsemach Tsamriyon, noted Israeli scholar of Judaic Thought, for his helpful suggestions regarding this commentary.

spectre," a world of "thistles and thorns," of trouble and travail, morally deficient and economically insufficient, a world of scarcity.

Upon this realization, he is driven from his Biblical utopia. He now knows how to distinguish good from evil. He understands that in order to get want-satisfaction he must be creative, he must conquer and subdue the inhospitable forces of nature as God originally commanded him to do; he must produce goods and services. This is a monumental task, but man accepts the challenge. He responds through work, expansion, and economic development. Thus, he and his progeny till the earth, raise cattle, practice division of labor, create new professions, build urban centers, form social institutions, expand horizontally and even vertically to the point of venturing to erect a "tower" to penetrate the very heavens — the ancient precursor of the modern "space program."

In this march of history, in its twists and turns, Barry Gordon observes a "chain reaction of major developments in the history of ideas" through trial and error, challenge and response, to the problems and perplexities of economic scarcity.

The People and the Land

Commencing with the migrations of a family, as presented in the Book of Genesis, Gordon focuses our attention on a central Biblical theme: the relationship of the people of God to the Land (Canaan) across its stormy centuries as "sojourners, possessors and dispossessed..." and finally as "out-journeying pilgrims." Moving from the simple to the complex, he canvasses Israel's religion, literature, and politics, and how they were instrumental in coping with the perennial problems of economic scarcity.

In this connection, Gordon insightfully observes that the category of out-journeying pilgrims "is applicable only in the context of the New Testament" (p. 1). According to this interpretation, the people are now moving out to become permanent pilgrims (p. 17). Severed from the Land, the solution to the economic problems must, therefore, be found elsewhere — in "the Kingdom." But to the adherents of the Torah, the Covenant with Abraham (Gen. 15:18–19, 17:8–9) and its later ratification at Sinai (Ex. 19:6) were considered irrevocable. The exile was thus viewed as a temporary aberration of Israel's national destiny, as manifested by Bar-Kochba's revolt in 132 c.e. and in numerous other ways. As a consequence, every national and/or natural event was now reinterpreted historically, and every historical event had retained at least a modicum of national significance. In this sense, and in Heine's words, the Torah became "the portable homeland" of the Jews in exile. With the Land fixed in their consciousness, they could still reason "as if" they were settled in the Land.

The Socioeconomic Linkage

Be that as it may, in ancient Israel, especially during the second Commonwealth, agricultural production constituted the basic and most significant sector of the economy. During that period most of the Israelites derived their livelihood from farming the soil.[2] The land was thus the center of all economic considerations which, in turn, exerted their influence both conceptually and materially, upon the other factors of production, such as labor and capital.

Even a glance at the biblical institutions and laws of *Shemitta* (the Sabbatical year) and *Yovel* (Jubilee) will reveal the existence of a close affinity between land, labor, and capital, human and/or beast. The very overlapping of those precepts indicates a special kinship among them. Those injunctions appear in Exodus 23:10–11, Leviticus 25, and Deuteronomy 15:1–11, and may be divided into three broad categories: cultivation, emancipation, and remission.

Thus, after six years of tilling the earth, the soil must rest so as to give it a chance to replenish its original vitality. After six years of servitude, a bondman must be released, to give him a chance to regain his human dignity. Debt obligations must be forsaken, to give the poor a chance to recover from economic depravity. Last, but not least, property that was expropriated must be returned at the time of the Jubilee to the original owner to restore a measure of socioeconomic equity. Even the welfare of the beasts is part of this scheme.

Clearly, there is a linkage between the prohibition of cultivating the ground on the seventh year, the remission of debt, and the emancipation of slaves. That linkage is of socioeconomic as well as ethical significance.

The Talmudic sages elaborated on these laws analytically both in *Halakha* (legal literature) and *Aggada* (homiletical). They emphasized a.o., the practical and the social connections between the various precepts of *Shemitta* and *Yovel*. Succeeding generations of scholars have been employing similar exposition. For instance, there appears to be a contradiction between Ex. 21:1–2 and Deut. 15:12 where it states that a Hebrew slave is to be released on the seventh year, and Lev. 25:39–40, where it speaks of his release on the Jubilee year.

To remove this contradiction, a contemporary scholar [Beck, 1966, pp.

35–36] suggests that the Pentateuch distinguishes between two types of Hebrew bondmen. The former statement (Ex. 21:1–2) deals with an Israelite who *voluntarily* sells himself as a slave, without a specific cause. In such an instance he must strictly abide by his contractual agreement and his social status is that of a slave, except that on the seventh year after the start of his servitude he must be released with a bonus.

The latter statement (Lev. 39–40) refers to a "brother" who is *forced* to sell himself because of unfortunate circumstances. In this case, Leviticus admonishes that he be treated "as a hired servant or as a settler," and not like a slave. Legally, he may quit whenever he desires, especially on the seventh year, when Hebrew slaves go free. However, since his expropriated land will be restored to him on the Jubilee which coincides with the release of all slaves, it is for his own good that he continue "like a hired servant" until he regains his economic independence.

The Mosaic Code has fascinated many. No wonder that Henry George (*Moses*, p. 8) wrote enthusiastically:

> It was not an empire...that Moses aimed to found...but a commonwealth in which none should be condemned to ceaseless toil; in which, for even the bond slave, there is hope; in which, for even the beast of burden, there should be rest.

> ...It is not the protection of property, but the protection of humanity, that is the aim of the Mosaic Code.... Its Sabbath day and Sabbath year secure, even the lowliest, rest and leisure. With the blast of the Jubilee trumpets the slave goes free, a redivision of the land secures again the poorest his fair share in the bounty of the common Creator.

The Iron Law of Life

An integral part of the institutions of *Shemitta* and *Yovel* is the biblical prohibition of all interest-taking. The Jewish Publication Society translation [1962] rendered *Neshekh* as "advanced interest" and *Tarbit* as "accrued interest," where the former is being deducted in advance and the latter at the time of repayment [*The Torah*, 1962, p. 230].

Interest-taking and loan-sharking were prevalent practices in antiquity, as attested by the *Eshmuna* code and Hammurabi's documentation, down to the neo-Babylonian and Persian empires [Baron, 1952, pp. 109, 69, 409]. So, too, was the practice of *antichretic* sales. It appeared in many forms and was known to the ancient Syrians, Babylonians, Egyptians, Persians, Romans, and Jews. Essentially, *antichresis* was an agreement by which the creditor had the right to use a pledge, be it real or personal property, for amortization of principle, or interest, or both [Cohen, 1950, p. 80]. As we have seen, this subject matter was well discussed by Barry Gordon.

Inasmuch as the Mosaic Code has categorically opposed interest taking, especially from the poor (Ex. 22:25–26, Lev. 35–37, Deut. 23:20–21, Deut. 24:6, 10–13), all those elaborate safeguards must have also made any form of antichretic loans virtually impossible. That there were lawbreakers in spite of all precautions, is no surprise. History provides more than sufficient evidence that dishonesty can flourish under any system, and it is more likely to occur in a system devised by idealists than in one devised by realists.

It appears, however, that the prohibition on taking interest was not generally observed and was honored more in breach than in practice (cf. I Sam. 22:2, II Kings 4:1, Isa, 50:1). An extreme manifestation of such violations of the biblical prohibition of usury is recorded in the book of Nehemiah 5:1–14. Although interest taking was illegal (cf. Deut. 23:20), it was nevertheless exacted and that against the demand for important capital as a pledge.[3] It was Nehemiah, by the sheer command of his moral stature and outstanding leadership, who caused a complete reversal of such practices. And yet, it was relatively short-lived.

That, too, is not surprising, for laws which ignore the forces of nature cannot work for a long time, even if they seem to be rationally perfect. That principle was well understood by the Babylonian Rabbis. They realized that when law and life are in conflict, life takes precedence (San. 74a). Accordingly, when they concluded that the laws regarding interest taking were no longer compatible with the economic needs of the community, they unceremoniously legalized antichretic sales which permitted the circumvention of the prohibition of interest-taking (Ket. 86a, Kidd. 47a). This was particularly the case during the Persian period.

Another such instance took place during the first century, c.e. when Hillel invented the famous institution of *Prosbul*, which practically nullified the Sabbatical release of debts (Deut. 15:1–2). The *Prosbul*, probably an abbreviation of a Greek expression, is a legal formula whereby a creditor could still claim his debt after the Sabbatical year, provided the bonds had been deposited in the court before the onset of *Shemitta* (Zeraim, Sheb. 10:3). By this act the court was empowered to collect the debt for the creditor. The text of that document reads: "I declare before you so-and-so, the judges of such-and-such place, that regarding any debt due to me, I may be able to recover any money owing to me from so-and-so at any time I shall desire" (Sheb. 10:4).

Moreover, by merely making this declaration, the creditor was no longer obliged to hand over the bonds to the court and in this way secured his debt against forfeiture. The ʾeason for this innovation was, as the Mishna states, that people should not refrain from extending loans to one another before the Sabbatical. It is noteworthy that the Talmud explains *Prosbul* as *pruz buli u-buti*, meaning an advantage to both the rich and the poor. In Rashi's words, the rich benefit since they secure their loan and the poor are enabied to borrow (Git. 36b–37a).

There is no need to discuss here the method which Hillel used to effect such a radical change, nor is it necessary to cite other examples of similar magnitude. Suffice it to mention that when the Rabbis "realized that under changed conditions a given law no longer served the high purpose of the Torah, they did not hesitate to modify it."[4]

It might have been tempting, however, to enter into an elaborate analysis regarding the intricate structural differences between *Shemitta* and *Yovel*, problems surrounding textual difficulties that agitate modern biblical scholarship, or perhaps a critique on the critics. The author of the chapter wisely resisted such temptation. Instead, he treated the subject matter with sufficient care and scholarly sensitivity, without the need to digress from his major goal.[5]

Faith, Wisdom, and Law

During their long colorful and historic odyssey, the Israelites' response to the perennial question of economic scarcity varied in method and application. From Abraham to Moses, from Jacob and Joseph to the Solomonic era, as possessors of the land and as dispossessed, down to the *Mishnaic* period, Gordon discerns, among others, three distinct solutions to scarcity: faith, wisdom, and law.

Accordingly, the Israelites have shifted their emphasis from one solution to another, depending on time and circumstance. It is to be noted that by using such expressions as "strategy" or "emphasis," Gordon seems to leave us with the impression that those different responses need not be looked upon as having been mutually exclusive of one another.

It is, however, easy to show that, from the Biblical point of view, all these seemingly different solutions not only worked on each other but also reinforced one another. We will demonstrate this viewpoint not merely with hints but with facts as they appear in the Pentateuch as augmented in the Biblical wisdom literature, and as developed in the Talmud.

The connection between "wisdom" and "law" is to be found in rather early Biblical sources. Both are viewed as vehicles leading to a better and nobler existence. Suffice it to mention that the book of law which Josiah, king of Judah, chanced upon (640–609 B.C.E.) and identified by many scholars with the book of Deuteronomy, views the Law and Wisdom as being identical in meaning and application.

A passage ascribed to Moses (Deut. 4:5–8) reads: "Here I am teaching you as the Lord my God commanded me, to observe statutes and ordinances in the land you are entering to possess. Keep them, obey them, for this is your wisdom and intelligence in the sight of the nations, that when they hear all the statutes they will say, 'This great nations is indeed a wise and intelligent people....'"

It is obvious from this passage that the wisdom tradition and covenant theology coalesce. Such interdependence is also manifest in Prov. 2:6, 9:10, Job 28:28, Psalm 111:10, and Jeremiah 8:8–9. It is also important to realize that these statements are not part of some esoteric philosophy geared toward a few intellectually gifted individuals, but have been an integral part of the very consciousness of the Jewish people for over 2,500 years.

Also in the *Hagiographa* (writings), *Hokhma* (wisdom) was conceived as God's creation even prior to the creation of the world. In Proverbs (8:22–32) "wisdom is fully conceptualized as a personal instrument of God in planning and implementation of the created order" [R.B.Y.S., Encycl. Judaica XVI, 262–63]. And since the Torah was thought of as a primordial manifestation of Divine wisdom, it subsequently led the Talmudic sages to *identify* wisdom with the principles of the Torah and thus firmly integrated wisdom and law into a single entity (Pes. 54a).

Again in the *Midrash* (Exposition), the rabbis employed a homily to compare God to a seasoned architect who would build a structure only when based on a blueprint. So, too, "God looked into the Law and created the world," the Law being considered the supreme source of wisdom (Gen. R.I.1).

It is noteworthy that etymologically the Hebrew noun *Amon* or *Uman*, as it appears in Prov. 8:30 and which is taken as "instrument" of an art or craft, and the Hebrew word *Amuna* (faith) are spelled virtually in an identical fashion and both stem from the same root *Amon* [Shoshan, 1966, p. 109]. In spite of the utilitarian character of its teaching, the Book of Proverbs emphasizes that true wisdom is associated with the fear of God (Prov. 1:7).[6]

Thus, if we are to apply this principle to the various biblical figures Gordon discusses, we find, for example, that Abraham was not only a man of supreme faith but also a skillful military strategist (Gen. 14:14–

15). This, then, shows the intermingling of faith and wisdom. Jacob not only dreamed of a flock that is "streaked, speckled, and grizzled" (Gen. 31:12) but also had a vision of a ladder standing firmly on the ground with its peak reaching to heaven, upon which angels of the Lord ascended and descended (Gen 28:12). Here, again, wisdom and faith mingle. And Moses was not only "a faithful servant of God" but also the lawgiver, par excellence. The same Israelites who, in the face of extreme scarcity in the desert, are sustained with "manna from heaven" are also commanded *not* to collect it on the Sabbath day (faith and law). One may respond to the demands of the moment in a particular way without losing sight of the other components.

In sum: in this view, faith is concretized in law and law is concretized wisdom. They must not be viewed as either/or but as both/and more, not as antithetical but as dialectical in the great human drama of challenge and response to economic scarcity.

In conclusion, Gordon's chapter on Judeo-Christian thought is a highly interesting and thought-provoking piece of work. Alas, the scarcity of space and the pressures of time have limited the scope of my comments. Having carefully studied the material at hand, I can say that his discussions of the New Testament and patristic literature as well as those of the Hebrew period are presented knowledgeably and ably.

It is certain that he, too, had to compress his comment on such a huge volume of literature in the available space. And yet his style is charming, his analysis cogent, and his scholarship admirable. Professor Gordon has rendered a valuable service to the economic profession in presenting a chapter on one of the most intricate periods in world history: "Biblical and Early Judeo-Christian Thought: Genesis to Augustine."

Notes

1. See Genesis 2:3. The Hebrew word *Laasot*, if literally translated, means "which God created to make" (Ibn Ezra, Abarbanel), i.e., the world is still unfinished and it is man's privilege to finish it (Soncino). See in particular Genesis Rabbah 11:6.

2. See G. Alon [1954, p. 93] for additional detail on this topic.

3. See *Rashi* on Nehemiah 5:7 who interprets this verse "...you are lending money against pledges of their sons and daughters, fields, vineyards, and houses." Rashi (1040–1105) is considered the foremost interpreter of the Hebrew Bible and the Talmud. See also *The Interpreters Bible*, its interesting commentary on the "Economic Problem," 1956, pp. 705–711.

4. See Lauterbach [1951, pp. 277–8]. See also *Encyclopedia Judaica* XIII [1972, pp. 1181–82].

5. It might be useful to present this material a bit more from a historical perspective,

perhaps in a footnote. For example, some important ancient documents like the "Nuzi Tablets" or the "Eshmuna" in Prichard's text could be discussed by way of comparison.

6. See Robert Gordis [1951, pp. 33–34 ff.], who makes the point when discussing "the religious ideas of Wisdom Literature."

References

Alon, G. *History of the Jews in Palestine During the Mishnaic and Talmudic Period* I. Tel-Aviv: 1954.

Babylonian Talmud (Heb.), Vilno, English translation. London: Soncino Press, 1938.

Baron, S. W. *A Social and Religious History of the Jews* I. New York: Columbia University Press, 1952.

Beck, Samuel Y. *From Sinai to Nebo* (Heb.). Jerusalem: 1966.

Cohen, Boaz. *Antichresis in Jewish and Roman Law.* New York: The Jewish Theological Seminary of America, 1950. p. 80.

Encyclopedia Judaica XIII, *Prosbul* pp. 181–82, *Wisdom* XI pp. 562–63. Jerusalem: Keter Publishing House, 1972.

George, Henry, *Moses.* New York: The Robert Schalkenbach Foundation, 1884, p. 8.

Gordis, Robert. *Kohelet-The Man and His World.* New York: The Jewish Theological Seminary of America, 1951.

The Interpreters Bible. Nashville: Abingdon Press, 1956, pp. 705–711.

Lauterbach, Jacob Z. *Rabbinic Essays.* Cincinnati: Hebrew Union College Press, 1951, pp. 277–8.

The Pentateuch, English translation and Commentary. London: Soncino Press, 1950.

Shoshan, Even. *New Dictionary* (Heb.). Jerusalem: 1966, p. 109.

The Torah, Philadelphia: The Jewish Publication Society (J.P.S.), 1962, p. 230.

4 ISLAMIC ECONOMIC THOUGHT

M. Yassine Essid

0311
0510

The brief reference to Ibn Khaldūn in J. A. Schumpeter's *History of Economic Analysis* [1954][1] gives little indication of the respect accorded him in the Muslim world and illustrates the difficulty of getting a coherent picture of Islamic economic thought from the piecemeal treatment it has received in Western literature. To understand the intellectual history of a current of thought developed outside Western culture it will be necessary to examine the contributions of each writer from the point of view of what they have written about questions commonly regarded as economic. However, the unevenness and repetitiveness with which economic subjects are treated in Muslim literature obscures the clarity of a cumulative development of ideas and may lead some to question whether Muslim thought emerges as a current sufficiently representative of commonly accepted economic notions to be included in a general history of economic thought.

From the beginning, Islam as a religion and also as a political system laid heavy stress upon the economic aspects of life. This emphasis reflected the leading role of economic activities, particularly mercantile ones, in the Meccan society of the prophet Muhamad's day. Without encouraging asceticism and while acknowledging the legitimacy of

77

acquisition, Islam sought from the start to create a moral attitude toward the use of money by laying down restrictions which would make wealth a source of community solidarity rather than of antagonism and division. The Islamic conception of a community was based upon an ideal and not abstracted from reality. The objective was to find an economic structure which would support such a social ideal, a commitment which still persists in the Muslim tradition.

Economics has never been regarded as a separate discipline in Islamic writings. The Muslim conception of the economy has been deeply embedded in visions of a social ideal and economic questions have been viewed in terms of their importance to the present and the future of the community of believers. For this reason, it would not be appropriate to ask whether certain economic formulations — for example, notions about price — are true or false but rather how Muslim authors have treated such ideas in relation to other statements or non-economic categories, particularly ethical and political ones. This approach involves an interpretation of an author's conception of society and is not an attempt to describe objective reality. Little attention will therefore be given to a comparison of Muslim and Western economic ideas. Instead, emphasis will be placed upon the way Muslim writers have perceived the role of the economy, whether accepting or rejecting it, and how such conceptions have fared when submitted to the ethical exigencies of a community idea.

Islam as a religion is characterized by a cosmic view of the world and human destiny in which there is no separation between spiritual and temporal realms, or between religious and secular practices. It is both a religion and a polity, a revelation and a temporal community of believers bound by the same faith. This unity expresses itself in a faith in God and His word revealed to his Prophet in a holy book, the Qur'ān. This revelation is completed by the Sunna, the Prophet's utterances and way of life which formed an ongoing commentary on God's revelation. The Sunna, combined with the Qur'ān, constitutes the Sharī'a, the "pathway par excellence," a body of norms which is both legally and morally binding on Muslims. Such is the institutional framework of the Muslim world in which daily life is permeated with a sacralization which radiates to every aspect of living.

Although not a treatise on political economy, the Qur'ān might be considered the first Islamic work on economic ethics. It is also, for Muslims, the fundamental conceptual reference for any thought about a communal way of life extending to both cultural and social levels. Since Islam sprang from a mercantile society and the Prophet himself engaged in commercial exchange, production for a market and trade were pictured in the Qur'ān as noble practices and merchants favorably portrayed. The commercial symbolism is even extended to God's relation with man.[2] Mention is made of bargaining, selling, buying, reward, lending, weight, and measure. Although the Qur'ān lauds the honest merchant, it does not fail to condemn the defrauder. Indeed, no action is more illicit, more reprehensive, and more vigorously condemned than one which is based on an unjust exchange. In a society which had institutions to scrupulously enforce justice in exchange, it would be natural for the market, on which the community of believers depended for daily necessities and which offered possibilities for fraud, to become a special focal point of legal concern.

In Islam there is no tradition of positive law derived from human reason. The law is derived from the Sharī'a, an expression of the divine willpower, and jurists and theologians develop ethical, social, and economic principles from that source. The power of the law is thus rooted in the subordination of the life of the individual to the communal one. In economic relations, the advantages associated with exchange will only accrue when property is protected and mutual benefit and redress guaranteed.[3]

The codification of the market rules into Muslim law and the development of jurisprudence (*fiqh*) originated in general discussions about exchange in a context of wider social relations. The development of Muslim cities and the increasing complexity of the exchange process gave rise, on the one hand, to a specialized literature, the *ḥisba* handbooks, and, on the other, to the appointment of an official, the *muḥtasib*, exclusively in charge of supervising markets. The *ḥisba* treatises are not only important documents related to the economic and social life in Muslim countries but are also sources of information about the history of economic thought.

In the beginning, the *ḥisba* literature was merely a collection of juridical advice and opinion on questions of public morality and market behavior. The compilation of this literature into handbooks for the use of market officials did not occur before the ninth century A.D. in the western Islamic world or before the eleventh century A.D. in the Orient. The handbooks indicate the variety and scope of the responsibilities of the *muḥtasib*. Some of the manuals treat religious and juridical duties, while others instruct market officials on technical aspects of supervising the crafts. The main crafts are listed in the handbooks and information given which will enable the market official to monitor the quality of manufactured goods and detect defects and malpractices. He was also expected to enforce standards for weights and measures, to check on the fineness of coins, and to prevent merchants from practicing usury. Ultimately, his responsibility was to assure good faith dealings in the market and to protect the customer from being cheated. Despite the fact that the *hisba* handbooks were primarily concerned with commercial matters, the reader will look in vain in them for any economic analysis of the market's mechanism. Instead, there are only restrictions, reinforced by references to the Qur'ān and the custom of '*Urf* derived from the revealed laws, upon specific activities which might threaten the survival of the community. The way in which questions about price are treated in these documents best illustrates the intellectual limits of the Muslim jurists.

Both the Muslim theologians and the *hisba* handbooks approached questions about price from the point of view of their administration in the market and did not attempt abstract analyses of the results of isolated two-party exchanges. Thus their concern was with the problem of *tas'īr*, a word which means, not price itself, but the action of evaluating by assigning a price to goods. As a result, *tas'īr* generated no theoretical discussions or economic analyses since the objective was not to establish fair prices in just exchanges and ultimately economic value, but simply to determine whether prices should be fixed by juridical or public intervention. Moreover, the Prophet's attitude as reported in a *hadīth* (sayings of the Prophet) did not encourage progress in this direction. When some buyers, during a period of high prices, asked the Prophet to set a price (in their favor), his answer was, "It is God who holds, gives, feeds and sets prices and I also would like to face my lord and no one would complain that I encroached upon his blood or money." What did Muhamad mean? In asserting that it is God who raises and lowers prices, did he reject the mechanism of the market as a price determinant or, in the consciousness that whatever answer he gave might determine the economic future of a mercantile society, was he simply giving a prudent answer to a controversial question? Or, in awareness of the rationalistic attitude of Muslim merchants, was he exhorting Muslims to adopt a fatalistic attitude toward price? We may also ask how it was that Muhamad, who had always lived in a mercantile society and who continually sprinkled his discourses with commercial terms, could ignore the *causes* of price movements, a question which will require further explanation.

In Islam, economic activity and the quest for profit have traditionally been viewed with favor, and trade has been placed on the same footing with Jihād, vigorous action in the cause of God. The Prophet himself is said to have heaped praise on the honest merchant by saying that he will be seated among the prophets in the shade of God's throne on the day of final judgment. In Muhamad's time, people felt close to the spirit of the new religion and lived in a palpable fear of God. In such an atmosphere, merchants' conduct was more likely to have been characterized by temperance and moderation, motivated by a concern for a satisfied soul. This may explain why the Prophet, when confronted with economic questions, did not wish to pronounce judgment. Relying upon the fervor of the believers in the new religion may have been a better course than an authoritarian ruling. Moreover, Muhamad's answer may be an indication that the high prices of the period were the result of market forces rather than the actions of greedy merchants. Forcing merchants through coercive procedures to sell at prices that resulted in loss could only impoverish the commercial class, destroy the market process, and put an end to trade. This course of action, from the point of view of the public good (*maslaha-al-'āma*), would strike a blow at the community of believers. In this context, Muhamad's attitude appears more realistic and may in fact reflect a faithful commitment to God's commandment, "O believers! Devour not one another's substance carelessly, rather than when it is the result of a mutually advantageous negotiation" (Women/29).

From an ethical point of view, forcing merchants to sell at fixed prices is unfair and, because the problem was serious enough, the Prophet was reluctant to create a system of case law by leaving to the judges the right to set prices. Saying that only God is entitled to set prices is to assert that the market price, under normal circumstances, is the just price conformable to God's will. Thus, from Muhamad's point of view, the natural regulation of the market corresponds to cosmic regulation. Prices rise and fall as the night follows the day or as the tides ebb and flow,[4] and imposing a price is not only an injustice to the merchants but results in a disordered state rather than the natural order of things. As noted by Max Weber [1975, p. 464], for someone with a unitarian vision of the universe "where social and cosmic events have a unitarian, ordained, and systemized end in view, human conduct must be directed accordingly and be modelled in terms of that ideal in order to assure salvation."

The issue of the naturalness of the market was discussed in greater detail in the *hisba* handbooks and disagreements over the question even divided *Mu'tazila* and *Sunni* [Gimaret, 1979]. Muslims several centuries removed from the simplicity of the economic life of the Prophet's times could no longer be satisfied with Muhamad's sketchy judgment. Responding to a more complex market while at the same time staying within the tradition handed down from the Prophet required efforts to eliminate trickery and abuse in the market without resorting to price regulation.

Ibn Taymiyya (1263–1328) [1973, pp. 19–49], an early fourteenth century Hanbalist jurist and theologian, asserted in his book, *The Hisba in Islam*, that price regulation may be either just or unjust, depending on the circumstances. According to him, prices reflect market conditions and price increases which result from a scarcity of goods or an excess in demand are caused by God. Since scarcity, which is the reason for rising prices, is within the domain of God, he argued, it would be unfair to penalize the merchant by setting arbitrary prices. On the other hand, monopolization, the action of creating an artificial scarcity in order to sell at a higher price, is by its nature an authoritarian fixing of price and against the welfare of the community. There follows a series of interdictions which are repeated in almost all of the *hisba* manuals. Most concern ways of dealing with interferences with the free play of the market, such as rules which prohibit merchants from selling at lower than market prices and interdictions against intercepting goods before they reach the market, called in Adam Smith's day "forestalling."[5] Throughout, the idea of protecting the merchant is very clear. Imposing a price, it is asserted, gives an advantage to the buyer at the merchant's expense. Efforts to assure a free competitive market should have one overriding concern: to protect the merchant's interests while at the same time causing no injury to the community of believers. Such a market was assumed to be the normal condition which will prevail if there is no interference with the "invisible hand of God" in guaranteeing just prices.

When Muslim authors, jurists, and theologians discuss economic questions, it is invariably from the point of view of a normative ethic in which each person, ruling himself, is expected to be guided by God's edict to "command the good and forbid evil," a principle also to be followed in the governance of the ideal city. Observing this principle will secure the foundation of a community and assure its future, while ignoring it will precipitate its collapse. Discussions of economic questions among Muslims have always been subordinated to larger political preoccupations, to the ideal of justice set forth in the Qur'ān, institutionalized in the Sharī'a, and put into practice by the Prophet and the first four caliphs, referred to in Muslim literature as the "Rightly Guided."

In a community founded on religious law, public concern was naturally oriented toward the legitimacy and qualifications of the ruler who would succeed the Prophet and enforce divine as well as human law in order to secure the well-being of the *Umma* (Muslim community) in this world and its salvation in the world to come. This is the reason why discussions about justice have, from the beginning, been couched in political terms. In this context, the ruler was considered by some as the axis of the social body, the center of a circle. Others pictured the ruler as serving the function of the brain in the human body or of the soul in an organism. The ruler was regarded as God's reflection on earth, the embodiment of His wisdom, and it was the Sultan who guaranteed justice on earth. Without a ruler, a country is doomed to be a victim of dissention, with the powerful oppressing the weak like fishes devouring each other. In the cosmic view of the Muslims, the ruler is the supreme power for justice on earth, just as God is the supreme ruler of the universe.

But such a high office, at the same time so feared and powerful, required from its holder qualities commensurate with the magnitude of his power, the most important of which was the quality of justice. This was not conceived as an absolute moral value but as a politically useful and necessary attribute of the head of the state. The art of just government was the object of great interest among Muslim writers during this period and gave rise to a genre of political literature of Persian origin called "Mirrors for Princes." This approach was well adapted to the use of absolute power which became more and more widespread in the Muslim empire, and resulted in a theoretical shift in the general view of the economy. No longer were actions couched in terms of the supreme interest of the community of believers but instead in the despotic conception of the state. Everything now is focused upon the palace of the sovereign, which becomes the center upon which converges all of the income of the state and from which emanates all of the manifestations of the ruler's power. In this context, justice is considered the bond by which the balance of the world is maintained, and its first function is to fill the coffers of the state. In this mythico-cosmological view of the world, the earth is a well-cultivated garden walled in by the state. The Prince, the head of state, is a shepherd who is assisted by an army maintained by public funds supplied by the subjects.

In the new view of the Muslim world, the state has become the center of the economy, serving as the distributor of goods. To answer questions put to him by the caliph Harūn Al-Rashīd, Abou Youssef Ya'koub (731–798) composed a legal treatise entitled *Manual on Land-Tax* (1921) which covered topics such as the reciprocal duties of the prince and his subjects, the distribution of land, the sharing of booty, the regulation of prices, and usurious and aleatory sales. To these technical discourses, to be used as a reference by the ruler, were added exhortations for the sovereign to be a good shepherd of the flock entrusted to his care and, through his actions, to choose the world to come rather than the one he now ruled. The sovereign as the administrator of distributive justice was the subject of another treatise written by an Andalusian thinker, Ṭurṭūshī (1059–1126). In his *Sirāj al-Mulūk*, he maintained that the power of a kingdom and the protection of the sultan rests upon public revenues, which guarantee their security. Taxes, he warned, must not be heavier than the subjects can bear and must be spent wisely and without extravagance. He admonished the ruler not to overwhelm farmers with taxes so burdensome they would abandon their land, for this would diminish the state's main source of income and make it impossible to pay the army. Unprotected, the sultan would fall under the attacks of his enemies. In this work, the circle of economic prosperity is represented, on one hand, by care for administrative and distributive justice and, on the other, by the maintenance of political stability which ultimately insures order and justice.

At first, the political art of government discussed by Muslim writers lacked a concept of economic administration. Later, the ancient Greek concept of *oikonomia*, the management of the household, would be passed on to the Muslim philosophers, the *falasifa*, who were the disciples of Plato and Aristotle, and *oikonomia* (*tadbīr*) would be used to designate management of the household (*tadbīr al-manzil*; administration of government (*tadbīr al-mudun*); and government of God on earth (*tadbīr al-'ālam*). *Tadbīr-al-manzil* is thus the name Muslim authors gave to one of the three subcategories of practical philosophy, falling between ethics and politics. Its objective, according to Shahrazūri (thirteenth century), is "the management of the household, which consists of husband and wife, father and children, and master and slave." Its practice, he maintained, will permit man to acquire virtue and avoid evil. This definition reveals the basic pedagogical character of the science.

The lost text of the neo-Pythagorean Bryson (1928), surviving only in an Arab translation, was copied and elaborated in more or less detail by a line of Muslim authors, like Farābī (d. 950), Ibn Sīnā (980–1037), Ghāzali (1058–1111), Tūsī (1201–1274), and Dawwānī (1427–1501). Some of them used nearly the whole text, while others copied long passages, sometimes modifying them to bring the text into line with Arabic social reality or with its ideological principles. This is illustrated by their discussions of the role of women in the family and their productive function in society. The vicissitudes of Bryson's treatise demonstrate, in the realm of economic ideas, the inhospitable climate in Islam for the Greek heritage. In the first place, Bryson's work did not give rise to new or original analysis. Second, his work was intended to explain the science of administration and production within an economic unit, the *oikos*, but his ideas were redirected by the *falasifa* to support their own political theories. Beginning as a treatise on household management, it was used as a reference for political economy. Thus, far from revitalizing Islamic thought, which lacked any theory of the production and distribution of goods, Muslim authors, by stressing the authoritarian structure of the household unit to reinforce their political ideas, missed the opportunity to use Bryson's work to enlarge their analytical perspective on the economy. The reason for this is to be found in the fact that, up to that time, political, ethical, and theological ideas in Islam had centered upon the community of believers and not on the *oikos*. In the non-Arabic Muslim world of Persia, however, Bryson's work fitted into a long tradition of wisdom literature dealing with practical daily life which was free of the authority of Arabic jurisprudence (*fiqh*) and receptive to anything of Greek origin. In this context, the total failure of Bryson's influence among Arab Muslims and its relative success among non-Arab Muslim thinkers is more understandable.

The writings of Farābī offer a good illustration of the redirection of the science of *tadbīr* into political theory. He undertook to create a model of society in which everything is rationally ordered with the ultimate objective of combining diverse elements into a coherent unity. Drawing on the principles of the administration and governance of the family household (*tadbīr*) to develop a theory of the state, he emphasized the similarities between personal rule in the household and that of the ruler of the state. Following Plato, Farābī argued that man's natural tendency is to seek the help of others and to form human associations. Thus are created communities, the smallest of which is the city, the ultimate end of which is happiness. But how should the city be ruled, made prosperous, and the life of its inhabitants reorganized to achieve happiness? This is the subject of Farābī's treatise, *Aphorisms of the Statesman* [1961]. Written in the style of the "Mirrors for Princes" literature, it asks the central question of the *falasifa's* political philosophy: what is the objective of human association? According to Farābī, the most important aspect of the family household is the associations which it fosters: husband and wife, master and slave, parents and children, owner and property. He who is asked to rule, arrange, and manage all of the parts is the master of the household. He is called ruler and his duties are like those of the ruler of the city.

Household management in Farābī's view is a political function like the government of the state, and its object is to lead the different members to a higher level of well-being. The analogy with the human body comes easily, with the people's happiness like a healthy body for the individual. Physical health requires also an enlightened brain to perceive the healthiest way to organize one's life and a heart to make the body respond to the intellect. The leader thus exercises both the functions of the brain and the heart (intelligence and leadership) in order to guide the citizens, who are like the limbs. All the parts are necessary to the body, but each one is adapted to a particular function. In carrying out their duties, both the ruler of the household and the ruler of the state must create perfect citizens by showing them the way to true happiness, which can be achieved by training individuals to fulfill their natural functions. This is the essence of justice, which is nothing other than the rationalization of forces, and rationalizing life is that to which every man should aspire. However, the rational ordering of one's actions should not be directed toward economic self-sufficiency but rather toward the achievement of ideal government.

After Farābī, Islamic political thought continued to follow the Greek tradition. Ibn Sīnā, taking his inspiration from Bryson's work, wrote a short treatise on *tadbīr al-manzil* in which he considered the elements of the political community, social organization, and the management of income and expenditure, dividing society into two categories: a leisure class and a class who must work in commerce and industry in order to supply the city with its means of subsistence. This stratification closely reflected the aristocratic social structure of the time. In this hierarchy, governmental functions have the highest status, followed by intellectual professions such as astrology and medicine and ending with the military nobility. Those in a privileged status must allocate part of their surplus to zakāt, a purifying tax used for the relief of the poor and one of the five pillars of Islam, and reserve the rest to provide for their future. Ibn Sīnā maintained that expenditures should conform to justice, which requires eschewing overindulgence and vice and following a middle way, the way of the *iqtiṣād*.[6]

The influence of Aristotle's *Nicomachean Ethics* and, to a lesser extent, Bryson's treatise, is evident in the work of Miskawayh (d. 1030), who substituted individual rationality for the traditional Islamic commitment to a community presided over by a prophet. Miskawayh identified reason as the source of truth and applied it to a determination of appropriate conduct, an approach which endorsed reasoned conclusions over blind obedience. He could have found in his society the same individual and collective behavior which Aristotle had found in his and carried them into a new systhesis, but, once again, the Aristotelian ideas expressed in the fifth book of the *Nicomachean Ethics*, as well as Bryson's, seem to have been destined to exert only a limited influence on Muslim economic thought.

Like his predecessors, Miskawayh's work offered little analytic refinement. His treatise did not deal with problems of production, exchange, or profit but was a kind of anthropology of happiness in which he sought to identify good and evil by deliberative reason free from dogmatism. In order to understand happiness or the good life, he said, one has to understand that man is ultimately composed of a body and a soul and that, as long as he is on earth, the two are inseparably linked. It follows that one cannot have a good life without external goods — power, fortune, and health — but such goods will soon become an impediment in the quest for happiness if one accumulates more than a sufficiency for the normal practice of virtuous activity. Man therefore needs reason in order to place limits on the two powers of his soul — the irascible and the affective. Reason is used to determine the temperate level of affective behavior, and this temperate balance is called justice. This notion of rational equilibrium was applied by Miskawayh to every aspect of human existence, and he tried to arrive at a golden mean in everything. "The truly just man," he asserted, "is he who strives for a just equilibrium in his deliberations, his acts, and in everything in which he is involved in such a way as to avoid any disproportion" [Arkoun, 1973]. Citing Aristotle rather obscurely, he defines money as a mean that which mutely achieves justice. Man, on the other hand, is endowed with the power of speech, and he uses it as a medium to evaluate all of his transactions in order to regulate them according to a system of correct and just proportions.

In his book, *Shawāmil*, he explained that it was the division of labor which gave rise to the need for a medium of exchange that could be used to purchase other labor. Because of its relative scarcity and durability, together with its ease of melting, gold has been preferred for this purpose above all other commodities. Silver, he maintained, serves as the deputy (*khalīfa*) of gold because of its divisibility. He then presents the strange idea that the value of gold is ten times — at the same weight — the value of silver because 10 and 1 are the extremes of the ten digits. In this discussion of prices, he asserts that if they "change from one good to another, it is in order that associations and transactions can be properly carried out and so that one can determine what to give and what to take. Money equalizes values by adding to one what it draws from the other to achieve a balance between them" [Brunshvig, 1967, p. 114].

Ghāzalī, who was outside the tradition of the *falāsifa*, also approached human conduct in the acquisition of money in terms of the golden mean. He advised seeking a mean between two excesses in all activities in order to cultivate the virtues of wisdom, temperance, courage, and justice. He therefore recommended that individuals not seek wealth for its own sake and that they not engage in commerce in search of opulence but only to satisfy reasonable needs. This is as far as Ghazālī goes in dealing with the ethics of the *falāsifa*, and he returns to the precepts of the Sharī'a in treating exchange relations from the point of view of true believer, stating that one who must earn his living should know what is and is not permitted in matters of sales. Monopoly is condemned as an inherent source of disorder. Influenced by a religious tradition hostile to the hoarding of money, he failed to recognize the functions of money as a store of value and as a reserve unit of purchasing power. Gold and silver currencies, which are not useful in themselves, exist, he said, to circulate as a medium of exchange and as common measures of value. He vigorously condemned as illegal the issuing of debased money, which he compared to robbery. This sin, he says, will fall on those who issue it, and he advised anyone receiving a debased coin to interrupt its circulation by throwing it into a well in order to limit the damages.

This brief survey of Islamic literature has indicated the way in which Muslim authors have approached economic subjects. We saw first the efforts of some writers to deal with economic subjects through the precepts of the Sharī'a and the difficulty they experienced in freeing their analyses from the grasp of religious tradition. At first, the traditional commitment to concepts of community interest overshadowed attempts to extrapolate economic principles from the market mechanism and prevented the emergence of a scientific economics. Even the *hisba* manuals continued to reflect this lack of development and were no more than catalogues repeating the same refrains about weights and measures. Thus the principle of economic rationality was not extended to an analysis of the public process or to a market mechanism but was confined to discussions of private commercial practices external to the Learned City.

We have also seen how the Mirrors for Princes literature, so rich in economic statements from the point of view of the management of the state's affairs through the political process, offered penetrating advice on public expenditures and their potential perverse effects, but failed, in the end, to free its orientation from confinement to the prince's interests and develop an independent economic discourse. On the other hand, the contact with Greek philosophy, if it liberated Muslim philosophers from the yoke of religious dogma, precipitated their willing submission to the masters of Greece. For the followers of Plato and Aristotle, the primacy of rationality replaced that of the holy scriptures, and Greek economic ideas, taken more or less unaltered, were applied to studies of ideal associations congenial to man as a political being. Thus, economic thought throughout this period was no more than a humble servant of politics.

The discussions about the ideal city and the analyses of its components and organization, though modelled on foreign patterns, never lost sight of contemporary reality. Farābī, for example, in thinking about the ideal state, had in mind the extinguished glory of the Abasside califate which he advocated reforming in the perspective of Plato's philosopher-king. The merit of the varied writings of the *falāsifa*, on the other hand, lay in their recognition of what the Greek tradition could offer in efforts to deal with the crisis of the Muslim city. In this setting, economic thought was elaborated within the limits of the status which Muslim thinkers gave to the theme of the ends of life and, with a paucity of ideas, many were content merely to repeat Aristotle and Plato. Committed as they were to speculative reason, these thinkers did not try to deal with concrete facts, and their writings represent a step backward from the thought developed by the theologians. As normative as the strictures of the theologians might have been, they had been developed in close contact with the religious, political, social, and economic life of the community, and they succeeded, more or less, in dealing with ideas fundamental to economic analysis. Having adhered more closely to reality, the theologians' concern with economic matters was a reflection of the practical situations faced by members of the community seeking to conduct themselves in conformity to the norms ordained by the Qur'ān.

Four centuries after Farābī, the califate was no longer an issue, and speculation on its reform in Greek terms had become irrelevant. By this time, another reality, the fragmentation of the Muslim medieval world, absorbed the attention of a thinker who was both a distinguished jurist trained in traditional Islamic beliefs and a man of action closely involved with the powerful men of that time. As one vitally concerned with the conditions of the Islamic *umma*, he was a privileged witness to the events shaking the Islamic community. This man was Ibn Khaldūn (1332–1406). Everything in this man's background predisposed him not to be a disciple of the Greco-Arab philosophy, for his philosophical outlook did not rest upon the same premises and was not oriented toward the same objectives. Although he did not reject the *falāsifa* principle that man exists in order to attain ultimate happiness, the author of the *Muqaddima* [1958] was knowledgeable in philosophical debate and hostile to abstract arguments divorced from social reality. Ibn Khaldūn was a chief justice, but he did not completely adhere to juristic tenets which required reality to submit to the exigencies of economic rules drawn from principles of law. He was neither a philosopher nor a jurist nor a believer in political ethics because, for him, moralizing solutions suit only societies not limited to force and violence but where there is also room for speech. There should, he felt, be reliance on discourse as well. These views led him ineluctably toward a new approach to explain the birth, the glory, and the decline of civilization, to which he gave the name of '*Ilm al-'Umrān*, or science of society.

Later commentators,[7] dazzled by the importance of Ibn Khaldūn's works, plunged into analyzing isolated aspects of his writings from the points of view of specific fields of knowledge and, in the process, fragmented its unity. As a result, there emerged Ibn Khaldun sociologists, historians, and economists, the latter by turns theoreticians of growth and development, of public finance, and forerunners of Marx and Keynes. One could make a selection of economic propositions from Ibn Khaldūn's works that could form a separate treatise, but separating his economic views from the rest of his works would not make Ibn Khaldūn an economist ahead of his time and would only confuse his ideas. In order to justify such a separation, that is to say, to be able to confer upon Ibn Khaldūn the title of forerunner in the development of economics, it would be necessary to find in his work economic analysis which can be understood as part of an economic system constituting a whole. This is far from the case, and expressions like *ma'āch* (means of subsistence) or *kasb* (acquisition of wealth) have general economic significance only when considered within the context of Ibn Khaldun's orientation. Moreover, his preoccupation with commerce and taxes, though relevant, was simply another approach to "matters of sovereignty" and, in this respect, merely another "mirror" for a prince woven into the web of history.

Ibn Khaldūn was conscious of what separated his approach from that of his predecessors. He asserted that Ṭurṭūshī's method was inadequate to penetrate the laws of society because it didn't go straight to the point. "Ṭurṭūshī," he said, "went round and round the subject...prowled around the issue without being able to discover it. He didn't understand clearly what he wanted to do." At issue were the incentives and mechanisms that underlie social development. The ideas of Turtūshī and the *falasifa* were inadequate, he said, because, like the reflections on political action and the conduct of sovereigns which have held the attention of thinkers throughout history, they did not grasp the realities of power. Only a knowledge of the relevant aspects of society — economic, political, ethical, and religious — would reveal the nature of power and guide political action.

According to Ibn Khaldūn, two different kinds of social milieu have characterized human development, the '*umrān al-badaoui* (nomad civilization) and the '*umran al-hadhari* (urban civilization). The difference between the two is based upon their *ma'āch*, a synthesizing concept into which is woven both the means of subsistence and the relationships between man and man, and man and nature. The social group is made possible by the productive activities which provide man's subsistence: farming, animal breeding, hunting and fishing, fabricating goods, and exchanging products, all of which are encompassed by *ma'āch*. This conception of *ma'āch* is central to Ibn Khaldūn's philosophy and comprehends the qualitative and quantitative differences between a natural economy oriented toward self-sufficiency and an unnatural one oriented toward the accumulation of unnecessary goods, the eager pursuit of profit, and a propensity for luxury. This dichotomy is reminiscent of Aristotle's distinction between *oikonomia*, the science of the acquisition of wealth oriented toward the good of the community, and *chrematistics*, the science of the unlimited accumulation of profit. But whereas Aristotle's conception is static, Ibn Khaldūn's is a dynamic one. Aristotle pictured a family unit in an ideal agrarian society, whereas Ibn Khaldūn's view encompassed the totality of human society in its historical development. On the one hand, Ibn Khaldūn dealt with the art of managing the production and distribution of wealth while, on the other, he developed a realistic analysis of the successive phases in the growth of human society. One can therefore understand why he had little regard for the science of *tadbīr* or *oikonomia* as a branch of practical philosophy, preferring instead his science of society which had a historical dimension. When he drew on juridical science or treatises on social relations, it was solely for the purpose of validating historical data or investigating the nature of society.

In elaborating the *'umran al-badaoui*, Ibn Khaldūn dealt with a natural economy oriented to production for the satisfaction of primitive needs, with economic activities based upon farming, fishing, and hunting. Neither money, taxes, market, nor state exists at this stage. Going hand in hand with these material conditions are the moral qualities of simplicity, courage, and independence. At this level, civilization is characterized as *'Aṣabīya*, a political force which will enable a tribe to become a conquering one and its chief the leader of a state. *'Aṣabīya* inhibits the emergence of the professional soldier, hence the absence of a standing army and a bureaucratic class. But this stage of social development will not last indefinitely because the tribal community will be transformed by changes in its means of subsistence. In this way it creates the conditions and contradictions which generate the destruction of its own characteristics. For men, in order to satisfy their needs, must cooperate, and the division of labor which results from cooperation leads them to produce more than is necessary. The resulting desire for wealth and the taste for comfort propels the tribal community toward urban civilization, a shift

from a self-sufficient natural economy, one oriented toward the satisfaction of basic needs, to a consumption-market economy.

Ibn Khaldūn thus counterposes rural and urban civilization, the first
being the primitive state of the second. A sedentary, urban economy
characterized by the birth of cities and the state emerges in the second
phase. As the city grows, so do its income and population. Production is
characterized by a greater division of labor to satisfy increasing demand
which, in turn, gives rise to more specialization and higher wages and
profits. Heightened economic activity requires the introduction of money
and production oriented toward the satisfaction of ever-increasing needs.
Developments in the sciences and arts now permit the labor force to
produce goods to support refinements of taste and improvements in
comfort, and urban people begin to build palaces fitted with running
water and to surround themselves with luxury goods. The virile and moral
virtues of the nomad are replaced by the depravity and vice of the
urbanite who, subverted by pleasure, luxury and idleness, lacks the
fortitude to defend himself. The vigor and solidarity which carried nomad
peoples to the urban stage of development disappears, the beginning of
the fall. Extravagant expenditures by the sovereign and the thirst for
well-being of the city's inhabitants exceed the revenues of the state. In
order to survive, the state is forced to increase its income by raising taxes
and seizing private property, measures which weaken the subjects and,
ultimately, the power of the sovereign. The economy now begins to
decay, markets wither, and urbanites abandon the city. Urban civilization
disintegrates and falls before the onslaught of a conquering people who
have the qualities of the nomand civilization.

The economy in Ibn Khaldūn's thought is not static. It changes, transforms itself, evolves along with the civilization it shapes. Its status, or the
one Ibn Khaldūn gave it, in the succession of stages in the development
of civilization denotes his low opinion of it. Whereas the economy plays
little role in the tribal and growth phases of human development, it is the
main cause of the phase characterized by decay and the fall of dynasties.

Ibn Khaldūn was a convinced advocate of royal authority and the
enhancement of its power, but he was confronted with a destabilized,
fragmented, and enfeebled Muslim world. His hope was to establish a
well-organized and just state with a powerful sovereign, a stable
monarchy that would endure. But the achievement of such a goal would
require overcoming the curse which comes with it, for it is this very
concentration of power which leads to the downfall of dynasties. Prevailing in the present only postpones disaster to the future. Ibn Khaldūn
was thus a man torn between the hope that a monarchy could establish

a solid base of power and his conviction that, in the end, economic development would frustrate that hope. For that reason, his "economic" thought was an attempt to understand and explain the operation of the economic mechanism in the urban phase, in which money, demand, trade, production, taxes, and consumption are characterized by the dimensions of the havoc they cause, undermining and perverting a society rather than strengthening it. Better knowledge of economic processes at this stage is what is lacking to enable the state to resist the forces which hasten its downfall.

This analysis of human history in terms of social and economic causes is found also in the work of Maqrīzī, an Egyptian thinker of the late fourteenth and early fifteenth century. A prolific author, he produced several encyclopedic historical works. Our interest, however, is in two of his books which were inspired by his own experience, his *Treatise on Famines* [1940] and his *Treatise on Money* [1930]. The author's professional career and the political power structure of the day, as well as a variety of scourges which devastated Egypt, all influenced the orientation of his works.

Muḥtasib of Cairo, Maqrīzī was in a position to observe very closely the functioning of the economy and to obtain precise information about exchange and monetary practices. The plague to which his daughter succumbed at the age of six probably led him to take a special interest in the causes of the natural calamities and social crises so widespread in his time, considered the darkest in the history of Egypt. Under the reign of Barquq, moral corruption and social repression accompanied the feudalization of the political system. Both political and economic power in this period were monopolized by a small minority who enriched themselves and created scarcity by their speculative activities. These machinations must have filled Maqrizi, a Muslim jurist, with feelings of outrage and revulsion. His status as *muḥtasib*, a position at the very center of political power, undoubtedly gave him an understanding denied to others of the events sweeping before him, and his talent as an historian enabled him to record and analyze them as probably no one else could.

He wrote his book on famines, he said, in one night, covering such crises from antiquity to the fifteenth century. He began by asking whether the severe famine of 1428 A.D. had any historical precedent. The popular mind, he noted, has a tendency to convince itself that its agony is unprecedented and has no remedy. He therefore decided to demonstrate that Egypt had repeatedly experienced horrors of the same kind and that their repetition proceeds less often from natural causes than from poor administration. He described a succession of famines in Egypt from pre-Islamic times to the advent of Islam, giving particular attention to the dreadful social repercussions which result from natural disasters, food scarcity, and high prices. Coming then to current crises, he maintained that their origin lay not so much, as commonly assumed, in natural events — devastating invasions of locusts, low average rainfall, or failures in the life-giving floods of the Nile — but in events of human origin, political as well as economic. To begin with, he pointed to the institutionalization of corrupt practices in the apparatus of the state and to the venality of administrative and religious officials which lead to increases in taxes, the impoverishment of the farmers, and to decreased production and rising prices, from which follow food scarcities and lower revenues. A second cause, he said, is the greed of state officials whose land speculation results in increases in ground rent and costs of ploughing and seed which, in turn, lead to land abandonment, lower production, and rising prices. Finally, he pointed to a third cause, the debasement of the money supply through the proliferation of copper currency.

Maqrīzī next turned to an examination of the stratification of Egyptian society in the fifteenth century, and listed the following classes: (1) government officials; (2) shopkeepers and the leisure class; (3) wholesale merchants; (4) farmers; (5) teachers and students; (6) wage earners; and (7) the poor. He ends the treatise with recommendations, both political and monetary, in the form of advice for rulers which, he felt, would remedy the evils that hung so heavily over his epoch.

In discussing the causes of crises, Marqrīzī dealt with questions concerning the monetary system, approximating theories recognized by modern economic science, such as the quantity theory of money, Gresham's law, and the difference between nominal and real price. However, little attention[8] has been given to the concepts associated with his new vision of reality, his interest in monetary problems, or his dynamic approach to social organization. Maqrīzī's originality lay in his rejection of determinism and his insistence upon the primacy of political and economic factors in the evolution of human society. He concluded that crises were not the result of divine wrath but grew out of political, social, and economic phenomena. His discourses reflect the interdisiplinary views of a thinker at once a jurist, historian, chronicler, and direct witness to the events he sought to analyze. He is an author who, unlike Ibn Khaldūn, was not a celebrity and whose works were known only to specialists. Writing outside the intellectual establishment, he introduced a new methodological approach that defied the straightjacket of disciplinary classification. He was not solely a historian, nor quite a sociologist nor an economist, but all of them at the same time. It is perhaps an exaggeration to credit him with the competence of a specialist in monetary theory since his treatment of monetary crises is not free from the powerful ethical and theological bias of the fifteenth century.

Maqrīzī lived in an epoch, a turning point in Egyptian history, which saw the inauguration of the monetary age but which had not yet freed itself from a religious orientation. The importance of monetary disorders in his theories reflects not only the sharpness of their impact on his consciousness but also his determined opposition to the debasement of gold and silver coinage. According to Maqrīzī, the history of economic categories is a drama in which unfolds extremely complicated ethical, metaphysical, and economic relationships. First came the genesis of money which, he asserted, coincided with the genesis of the universe. "It is reported," he wrote, "that it was Adam who first minted the *dinār* and the *dirham*," and he added that "subsistence was only assured with the beneficial circumstances made possible by those two coins." In all the cities of Egypt during both pre-Islamic and Islamic reigns, he wrote, gold had never ceased to serve as the exclusive monetary standard for evaluting labor and prices. There is thus a historical justification for the power of gold which, in spite of the passage of time, always managed to keep its value. From this pure ideal form of currency one can only turn to a corrupted, spoiled form. From the alchemical perspective, pure gold becomes also the guarantee of the perfection of sovereignty, and Marqrīzī tells the story about Ibn Ṭūlūn's discovery of treasure with a text in hieroglyphics which he deciphered as follows. "I am Mr. So-and-So, son of So-and-So, the king who separated gold from its alloys and impurities. Whoever wishes to know the superiority of my reign over his must consider how much the standard of fineness of my gold coins is superior to his. For he who refines gold from its alloys is purified himself during his lifetime and after his death."

The quasi-sacred status attributed to gold emphasized the dimensions of the disaster which the Egyptian author envisages when gold currency is replaced by copper,the reign of simulacrum. When Maqrīzī recounted the historical context in which copper coinage had been introduced to serve "to calculate exchanges when it was necessary to deal with mercandise of a very small value beng sold for a *dirham* or for a fraction of a *dirham*," he wondered that an odd money chosen for its divisibility could serve as a substitute for gold and silver coins and its circulation, as a result of the favor it gained among the people, expand so much in the reign of Barqūq "that it became the major currency of the country." So here is the bad money driving away the good, but this principle (later to became Gresham's law), according to Maqrīzī, is not limited to currencies

but applies as well to the political sphere, where the same cyclic retro-
gression takes place. For the golden age and the gold currency of Ibn
Tulūn were driven out by the silver money of Saladin, which in turn was
replaced by the copper coins of the age of Barquq. The reign of bad
money evicts not only two other currencies but destroys as well all of the
social, religious, and moral values that form the foundation of the city.

Thus Maqrīzī formulated a generalized Gresham's law applying to
all facets of life. "I would have you know," he wrote, "that the final
stabilization of the standard of living of the population on Egyptian
territory has been achieved simply by creating copper coinage to serve as
a counterpart to all articles for sale and all sorts of food...." [These
coins] are used for farm rents, for interest on commercial capital, for all
state taxes and to fix the cost of labor, of whatever kind. For, to the
Egyptians there is nothing but that currency to evaluate all their
wealth...." But he asserted that "it is a recent innovation, a disaster
which has just been invented, which has no foundation in any nation
which has received the word of a prophet, an enterprise without legal
sanction.... No doubt," he added, "he who invented it was following
neither ancestral tradition nor the ideas of any human being." And he
went on, "This change has caused the disappearance of joy and the
suppression of beauty in the world, reducing fortunes to nothing and
spoiling their pleasure. The public drifts toward mediocrity while the
community is in danger of being exposed to want and humiliation." It
would be hard to imagine a stronger indictment of the dominance of
felous (copper coins). "Gold and silver currencies," he writes, "are the
primary legal forms of money, while the *felous* is merely an accessory
which takes on the appearance of the real thing. Thus that which was
made an accessory has become the principal."

In this manner Maqrīzī sets in opposition money which coincides with
nature and that which is given its value by law, natural value as opposed
to nominal value. He argues that copper coinage is totally dependent
upon legislative action, a dependency so total, so absolute, so complete,
that it may be likened to a kind of servitude to the despot. Thus, the
circulation of the *felous*, like power, is a form of despotism, and this
correspondence between the reign of arbitrary money and its political
equivalent is a theme that runs throughout his treatise on famine. "If one
considers the prices of goods in terms of gold and silver," he says, "they
will be found to be very little higher, but if one takes account of the
swindle by which the people have been victimized by the influx of copper
coinage, no greater catastrophe or frightful reality could be imagined.
This is what has caused the general situation, what has disarranged the

conditions of life and has led the people, little by little, to decline and ruin."

Maqrīzī's treatise is a symptom of the collapse of the profound ideological connections between economic concerns and other aspects of life. Existence seems to reduce itself to economics. There is a political economy of the totality of life. Thus the ideas of this critic of copper money take on an economic significance for the economist, but this in itself is a reflection of an existential situation. Crises were becoming more frequent and their effects cumulative. Beginning with the crisis of his time, Maqrīzī drew up an inventory of past catastrophes, no longer accepting versions based on conventional wisdom any more than he accepted the tyranny of copper money. Instead, he went further in search of fundamentals, for the source of intrinsic value, to gold, the historic standard of measure. From the beginning, history is for him nothing but a long descent, and the only solution he could conceive of was to return to the gold standard.

We note from this account that there was no break between Maqrīzī and his teacher, Ibn Khaldūn, regarding the latter's conception of the link between the economy and the progress of civilization. Both treat economic changes as inextricably bound up in the evolution of Muslim society and its "progress" as nothing but a long decline toward a worse situation. For both, salvation lay only in a return to the past. In Ibn Khaldūn's thought this return is to a strengthened power of the state through better understanding of economic mechanisms, while in Maqrīzī's it was to a monetary system based on gold consistent with its ancient status. Together they presided, each in his own way, over a crucial period in the history of the Arab-Muslim world, the beginning of its downfall. That period is important not only for a better understanding of the past, but in a very significant way, for the present as well, because the current high favor that surrounds Ibn Khaldūn and, to a lesser degree, Maqrizi, is not justified so much by the modern character of their works as by the medieval aspects of the contemporary Muslim world which seem to find in their analyses a realistic image of the conditions prevailing in the Medieval Islamic world.

Contemporary Islamic Economics

The last 30 years have witnessed the emergence of numerous independent Muslim states. However, their continued reliance upon Western political and economic models for the achievement of economic prosperity, well-being, and the establishment of social justice has not produced anticipated results. More recently, to the more marked socioeconomic problems have been added new ones: growing regional, national and international disparities, a wider and wider technological gap, the tapping of nonrenewable resources on an enormous scale, cultural alienation and dependency, and many others. This painful situation, reinforced by feelings of powerlessness in taking up the challenge of modernity, has impelled the elite as well as the masses to draw on Islam as a religion in order to restore to the Islamic way of life and tradition of thought a vitality appropriate to accelerated economic development. From a focal point for political mobilization against colonial aggression, Islam has now become an ideological refuge for the accomplishment of a variety of tasks. It is in this framework that a contemporary current of thought has sought in Islam inspiration for economic models for the building of a new social and economic order which would find their reference in a religous heritage in which the material and the spiritual are unified.

What is now called "Islamic economics" is an offspring of the reformist thought of the first half of the twentieth century developed in several countries of the Muslim world and has for pioneers well-known thinkers such as Afghani, Ikbal, Bana, Said Kotb, and others. In analyzing the social, economic, and political conditions in their respective countries, which were dominated by the Western colonial world, these writers concluded that the backward state of the Muslim world, compared to the Western world, was a result of economic factors and that a choice would have to be made among the economic systems that have assured progress elsewhere. Viewing their own countries as victims of capitalist expansion, they could only reject the principles upon which it is founded. Although socialism promised to satisfy some of their aspirations, many of its ideological principles were objectionable. In any case, they didn't wait long to distinguish between socialism and communism. Though tolerant toward the former, they have been openly hostile to the latter. The objective became to find an original economic course different from both liberalism and communism which would combine modern methods of management with the resources and values of Islam, the abandonment of which was seen by some as the cause of the unfavorable conditions in the Islamic world.

Since the beginning of the 1960s, a generation of professional economists,[9] many funded by government grants, has conducted research with an exactness claimed to be scientific in a new discipline which, on the one hand, offers an Islamic critique of Western economics and, on the other, seeks to develop economic theories that reflect Islamic principles and values. The change has been from a simple exposition of the economic teachings of Islam to what has come to be called "Islamic economics" in which *homo Islamicus* has replaced the sovereignty of the neo-classical *homo economicus*, that is to say, the substitution of a responsible and altruistic attitude for a selfish one dominated by the desperate drive for profit. Starting from the assumption that, in Islam, ethics commands economics, Islamic scholars have under consideration a model where individuals are guided in their decisions about production, exchange, and consumption by certain norms of behavior [Kuran, 1983] and they expect that some of the problems related to efficiency and equity will be solved if individuals are induced to follow these norms. They have included also in the management of the state's finances the precept of zakāt, a tax on wealth and income, and the prohibition of interest. From this brief description, it will be clear that behind this model lies the conviction that Islam constitutes, for these scholars, the ideal life as they conceive it through the example of the Prophet and the four caliphs.

The return to the Qur'ān and the Sunna as guides to economic conduct in the modern world, in spite of the fact that these scriptures do not contain economic theories and that even during the Prophet's time a system of restrictions had to be developed to lessen the impact of conflicts, an indication that even at the beginning of Islam reliance on norms of behavior was ineffective, raises the question as to whether Islamic thinkers are involved in a debate in which they confuse myth and history.

Whereas Western political economy formulated its concepts on the foundation of historical reality, Islamic economics appears as a nebula with no connections with reality except its ties to the precepts of the Qur'ān, the injunctions of the Prophet, and the idealized conduct of the four enlightened caliphs. When they deal with practical problems, the new economists of modern Islam, without passing their theories through the sieve of critical analysis, tend to leave ethics to politics. Conscious that the introduction of moral values into the sphere of economics will not be achieved with the wave of a magic wand, they have turned to education as the way to inculcate ethical values in children. It is thus the state which must see to the transformation of the individual to the end that he will adapt to the model. One is torn in these multiple contradictions between the ideals of justice, equity, and liberty and the constraints which often oppose their achievement.

Conclusion

In their efforts to build an original and living model, contemporary Muslim economists are but reproducing, at a few centuries' removed, the bitter conflict which has never ceased to put in opposition in the Muslim city economic imperatives, on the one hand, and the ethical, political, and social values of Islam, on the other. In reviewing the history of Islamic economic thought, we have tried to identify the place it has been accorded in Muslim society and the attitudes adopted by Muslim thinkers on the problem of man's livelihood.

If, in the beginning of Islam, Muslim society reflected the image of the ideal city in action, the expansion of the empire, the increase in economic activities, and the complexities of urban life led to inevitable changes. The *hisba* handbooks provide us with a useful reference not only to the way Muslim society has perceived the economy but also to the way it has tried to make the economy, which tended to become uncontrollable, conform to the revealed law. In the Mirrors for Princes literature, a widened perspective on the economy led to a discourse on justice as a guarantee of the permanence of the state and the power of the sovereign. The *falāsifa*, inspired by the Greeks, sought to incorporate the economic domain into their theories on the way to make the perfect man fit the ideal perfect state. With Ibn Khaldūn and Maqrīzī, who reflect the new conditions of the Muslim world, economic forces appear as fundamental elements in the analysis of the problems of the state and emphasis is placed on the need to control their effects. Finally, modern Muslim economists, still obsessed with the view of the economy that is so characteristic of Islamic thought, see in the return to the ideal of Islam the best way to adapt the individual to ethical norms.

Notes

1. Schumpeter [1954] mentions Ibn Khaldūn twice [pp. 136, 788].

2. "In that manner," says Charnay [1978, p.99], "a commutative pact would be the foundation of the Muslim social fabric and the fundamental mover of its dynamic, of the genesis and birth of the social relations. The personal relations humanizing the institutions would be the projection of that archetypal relation founded on calculating realism and leading to an agreement between two parties..." [see Torrey, 1892].

3. My interpretation here follows Gardet [1978, p. 330]. It is a matter of solidarity and collectivity, concepts which stress cooperation and mutual aid, not only within the framework of the family and the craft guild but within the framework of the production and consumption of goods. The farmer and the craftsman must consider themselves associates rather than adversaries of those to whom they sell the product of their labor.

4. Miquel [1973, I, p. 109] cites Mā-shā-Allāh [770–820], a Jew who wrote a book in which he developed an astrological theory of the mechanism of prices.

5. The purpose of such rules was to prevent unscrupulous persons from obtaining goods at too low a price by persuading vendors coming to the market that the current market price would not make worth their while carrying their wares farther.

6. Synonym for justice meaning the middle way, *iqtiṣād* has come to mean economic knowledge and management in the contemporary Arab world.
7. Spengler [1963–64], Somogyi [1965], Haddad [1977], Andic [1975], and Abdus-satar [1973].
8. Oualalou [1976].
9. For example, Naqvi [1981], Rahman [1974–76], Awan [1983], and Abdulmanan [1981].

References

Abdulmanan, M. *Institutional Setting of Islamic Economic Order*. Jeddah: International Centre for Research in Islamic Economics, 1981.

Abdus-satar, M. "Ibn Khaldūn's Contribution to Economic Thought." In *Contemporary Aspects of Economic Thinking in Islam*. Gary, IN: American Trust Publication, 1976, pp. 121–29.

Andic, S. "A Fourteenth Century Sociology of Public Finance." *Public Finance* 1:1965, 22–44.

Arkoun, M. *Contribution à l'étude de l'humanisme arabe au IVe/Xe siècle: Miskawayh philosophe et historien*. Paris: Vrin, 1970.

Awan, Akhtar A. *Equality, Effiency, and Property Ownership in the Islamic Economic System*. Lanham, MD: University Press of America, 1983.

Brunschvig, R. "Les conceptions monetaires chez les juristes musulmans." *Arabica* 14:1967, 113–43.

Charnay, Jean Paul. *Sociologie religieuse de l'islam*. Paris: Sindbad, 1978.

Dawwānī. *Akhlāk-I-Jalālī*. Trans. from the Persian by W. F. Thompson as *Practical Philosophy of the Muhammadan People*. London: Oriental Translation Fund of Great Britain and Ireland, 1839.

Dimasqi. *Kitāb al-Ishāra ila Mahāsin al-Tijāra* (The Book of Knowledge of the Beauties of Commerce and of Cognizance of Good and Bad Merchandise and Falsifications). Cairo: Matba'at al Mu'ayid, 1977. Trans. into German by H. Ritter as "Ein arabishes Handbuch der Handelswissenschaft." *Der Islam* 7:1917, 1–91.

Farābī. *Fusūl al-mandani* (Aphorisms of the Statesman). Ed. with English translation, introduction, and notes by D. M. Dunlop. London: Cambridge University Press, 1961.

Gardet, Louis. *Islam: religion et communauté*. Paris: Desclée de Brouwer, 1978.

Ghazali. *Ihyā ulūm al-Dīn*. 4 vols. Cairo: Matba'at al Sarkyya, 1932.

Gimaret, Daniel. "Les théologiens musulmans face à la hausse des prix." *Journal of the Economic and Social History of the Orient* 3:1979, 330–38.

Haddad, L. "A Fourteenth-Century Theory of Economic Growth and Development." *Kyklos* 30:1977, 195–213.

Ibn Khaldūn, A. *An Introduction to History*. 3 vols. Trans. by F. Rosenthal. London: Routledge & Kegan Paul, 1958.

Ibn Sīna. *Kitāb-al Siyāsa*. Published with an introduction by Louis Cheikho in *Al-Mashriq* 21, 22, 23:1906, 966–73; 1037–43; 1073–78.

Ibn Taymiyya. *Al Hisbatu-fī-l-Islām*. Kuwait: Maktabat dār-L-argam, 1973.

Kuran, T. "Behavioral Norms in the Islamic Doctrine of Economics: A Critique." *Journal of Economic Behavior and Organization* 4:1983, 353–79.

Kurshid, A., ed. *Studies in Islamic Economics*. Leicester: University of Jeddah and the Islamic Foundation, 1980.

Maqrizi. *Kitāb Shudhūr al-'uqud fi dikr al-nuqūd* (Treatise on Money). Constantine, 1930. Trans. into French by Daniel Eustache as "Les perles des colliers; étude de numismatique et de metrologie musulmans." *Hesperis Tamuda* 10:1969, 95–189.

————. *Ighāthatu-l-umma bi kashf-l-ghumma* (Treatise on Famines). Cairo: Ziada et Sayyal, 1940. Trans. into French by Gaston Wiet as "Le traite des famines." *Journal of the Economic and Social History of the Orient* 5:1962, 1–90.

Miquel, André. *Geographie du monde musulman*. 2 vols. Paris: Mouton, 1973.

Naqvi, S. N. H. *Ethics and Economics, An Islamic Synthesis*. Leicester: Islamic Foundation, 1981.

Oualalou, Fathallah. *La pensée socio-économique d'el-maqrizi*. Rabat: *Bulletin economique et social du maroc*, 1976.

Plessner, M. *Der Oikonomikos des Neupythagoreers "Bryson" und sein Enfluss auf die Islamische Wissenschaft*. Heidenberg: C. Winter, 1928.

Rahman, Afzal-ur. *Economic Doctrines of Islam*. 3 vols. Lahore: Islamic Publications, 1974–76.

Rosenthal, E. I. J. *Political Thought in Medieval Islam, An Introductory Outline*. London: Cambridge University Press, 1958.

Schumpeter, Joseph A. *History of Economic Analysis*. Ed. by Elizabeth B. Schumpeter. New York: Oxford University Press, 1954.

Somogyi, Joseph. "Economic Theory in Classical Arabic Literature." *Studies in Islam* (Delhi) 2:1965, 1–6.

Spengler, J. J. "Economic Thought of Islam: Ibn Khaldūn." *Comparative Studies in Society and History* 16:1963–64, 268–305.

Torrey, C. Charles. *The Commercial and Theological Terms in the Koran*. Leyden: E. J. Brill, 1892.

Turtūshī, Abu Bark Muhammad. *Sirāj-al-mulūk*. Ed. and trans. into Spanish as *Lampara de los principes* by M. Alarcon. 2 vols. Madrid: Instituto de Valencia de don Juan, 1930–31.

Tusī, Nasiruddin. *Akhalāk-I-Nāsirī*. Trans. from the Persian by G. M. Wickens as *The Nasirean Ethics*. London: Allen & Unwin, 1964.

Weber, Max. *Économie et societé*. Paris: Plon, 1975.

Ya'koub, Abou Youssef. *Kitāb-al-kharāj*. Trans. into French by E. Fagnan as *Livre de l'impôt foncier*. Paris: Geuthner, 1921.

Commentary by Timur Kuran

Continuity and Change in Islamic Economic Thought

I

Most contemporary economists draw their ideas and inspiration from schools of thought founded within the last three centuries. Among the oldest works they consult are Adam Smith's *Wealth of Nations,* published in 1776, and Karl Marx's *Capital,* published between 1867 and 1894. In striking contrast, Islamic economic thought originated over 14 centuries ago. Moreover, the primacy of the Qur'ān and the Sunna — recollections of Prophet Muḥammad's words and deeds — has been a persistent theme in its development. Not that Islamic economic thought has been an entirely static endeavor; it has exhibited a measure of dynamism, substantive as well as methodological. From the very beginning, however, innovations generated conflict. To this day, major controversies remain unresolved, and Islamic thought continues to harbor a variety of viewpoints and methodologies.

To appreciate the elements of continuity and change in Islamic economic thought, one must first understand the historical context in which it arose and endured. Seventh-century Arabian society was plagued by numerous socioeconomic problems, involving such issues as credit, inheritance, taxation, income distribution, and interpersonal trust. Muḥammad, the founder of the first Islamic community, was a successful merchant who then also became a statesman and administrator. The scores of socioeconomic precepts in the Qur'ān, which the Prophet transmitted into writing over a period of 22 years, address the problems that he and his community grappled with. Yet the precepts appear not as ephemeral solutions applicable to one particular society, but rather as elements of a divinely ordained, eternal social order. Significantly, one hears a single voice in the Qur'ān: that of an omniscient, omnipotent God. This voice articulates very general precepts, without reference to the particularities of seventh-century Arabia.

In many respects, however, the Islamic community underwent momentous changes during the period in which the Qur'ān was being written. These are evident in the evolution of the Qur'ānic precepts. Consider, for instance, the requirement to help one's brethren in their time of need. The early chapters of the Qur'ān, which were produced before the still minuscule community migrated from Mecca to Medina,

called on Muslims to care for one another — without, however, speci-
fying ways in which altruism should be displayed. Formal precepts of
altruism appear in chapters put into writing after the community's re-
settlement, which induced an enormous growth from about 80 people to
many thousands only a year later. One such precept is zakāt, an obligatory tax-cum-subsidy scheme which requires Muslims to donate a portion
of their wealth to the poor and disadvantaged.

The genesis of zakāt is undoubtedly linked to the community's growth
pattern. In a small community, where members live in close contact, have
common experiences, and develop similar preferences, community-wide
sharing tends to emerge even in the absence of formal requirements. In a
large, heterogeneous community, however, community-wide sharing
generally requires some form of coercion; without this, the average individual remains indifferent to the well-being of most members, even
though he may pay lip service to the ideal of religious brotherhood.[1]

Of course, this rationale for the emergence of zakāt is nowhere to be
found in the pages of the Qur'ān, which is not, after all, a treatise in
political economy. Nor does the Qur'ān provide details regarding
practices and institutions it mandates. In practice, therefore, the Islamic
community had considerable latitude in structuring the social order.

In the early years, the Prophet himself played a leading role in matters
of interpretation and implementation. In this connection, he determined
the scope of zakāt and distinguished between just and unjust market
practices. On both counts the record indicates that he took a pragmatic
approach. For instance, he exempted from taxation some indivisible
commodities, including horses and certain jewels, whose market value
could not be assessed easily under conditions of the time.[2] And after
prohibiting the exchange of fresh dates for dry dates, on the grounds that
this might entail exploitation, he reversed his decision in response to
protests.[3]

II

The Prophet's death in 632 A.D. set the Islamic community on a new
path. The Qur'ān was now a closed book, and it could not be interpreted
and reinterpreted as freely as before. Unencumbered by tradition, the
Prophet had routinely broken with the past, on occasion reversing his
own judgments. The leaders who succeeded him, on the other hand,
found that when they introduced changes they risked being accused of
failing to uphold the Prophet's legacy, which was becoming enshrined as
the Sunna. With rival factions trumpeting their loyalty to the Sunna as a

credential for leadership, a consensus started to form among Muslims as to the impermissibility of tampering with the established order.

At first, though, the possibility of legitimate change was not completely blocked. The initial four caliphs, each of whom had been a close associate of the Prophet, were able to develop the Islamic order as a living tradition. This continued to be the case, although to a lesser extent, with their successors over the next two centuries or so. Revealingly, the second caliph, 'Umar I, succeeded in extending the coverage of zakāt to horses when there was a surge in the volume of horse-trading.[4] At the same time, decisions of the early caliphs influenced the evolution of Muslims' beliefs about the nature of the Islamic order. When they introduced innovations, they established precedents that gained sanctity in the eyes of the pious. When they preserved the status quo, they reinforced the sanctity of the existing order.

Meanwhile, the petrifying ideals of Islam were increasingly ignored in practice. As the community grew by leaps and bounds, its bonds of brotherhood proved nowhere strong enough to hold it together: it was engulfed by factionalism, of which the Sunni-Shī'ī split was only one manifestation. Where once the cooperative spirit had held sway, coercive practices gained ascendancy, following the usual pattern in societies that grow dramatically. Rulers sought more revenue to manage and defend their territories — and, of course, to enrich themselves — so they imposed a variety of new taxes, some on nascent sources of wealth and income. Certain groups that formed along tribal, regional, or occupational lines won special privileges; these included price controls and entry barriers, both of which Islamic doctrine had generally rejected. At the same time, economic restrictions that had been accepted as absolutely essential — for instance, the ban on interest — came to be violated routinely.[5]

The crucial question is this: how did the scholars of Islam, the 'ulamā, react to the immense discrepancies between ideal and practice? One can distinguish two types of responses, each of which, touched on by Mr. Essid, is addressed below.

III

The first response was to strive for a recreation of Islam's "Golden Age," which according to Sunni consensus, covers the brief period up to the death of 'Alī, the last of the four "rightly-guided" caliphs. Underlying this response were two articles of faith. One, that during this period all problems of the Islamic community were solved with the utmost efficiency

and in an impeccably just manner; and two, that the ideal order emerged
all at once in unalterably perfect form. For those who accepted these
articles, it seemed patently obvious that the perceived illnesses of Muslim
civilization could be remedied only by turning back the clock — by
eradicating, that is, every element of the social order not already present
in Islam's earliest years.

The emphasis in this backward-looking campaign was on fidelity to
Islam's behavioral norms. If only people would abide by these norms,
it was thought, the blissful social order would be reestablished. This
line of reasoning, which received a forceful treatment from Ghazālī in
the eleventh century, implies that the preferences of individuals are
immaterial, in that the community's welfare does not depend on them.

The mission of the 'ulamā thus came to be defined as rediscovering and
elucidating Islam's ideal way of life through study of the Qur'ān and the
practices of early Islam. Convinced that this way of life suits all people in
all societies at all times, they could not entertain the possibility that
certain precepts of the Qur'ān and practices of the early Muslims might
have or one day might become irrelevant. Their writings tended to
feature broad abstractions, designed to be impervious to local circumstances and historical particularities.

Believing as they did that the model of the ideal order they developed
in these writings was the manifestation of God's message to mankind, the
orthodox 'ulamā were unequivocally opposed to transforming it. Accepting that transformation could bring improvement, they reasoned, would
be tantamount to acknowledging that the model was imperfect. But this
was an unthinkable proposition if only because it would cast a shadow on
the achievements of the early Muslims, including the Prophet and his
disciples, who, they were convinced, had relied on this model for governance. The orthodox current became increasingly powerful over time. By
the end of the ninth century, it was able to quash philosophical debate
and speculation, effectively arresting the growth of knowledge within the
Islamic tradition. From this point on, it was legitimate to assimilate,
classify, and transmit ancient ideas, but illegitimate to modify or trans-
form them. Only the hardiest independent thinkers would attempt openly
and explicitly to challenge them.

IV

While Islamic thought turned into a celebration of the permanent, it did
not stop evolving altogether. In fact, the very 'ulamā who equated

novelty (*bid'a*) with heresy actually introduced and encouraged numerous adaptations. Moreover, they conferred legitimacy on a variety of practices and institutions at odds with early Islamic doctrine. In reality, therefore, their conception of the ideal order was dynamic, although this was cleverly concealed by their methods of adaptation. These methods form the *'ulamā's* second type of response to discrepancies between ideal and practice.

One method was to trace the origin of a new practice or institution either to a textual source or, through a series of oral transmissions, to the opinion of a venerated early Muslim. Frequently, this early Muslim was none other than the Prophet himself. Centuries after his death, scores of words and deeds were attributed to him, many of which addressed issues that had not yet arisen in the seventh century.[6]

Various groups benefited from these surreptitious adaptations of Islamic thought. A case in point is the legitimization of the guild regulations, beginning in the eleventh century when the urban guilds were gaining strength. As noted by Essid, this was accomplished through the ḥisba manuals. These manuals, whose authors include Māwardī, Ghazālī, and Ibn Taymiya, provided Islamic justification both for controlling the guilds' activities and for shielding them from competition. These two pursuits were not always congruent, which imparts a measure of tension to the literature. But this tension does not take the form of a clash between theories about the workings of markets. It involves, rather, disagreements over the meaning of Qur'ānic precepts and the interpretation of the Prophet's words and deeds.

Despite this tension, many economic practices and institutions that emerged after the Golden Age — not only guild regulations but also taxation policies, financial restrictions, and inheritance laws — were identified with Islam in the belief that they had been part of the Islamic way of life from the very beginning. This dynamic identification process, which concealed the evolution of Islamic thought, was facilitated by the community's "consensus doctrine." According to this doctrine, which the *'ulamā* bolstered through numerous Qur'ānic verses, the opinion of an individual Muslim is fallible, but that of the Muslim community is not.[7] Its widespread acceptance accorded a nimbus of justice and authority to any arrangement perceived as enjoying the Muslim community's approval. When an arrangement was thus infused into Islamic tradition, it became essentially immune to explicit criticism.

Another method of adaptation involved ruses (*ḥiyal*), which the *'ulamā* developed or ratified to bring customary practices into line with the letter of Islamic injunctions. As an illustration, consider the law that dictates each child's share of his parent's estate. A parent wishing to violate this can do so by following the ruse of declaring, before his death, that he owes some person a certain sum of money. Since all his debts must be paid off before his estate is split, the parent ends up allocating his will as he pleases — assuming, naturally, that the designated creditor faithfully transfers the money he receives to the favored child. Another widely used ruse was devised to legitimize violations of the presumed Qur'ānic ban on interest. To lend person B $100 at 10% interest, person A simply sells him an object for $110, to be paid after a year, and then buys it back for $100, payable immediately.[8] Each of these ruses enables the concerned parties to circumvent a cherished Islamic precept, while conforming dutifully to its literal meaning.

V

Maintaining as they did that Islamic thought could be based essentially on the Qur'ān and the Sunna, the orthodox 'ulamā did not consider rationalism a legitimate approach for finding the ideal social order. Yet in the early years of Islam, there had been a significant number of thinkers who upheld it. Among them were the Mu'tazila, whose popularity and strength peaked in the eighth century. While not denying the validity of the Qur'ān and the Sunna, the Mu'tazila tried to accord reason a systematic role in discussions about the social order. Considered for this a threat to Islam, they were persecuted and their writings destroyed. What little we know about their specific views is based on summaries provided by their critics.

Given this background, the late fourteenth and early fifteenth century writings of Ibn Khaldūn and Maqrīzī look very impressive.[9] To be sure, and as Essid aptly points out, both of these writers entertained the notion of a Golden Age. Moreover, they saw in the history of Islamic civilization a long period of degeneration and decline. At the same time, they *explicitly* rejected the suggestion that the Golden Age could be reestablished merely through propagation of Islamic ideals. After all, this had been the preoccupation of many renowned writers of the previous seven centuries, and the results seemed anything but laudable.

Ibn Khaldūn and Maqrīzī held that by nature people are selfish and oppressive. A major manifestation of this, they maintained, was that state officials, from the rulers on down, used their power for self-glorification and enrichment, rather than in the service of Islamic goals. Matters could be rectified by putting officials under the rule of the law. But this law could not be the one to which Muslim societies were accustomed: its vulnerability to abuse seemed obvious from the historical record. They themselves, on the other hand, were at a loss to offer a viable substitute. To do that, they felt, one had to know much more about the way society operates.

It is in this spirit that they undertook their deservedly famous investigations of socioeconomic processes. I shall comment on Ibn Khaldūn's theory of growth and development, both because this constitutes a most profound contribution to the social sciences in general and because I do not concur entirely with Essid's evaluation of it.

Ibn Khaldūn recognized that the administrative entity known as the state has a limited life span. Created in the first place by people's shared interests, it is eventually torn asunder by assaults from within — assaults perpetrated, partly in response to corruption and mismanagement, by nomadic tribes. With the fall of a state, the people under its wing find themselves in the throes of intolerable conflict, from which they then extirpate themselves by founding a new state. Two forces, according to Ibn Khaldūn, underlie the cohesive and divisive tendencies that cause states to rise and fall: religion, which is cohesive, and 'aṣabīya, which although destructive by itself, can also, when combined with religion, generate a cohesive unity of purpose.

To a modern reader, the social dynamics postulated by Ibn Khaldūn raise more questions than they answer. It is difficult, in particular, to make complete sense of the interplay between religion and 'aṣabīya. Notwithstanding this weakness, the theory contains the immensely valuable insight that social structures carry within them the seeds of their own destruction. Variants of this idea appear much later in the works of a number of extremely influential thinkers, including Marx and Schumpeter. The idea also forms the basis of Mancur Olson's celebrated *Rise and Decline of Nations* [1982] — although, I might add, Olson fails to cite Ibn Khaldūn among the originators of his thesis.

It is remarkable that Ibn Khaldūn escaped being branded as a heretic, even though his thesis can easily be construed as directly conflicting with the orthodox position. Indeed, the notion that the administrative units within Islamic civilization are afflicted by seemingly unavoidable cyclical swings in fortune contradicts the belief that if only people would be good Muslims, a crisis-free order would reemerge. The reason Ibn Khaldūn's works were tolerated is undoubtedly linked to the fact that he consistently characterized "true" Islam as a unifying force. Whatever the complete explanation, it is possible that Ibn Khaldūn sought deliberately to disguise the revolutionary nature of his thesis. In this connection, it has been suggested that a number of medieval writers — including Ibn Rushd (Averroes) — used elaborate methods for hiding their true opinions from orthodox eyes.[10] To suggest that Ibn Khaldūn also practiced dissimulation is, of course, sheer speculation, but the matter deserves investigation.

Ibn Khaldūn did not succeed in discovering a formula that would stabilize the political structure of the Islamic community and bring back conditions of the Golden Age. He remained pessimistic in this regard, which makes it appropriate, I think, to categorize him as an "Islamic realist." Significantly, his works never entered the mainstream of Islamic thought. Although a few modern reformists have looked to them for inspiration, they have had little influence, substantive or methodological, on dominant intellectual currents.

VI

A dramatic development over the last few decades has been the emergence of economics as a distinct branch of Islamic social thought. There now exist "Islamic economists" who have assumed the responsibility, held heretofore by the *'ulamā* collectively, for guiding the faithful on economic matters. The Islamic economists have generated a staggering volume of writings in diverse languages.[11]

The vast majority of these writings are concerned with three broad issues. Most important is the identification of a set of behavioral norms to guide Muslims specifically in their consumption, production, and exchange activities. Refining and adapting the time-honored orthodox argument, the Islamic economists maintain that *economic* problems, including poverty, low productivity, and inequality, can be overcome by ensuring that Muslims abide by what they consider to be Islam's behavioral norms in the economic sphere. The other two issues are zakāt, viewed as the basis of Islamic fiscal policy, and the prohibition of interest, regarded as the centerpiece of Islamic monetary policy. Almost all Islamic economists consider this trio — the norms, zakāt, and the prohibition of interest — to be the pillars of the ideal economic system.

From a methodological standpoint, some serious tensions are evident in the literature. According to many writers, Islamic economics already exists in the religion's heritage and is merely waiting to be discovered by contemporary scholarship. Like generations of *'ulamā* before them, these writers devote their efforts to comprehending and interpreting the

Qur'ān, the Sunna, and medieval Muslim teachings. This limited focus causes them to ignore such issues as unemployment, overpopulation, natural resource management, and international debt — each of which is high on the public agenda in many Muslim countries.

For other writers, all that Islam provides is a few requirements such as zakāt, zero interest, and the elimination of speculation. The Islamic economist's task, they hold, is to construct a theory and an economic blueprint consonant with these requirements. They believe that while 'ulamā of the past made useful contributions to this task, much work remains to be done. In this regard, some are finding use for a number of tools of non-Islamic origin — for instance, the optimization techniques of neo-classical economics. As a rule, however, they do not acknowledge such borrowings, which helps sustain the myth that Islamic economics draws only on Islam's own resources.

As in the past, it is proving difficult to implement some of Islam's perceived economic requirements. A case in point is the ban on interest, which constitutes the *raison d'être* of the Islamic banks that have mushroomed throughout North Africa, the Middle East, South Asia, and elsewhere. These banks have eliminated interest only in name: they use a panoply of practices that can only be characterized as interest in Islamic garb. Although the matter is shrouded in controversy, a number of Islamic economists have sought to legitimize these practices.[12]

Positive economic analysis, which involves forming, testing, and if necessary, abandoning hypotheses, remains a neglected pursuit. Very recently, however, a few Islamic economists have taken some cautious steps in this direction. For example, two Islamic economists from Malaysia have shown, using econometrics, that Malaysia's recently-imposed zakāt scheme actually accentuates inequality.[13] It remains to be seen whether results of this sort will generate a readiness to reopen issues that have been closed to discussion for centuries. What we do know is that Islamic modernists, who, like the Mu'tazila of early Islam, support independent thinking and seek to liberate Islamic scholarship from the obligation to follow past consensus, enjoy the esteem of very few Islamic economists. Muhammad 'Abduh, the co-founder of the Sunni modernist school, is considered a heretic, partly because he saw nothing wrong with depositing money in interest-bearing bank accounts.[14]

A potent controversy in the contemporary literature involves private ownership. In accordance with past consensus, all Islamic economists agree that Islam does not object to private ownership per se. At the same time, many of them feel that the public interest may necessitate limits. A minority have gone so far as to advocate collective ownership of key economic resources. Since all sides in the debate have bolstered their arguments with Qur'ānic verses, it appears that the issue will not be resolved easily.

Notes

1. For details of this thesis, see Kuran [1983, 1986].
2. See Tuğ [1963, p. 56] and Aghnides [1961, pp. 236–9].
3. See Muslehuddin [1974, p. 68], who attributes the example to Ibn Qayyim Jawziyya.
4. See Aghnides [1961, pp. 236–9].
5. For more on the practices of the early Islamic community, see Rodinson [1973, ch. 3] and Kuran [1986].
6. See Goldziher [1971] and Schacht [1959]. The authenticity of the Sunna has also been questioned by a few modernist scholars. See, in particular, Rahman [1982, p. 120].
7. On this doctrine, see Hourani [1964, pp.13–60].
8. On these and other ruses, see Khadduri [1984, pp. 149–55] and Rodinson [1973, pp. 36–7, 44–5].
9. Of these, the most essential is Ibn Khaldūn's *The Muqaddimah: An Introduction to History* [1958].
10. See Keddie [1963].
11. Recent bibliographies include Siddiqi [1981] and Nienhaus [1982]. For critiques of the literature, see Kuran [1983, 1986] and Pryor [1985].
12. See, in particular, Council of Islamic Ideology [1983].
13. See Salleh and Ngah [1981].
14. See Khadduri [1984, p. 200].

References

Aghnides, N. *Mohammedan Theories of Finance*. Lahore: Premier Book House, 1961.
Council of Islamic Ideology. "Elimination of Interest from the Economy." Ed. by Z. Ahmed, M. Iqbal, and M. F. Khan, *Money and Banking in Islam*. Jeddah: International Centre for Research in Islamic Economics, 1983, pp. 103–257.
Goldziher, I. *Muslim Studies*, vol. 2. Ed. by S. M. Stern, transl. C. R. Barber and S. M. Stern. London: George Allen and Unwin, 1971; first German ed., 1889.
Hourani, G. F. "The Basis of Authority of Consensus in Sunnite Islam." *Studia Islamica* 21:1964, 13–60.
Ibn Khaldūn. *The Muqaddimah: An Introduction to History*, 3 vols. Transl. F. Rosenthal. New York: Pantheon, 1958.
Keddie, N. "Symbol and Sincerity in Islam." *Studia Islamica* 19:1963, pp. 27–63.
Khadduri, M. *The Islamic Conception of Justice*. Baltimore: Johns Hopkins University Press, 1984.

Kuran, T. "Behavioral Norms in the Islamic Doctrine of Economics: A Critique." *Journal of Economic Behavior and Organization* 4:1983, 353–79.

Kuran, T. "The Economic System in Contemporary Islamic Thought: Interpretation and Assessment." *International Journal of Middle East Studies* 18:1986, pp. 135–64.

Muslehuddin, M. *Economics and Islam*. Lahore: Islamic Publications, 1974.

Nienhaus, V. *Literature on Islamic Economics in English and German*. Köln: Al-Kitab Verlag, 1982.

Olson, M. *The Rise and Decline of Nations*. New Haven: Yale University Press, 1982.

Pryor, F. L. "The Islamic Economic System." *Journal of Comparative Economics* 9:1985, 197–223.

Rahman, F. *Islam and Modernity*. Chicago: University of Chicago Press, 1982.

Rodinson, M. *Islam and Capitalism*. New York: Pantheon, 1973.

Salleh, M. S. and Ngah, R. "Distribution of the Zakāt Burden on Padi Producers in Malaysia." Ed. by M. R. Zaman, *Some Aspects of the Economics of Zakah*. Gary, IN: Association of Muslim Social Scientists, 1981, pp. 80–153.

Schacht, J. *The Origins of Muhammadan Jurisprudence*, 3rd ed. London: Oxford University Press, 1959.

Siddiqi, M. N. *Muslim Economic Thinking*. Leicester: The Islamic Foundation, 1981.

Tuğ, S. *İslam Vergi Hukukunun Ortaya Çıkışı*, Ankara: Ankara Üniversitesi İlahiyat Fakültesi Yayınları, 1963.

5 SCHOLASTIC ECONOMICS

Odd Langholm

0 3 1 1

The first European universities were founded in the twelfth century, and from then on economics came into the hands of university professors. There had been cathedral schools even earlier, but their teachings were mainly derivatives of patristic thought. In the high Middle Ages a number of external events and inventions drew attention to economic phenomena from a theoretical point of view. The crusades had opened up the world, towns and markets were expanding with the growing economies, new commercial techniques were being introduced. Simultaneously, those searching for norms to guide behavior in this increasingly important area were helped by the re-examination of the economic arguments of the ancient world, as documented in Roman law and in Greek philosophy. The thirteenth century saw the emergence of that famous synthesis known as scholasticism, in which these elements were fused with the patristic tradition, and of which economics is only a very small part.

Most of what there is of economics must be dug out in small segments from learned tomes of philosophy, theology, and law. The civilians (Roman law doctors) commented on the *Code* and *Digest* of Justinian, the canonists on the *Decretals* of Pope Gregory IX. Some patristic material went into the *Sentences* of Peter Lombard, the most widely

115

used textbook on theology in the Middle Ages. They might also publish theological *summae* or collections of disputed questions (*quodlibeta*). All this provided the doctrinal basis for the more practical handbooks for confessors, which often contain rules of economic behavior. Among the ancient philosophical texts translated in the thirteenth century, food for economic thought was primarily to be found in the *Ethics* and *Politics* of Aristotle. Amidst this enormous mass of general literature there are a few slimmer tracts devoted specifically to buying and selling, to money, or to usury. The first great flowering of scholastic economics lasted for no more than a century, from the translation of Aristotle's *Ethics* shortly before 1250 to the first outbreak of the Black Death before 1350. Coinciding with the effects of war and famine, the ravages of the epidemic left a gap in primary sources which speaks eloquently of the sensitivity of intellectual effort to material conditions. Threads were picked up again in the fifteenth century, and some of the late scholastics have become famous as economists, but recent research has shown that they were often copying verbatim from previously forgotten pre-plague sources. Pockets of scholasticism survived (e.g., in Spain) to produce some important contributions to economics until well into the seventeenth century. But long before that, the Renaissance and the Reformation, the invention of printing, and the great discoveries, had combined to shatter the unity of the intellectual world, alter its means of communication, and weaken the basis in faith and morality on which scholastic social philosophy sought to build.

In a number of books the French philosopher and historian, the late Étienne Gilson, drove home three facts which now, largely because of him, seem obvious: that (1) recent philosophy is in great debt to the philosophy of the Middle Ages; (2) the dominant characteristic of medieval philosophy is that it is a Christian philosophy; and (3) the concept of a Christian philosophy is not a contradiction in terms. It may be useful to apply these propositions to medieval economics. It is likely enough that the concept of a Christian economics will look like a contradiction to many. The Gospel message is to shun worldly riches and cares, trusting in God to provide, and above all to love one's neighbor as oneself, whereas economics is the art of providing as best one may for one's material needs, often by making a profitable deal with one's neighbor. There can be no question but that this sense of contradiction weighed heavily on the scholastics when they wrote about economics. It has often been suggested that economics proper is the product of a new philosophical outlook which, rather than repressing human nature, accepts it for what it is and seeks to guide it toward socially useful ends. It is true that very much of scholastic economics consisted in preaching against worldliness and greed. But commercial institutions and functions were recognized as necessary, and a realistic attitude to human *incentive* had to be taken. Thus Peter Olivi (d. 1298), the author of a much copied treatise on economic contracts, while explaining why it is reasonable to allow prices to rise in case of a general scarcity, states openly that unless one does this, those with supplies in stock will be less inclined to part with them, to the detriment of all those who need them.[1] This is by any account an economic proposition, but it may be argued that it is so because it admits of sentiments which are hardly Christian.

Those who take this point of view may claim that recent *reactions* against dominant trends in modern economics also have something in common with scholastic thought. The common approach, now more often codified in positive law, relied then mostly on moral and religious sanctions. Realizing the futility of merely preaching *charity*, yet disinclined to rely on the social benefits of "loosening the bridle on cupidity," as one scholastic put it,[2] the aim was rather to ensure some benefits to individuals and community by imposing norms of *justice* on economic relationships. In scholastic thought this orientation is largely explained by its dependence on canon law, and it was strongly reinforced by the appearance of Aristotle, much of whose discussion of economics is to be found in a chapter on justice in the *Ethics*. It is sometimes alleged that this moral and legalistic orientation prevented the flow of genuine analysis and thus the advance of explanatory and predictive theory. There is certainly a danger of this if argument is used mainly to back up preconceived moral positions. But this was by no means always the case with scholastic economics. Frequently, in order to develop good and workable norms of justice, it would be necessary to go beyond superficial appearances of equity and reason out how alternative rulings would affect individuals and community in the long run (often reluctantly admitting the likely reactions of men as they are, not as they ought to be). It is in the course of this kind of "value-neutral" reasoning supporting norms of justice that the scholastics contributed to the development of economics.

Before the industrial revolution, production was a rare subject in economics; it dealt mainly with exchange. Rules of justice in exchange will reflect ideas about the nature and extent of *property*. Since the physiocrats, the prime economic argument in favor of private property has been that it provides incentive for productive *efficiency*. Some of the scholastics repeated a similar argument from Aristotle's *Politics*, but they did not much favor this kind of reasoning and tended to give more wholehearted assent to some other arguments proffered in the same context. First, according to Aristotle in *Politics*, II, arguing against Plato, common ownership of productive resources is bound to cause dissension over the distribution of products because some will take more than their share. This is akin to the argument from peace on which modern political science has been based since Hobbes. It has a number of roots. Thus the catchword (sometimes attributed to Hobbes) that "communality is the mother of discord" is a medieval legal dictum. For the scholastic theologians it was also natural to associate Aristotle with the Church Fathers, who explained property as an institution made necessary by man's sinful nature. After the Fall men will no longer live peacefully together but will quarrel over goods actually granted by God to mankind in common; hence the need for private property and for laws to protect it.

In the Aristotelian version the argument from peace may sometimes implicitly contain an argument from *labor*. Seeking to explain *why* communism leads to quarrel, Albert the Great (d. 1280), in commenting on the *Politics*, points out that when some claim a larger share in the common product than what corresponds to their labor input, then those who have worked more and get less will find this unjust, and this is what stirs up trouble.[3] The right to the fruits of one's labor is the property argument associated with Locke in the seventeenth century. It is sometimes alleged that it did not play any significant part in political theory before Locke and that the Smithian labor theory of value rests on the Lockean labor theory of property. The first assertion is questionable. A large part of Roman law dealt with property and the medieval civilians often addressed themselves to settling disputes between conflicting titles of acquisition, among which acquisition by labor was well recognized. As to whether the labor theory of value rests on the labor theory of property or vice versa, this seems a moot point as long as both exist side by side. In the scholastic tradition they did so owing to Albert the Great, whose commentary on the *Ethics* emphasized labor as a determinant of price.

In addition to the socioteleological arguments from peace and efficiency, Aristotle is swayed towards private property by the consideration that it is necessary for a full and *virtuous life*. Specifically, the virtuous man is a liberal man, and unless he has something to be liberal about, such as property, he is unable to exercise this virtue. This could readily be restated in terms of such Christian virtues as compassion, charity, and mercy. It led to the introduction of two motifs. On the one hand there was a tendency in scholastic thought to accept the social order and invite poor and rich alike to view their God-given roles as opportunities to exercise Christian virtues: humility and self-denial on the part of the former, charity and compassion on the part of the latter. Kinship with the

Aristotelian liberality argument is here evident. On the other hand, the scholastics would not be content to welcome the *opportunity* to exercise charity merely on account of its beneficial moral effects on the giver. The patristic tradition had strengthened an element of social consciousness always present in Christianity. Charity had become an *obligation* because of its benefits to the receiver. Aristotle himself said that liberality combines private ownership with common use, an idea readily assimilated with the patristic notion of *stewardship*. God created the world and is by rights the owner of all creation. Man's fallen nature made some property arrangements necessary, but these grant man, as God's steward, no absolute moral right to retain for himself a surplus which others need. This *duty to share* involves not only the function of charity (*eleemosyna*) and the virtue of charity (*caritas*). It extends to the function of economic exchange of property and to the virtue of justice in exchange.

This qualified concept of property rights clashed with the more liberal standpoint of the Roman law. It was this that won through in the long run, but an effort to modify it is an important theme in scholastic economics. To some extent the medieval civilians themselves contributed to this effort. According to *Code* 4, 35, 21, everybody is "moderator and arbiter of his own goods," which seems to imply that the owner may keep them or sell them as he pleases and demand any price he likes; while *Digest* 39, 3, 9, 1 states that "a willing party is not injured," implying that if someone has voluntarily consented to the terms of exchange, he cannot reasonably complain that they are unjust. It follows from these principles that "a thing is worth what it can be sold for," a frequently quoted maxim in legal sources. If it is accepted as it stands, the concept of a *just price* becomes meaningless. Justice will pertain only to keeping or breaking a contract according to its terms, not to the terms as such. The scholastics persisted in the belief that just terms of contract is a meaningful concept.

However, this should not be understood to mean that they set themselves the task of working out exact and universal just-price formulae. Several criteria of fair pricing were recommended, but they were rough rules of thumb only, allowing for "great latitude," as John Duns Scotus (d. 1308) put it.[4] Nor were they meant to apply to all exchanges. The scholastics on the whole favored government price regulations, and some medieval prices were in point of fact fixed by guilds and other corporations. But the majority of exchangers must needs be left to their own devices, and the most that could be hoped for was that they would take some heed of just norms of their own volition. Anyhow, as long as terms of contract were truly voluntary on the part of both parties to an exchange, there would be no reason for any moral authority to intervene.

Just price criteria were useful as *correctives* to the bargaining process in exceptional cases or as *checks* on that process, by arresting cases where free bargaining seemed to have been violated.

The operative word here is *free* bargaining. Valid contract presumes *consent*. The medieval civilians carefully conditioned their value maxim on the basis of that principle. A thing is worth what it can be sold for provided the buyer *knows* and *understands* what he buys, said Alessandro Tartagno (d. 1477) in comment on *Digest* 36, 1, 1, 16, adding the last of the italicized words to a modified formula due to the great Bartolus of Sassoferrato (d. 1357). Provisions like these seek to ensure true consent by arresting fraudulent withholding of information about product and sales conditions, exploitation of immature and mentally incapacitated persons, etc. They come in addition to violation of consent by physical force and blackmail. But the scholastics were not prepared to leave the issue there. They went a step beyond the lawyers. Even if physical and moral power is ruled out, there remains the kind of power which is *sui generis* to economics itself, namely *bargaining power*. Coercion rendering contracts invalid might include *economic coercion*, if one party to a contract were in the *economic power* of the other party and this power were wielded to obtain unjust terms of exchange.

Aristotle provided the textual basis for an analysis of the voluntary. In *Ethics*, III, there is a discussion of man's moral responsibility for actions performed under duress. In certain situations an agent may be said to act willingly within the limits of choice imposed by circumstances but unwillingly insofar as acceptance of these strictures is concerned. One example given is that of a captain who jettisons cargo from a ship in storm. To the scholastics this provided authority for the principle of *conditional consent*. They turned Aristotle's context around and applied his principles to the moral responsibility of agents exploiting duress imposed on others. Recognizing that economic duress can influence price even in the absence of fraud and force in the legal sense, the scholastics would concede no difference in principle between taking advantage of duress and actively applying it. The distinction between *compulsion* by impersonal force of circumstances and *coercion* by a human agent was irrelevant to Aristotle's own discussion, and the scholastics were disinclined to make any such distinction as might relieve a contracting party from blame by reference to economic conditions imposed by suprapersonal forces. While circumstances may permit a seller to drive a very hard bargain, he does not have to do so. The price demanded is in the final analysis subject to his own decision, for which he is morally responsible, whatever power the situation lends him. From this viewpoint economic duress due to unequal bargaining powers is always personally inflicted.

How then to decide when terms of exchange entered upon are truly voluntary and thus valid and when consent is conditioned by force of circumstances? There is no logical distinction possible, since in every decision there is *some* freedom of choice but not *as much* as one would have wanted. However, this does not mean that the problem of conditional consent is not ethically relevant. Briefly, what the scholastics did was let the question of compulsion in a formal sense rest and rather concentrate on evidence of *need* in a substantive sense. Thus Olivi, conditioning the value maxim, states that a contract is invalid if it issues from such feebleness of mind or from such duress as to rob it of legal force, or if consent is given owing to such *poverty or other necessity* that it cannot be said to express free will.[5] While the injunction against exploiting general poverty was universal, the scholastics after Olivi would mainly find evidence of conditional consent and blameworthy economic duress under *certain types of market conditions* and in the exchange of *certain types of product*. We shall return to the market criterion below. As to product, the Roman law provided some precedent for concentrating just price teaching on necessaries, while leaving luxury prices free to find their own levels. As Baptista Trovamala (d. after 1494) states in his *Summa* for confessors, the seller is wholly and entirely the moderator and arbiter of his goods in the case of jewels and gems and similar articles not necessary for life but rather for pomp and ornament.[6] This does not mean that luxury markets were ignored. On the contrary, precisely because economic forces were there permitted to play freely, they provided the best object lessons on which those interested in economic *analysis* might base their economic ethics.

Some medieval manuals provide elaborate check-lists itemizing what the merchant should look for and what he should avoid when computing prices. A good example is John Nider's (d. 1438) handbook *On the Contracts of Merchants*. Other works went more deeply into the philosophy supporting such items. Generally speaking, just prices were prices which would have established themselves in the absence of fraud and force of all kinds and under otherwise normal conditions. This means that some of the reasoning underlying the criteria of just pricing can tell us how and how far the scholastics understood the mechanisms involved in price formation. Some of the best evidence is to be found in the commentary tradition on Aristotle's *Ethics*. In the fifth book of that work the author discusses justice and devotes a chapter to justice in the exchange of commodities, with or without the medium of money. Justice in

exchange consists in *proportionate reciprocity*, says Aristotle. If a builder
enters into exchange with a shoemaker, then this condition is fulfilled if
"the builder is to the shoemaker as the number of shoes is to the house."
This cryptic saying has inspired much fanciful speculation. It clearly
invites the idea, quite common among modern interpreters, that the
exchange ratio should reflect the relative social status of the exchangers.
It is possible to trace this idea back to the early humanist tradition on the
Ethics. But it is clearly economic nonsense, and the scholastics looking
for economics in Aristotle never propounded it. Instead they elaborated
two other ways of interpreting the ancient text.

Albert the Great, who commented twice on the *Ethics*, was active in
launching both traditions but is best remembered for his *labor and cost*
interpretation of Aristotle. The number of shoes to be exchanged for a
house should reflect productive effort and expense. This is a much older
idea. But there is something in Albert the Great's statement of it which in
the forwardlooking perspective of the development of economics is highly
significant. In some (older as well as newer) versions of the labor theory
of value (and of property), labor can claim its reward because this is in
some sense inherently or *a priori right*, but in Albert's explanation it is
right because it is *socially necessary*. Unless there is justice in exchange,
says Aristotle in *Ethics*, V, "arts will be destroyed." For this very general
proposition Albert the Great suggests a more specific interpretation.
Unless the carpenter gets as much in exchange for a bed as it has cost him
to produce it, says Albert, he won't make any more beds in the future,
and thus "the art of making beds will be destroyed."[7] It is futile to
impose as just a price which will cause the product in question to disappear from the market. This is an aspect of economic ethics which the
scholastics (being all disciples of Albert the Great) kept firmly in view. It
provides the basis for a *principle of indemnity* which was applied consistently both to the exchange of commodities and to the lending of money.

If Albert's interpretation suggests one-half of the formula stating the
conditions of market equilibrium, there is something in the *Ethics* also to
invite the other half. When Aristotle explained what causes builders and
shoemakers and other artisans and professionals to enter into exchange
with one another, he used the word *chreia*. The first Latin translation of
the *Ethics* rendered this as *opus*, i.e., the *need* or *want* which these agents
have for each other's products. Now *opus* in Latin also has a different
meaning unrelated to the Greek *chreia*, namely *work*, and this may be
what set on foot the Albertian labor theory of value. For it is suggested in
the ancient text that *chreia* is not only the cause of exchange; it is also (as
Aristotle puts it) a *measure* of goods in exchange. The scholastics took

this to mean a measure of *value*. In an early revision of the translation, *opus* was replaced by *indigentia*. This permits of connotations not present in the original word; suggesting a more active kind of need, it points toward our concept of *demand*. Thomas Aquinas used a copy of the *Ethics* in this new version. Prices of things are determined, said Aquinas, according to how much men need (want, demand) them (*indigent eis*).[8]

One commentator who picked up both these traditions was Henry of Friemar (d. 1340). Two further developments are evident in his work. First, scarcity is added to the price formula. *Indigentia* is not only need or demand as a psychological phenomenon independent of external conditions; rather, it is taken to include conditions of supply as well. It is demand given by need in the face of scarcity. Next, it is not particular demand that determines price, but common demand (*communis indigentia*).[9] These are both analytical steps of major importance, albeit the failure to separate supply and demand explicitly as variables is an unfortunate dead end. Writing a few decades later, John Buridan (d. after 1358) crowned the scholastic Aristotelian tradition with a number of commentaries in question form. In one of his economic questions on the *Ethics* he added yet another refinement to the concept of *indigentia*. According to Buridan, the concept must be extended from "the needs of the poor" for necessaries to include also "the needs of the rich" for luxuries, in fact, to comprise any desire backed by ability to pay.[10] In the course of less than a century since the Latin translation of the *Ethics* the Aristotelians had thus arrived at a workable concept of effective demand.

Starting in the late nineteenth century, scholars looking back on scholastic economics from opposite camps of a modern ideological conflict were bound to see the labor and demand theories of value and the just price as mutually exclusive and conflicting as well. Different historical schools sprang up, and they have persisted to this day, each interpreting the evidence in favor of modern positions. According to one school, the scholastics attributed value entirely to labor. According to the other, more in vogue at present, they derived value from demand; labor hardly entered into it at all. But each of these interpretations can be maintained only on the basis of very selective reading of the texts, since most scholastics repeated fragments of both theories. The conflict between them is anachronistic. In point of fact, labor and demand served as mutually supporting criteria of fair pricing just as, from a modern analytical viewpoint, they can be seen as alternative ways of stating one and the same theory of value. Some of the scholastics must have come very close to that important insight.

One of Buridan's sources was Gerald Odonis (d. 1349), whose treatise on economic contracts is a critical paraphrase on Olivi's work. Later Odonis also composed an *Ethics* commentary whose chapter on exchange is similarly inspired. Several prominent later works bear the same stamp, notably the economic sermons of Bernardino of Siena (d. 1444), whose considerable fame as an early economist rests partly on verbatim quotes from Olivi and Odonis. Olivi's treatise consists of a series of questions. His very first question contains a brief catalogue of factors influencing value. They drew attention as Bernardino's *raritas* (scarcity), *virtuositas*, and *complacibilitas* (roughly: objective and subjective utility).[11] But these words appear first in Bernardino's hand as marginalia in a copy (still preserved) of Olivi's treatise.[12] It was Peter Olivi who first split the composite concept of *indigentia* into the factors of *utility* and *scarcity*. However, the following question contains a longer list of value determinants. It also includes utility and scarcity, but leans more heavily on the cost side, suggesting labor, risk, industry, and productive skill.[13]

The analysis of practical knowledge and skill (*peritia*) is particularly important. In the labor version of Aristotle's exchange model it cannot be taken for granted that proportionate reciprocity will correspond exactly to the number of hours required to make a house compared to a pair of shoes or to the amount of labor according to some other physical (value-independent) measure. Relative values of different units of labor must be taken into consideration, and these relative values are also dependent on demand. Certain higher professions, says Odonis, can ask higher prices for their services because these services will be scarce. Common work, less scarce, commands lower wages.[14] The choice of professional services as examples, rather than physical commodity production, may fail to reveal how close this comes to a true statement of the "circle of value." Modern value theory centers upon an equilibrium proposition according to which factor and product value determine one another simultaneously. A professional service is product and factor both. Focusing on this type of example leaves out complementary factors and thus falls short of an explanation of factor substitution, albeit Olivi refers to investment in training as one particular cost factor involved in skilled crafts. Another drawback may be that the explanation tends to stop short with wage *differentials* due to scarcity rather than proceed to the crucial point concerning labor in the formation of product value, *viz.* that *all* labor that brings forth a needed product will be scarce. However, in the Aristotelian commentary tradition the Albertian generalized concept of labor kept rubbing against the demand concept from Aquinas. Odonis inherited them both and all but stated explicitly their essential relationship.

Olivi's and Odonis's skillful artisans will often provide mainly for

Buridan's "needs of the rich." Returning now to necessaries and to rules of just pricing, we find that Henry of Friemar's "common need" (*communis indigentia*) points up an important distinction. It was usually held that prices reflecting common need might be charged; what was not to be exploited was particular need. This principle may have been borrowed by the Aristotelians from the legal tradition. The early manuscripts of the *Digest* contain a note at 9, 2, 33 sometimes attributed to the glossator Azo (d. ca. 1230): "A thing is worth what it can be sold for — commonly, that is." From then on, *communis aestimatio* became one of the safest bases of the just price. It might signify the deliberate consensus of several knowledgeable persons, the agreed price of a craft guild, or the like, but quite early on it came to mean specifically the kind of estimate which the total community makes unintentionally through the impersonal working of the economy. Bartolus, commenting on *Digest* 13, 1, 14, states: "A thing is worth what it can be sold for, that is, commonly and in a public place, to many people, over several days." These are, of course, the characteristics of the regular, competitive market. Said Antonio of Butrio (d. 1408), the canonist: "A thing is worth what it can be sold for *in mercato*."[15] There are many similar statements to be found in the philosophical literature.

The normal competitive price, then, i.e., the common estimate of common need as established under normal market conditions, is the just price. This is at present a much favored interpretation. But it may be wise to stop for a moment and ask *why* such a market price is morally acceptable. What does *common* actually mean here and why is the common just? Now *communis* in Latin, just like *common* in English, has two related but distinct meanings: they can mean *joint* or they can mean *usual*. The *common estimate* of the scholastics may be somewhat flavored by both meanings. As well illustrated by the quotation from Bartolus, just value presupposes aggregation as well as a temporal average. What would be wrong, however, is to ascribe to the scholastics the entirely modern notion that the market price is just because it serves to *allocate joint social resources optimally*. To them the joint would be just for somewhat the same reason that the usual is just, namely because each *prevents exploitation by force of singular circumstances*. The competitive market rules out duress, or at least the kind of duress that can reasonably be claimed. It offers as much protection against merely conditional consent as can well be required of a system of justice in pricing. In the market, no one can be made to pay more than everybody else must pay. It is in singular exchange situations, in the absence of a market or under abnormal market conditions, that the needy can be induced to pay more than he ought to.

Note that there is no difference in principle here between exploiting a
single buyer in need and exploiting a community by withholding supply.
General scarcity may be a legitimate price determinant, but to *create
scarcity* is one of the worst of economic sins. Buyers may compete for
what little is released and thus drive the price up to a level which may
well be said to be a *joint* price but which includes profit from the *unusual*
conditions prevailing, hence the general condemnation of *monopoly*.

The fact that normal cost must approximate competitive price in the
long run and that this is the just price, does not mean that a seller is
always obliged to sell at that price. It was agreed that if the seller's actual
costs had been for some reason exceptionally high, he was permitted to
keep himself *indemnified* by charging a higher price (provided, of course,
that the buyer was prepared to pay it, which under competitive conditions
he might not be). "Costs" in this connection might even include profit
forgone or utility lost in parting with the commodity. If, on the other
hand, no such extraordinary cost or utility intervened on the seller's part
but a potential buyer was still prepared to pay the higher price (owing to
the commodity's extraordinary utility for *him*), this was not permitted.
Such preparedness to pay more than the just price could only be conditional; it was evidence of coercion. It meant selling something which did
not belong to the seller, said Aquinas, who first stated this "double rule"
of just pricing.[16] It was subsequently taught by a number of scholastics,
including Peter Olivi and John Duns Scotus.

The Thomist double rule of just pricing provides a convenient avenue
of approach to the scholastic theory of *usury*, which applies the rule in
strict analogy. No part of medieval economic doctrine is more controversial than the ban on profit over and above the principal on money
loans. This is usury, an economic sin worse even than monopoly. The
ideological basis of usury doctrine is mainly Biblical and patristic, but its
logic is very largely Aristotelian. Contrary to the view held by some
modern critics, just-price and usury theory apply a number of common
principles. Prominent among these is the principle of indemnity. From
very early on in the scholastic tradition it was agreed that if a lender can
show that parting with money will involve elements of cost or loss to him,
he can justly demand indemnity for this from the borrower. Such *extrinsic
titles to interest* came to embrace both actual loss (*damnum emergens*) and
forgone gain (*lucrum cessans*). This corresponds closely to the first half
of the double rule of just pricing. The second half of the rule found its
counterpart in the rejection of any claim based on the apparent utility
derived by the borrower from having money at his disposal for a period
of time. This utility is no business of the lender's; however the money

is used. If usury is charged on this basis, says Scotus (echoing Aquinas on commodity exchange), the lender sells something which does not belong to him.[17]

What he does sell, according to Aquinas and Scotus, is the borrower's *industry*. Whenever the use of borrowed money seems to be profitable, it is an illusion to attribute this profit to money; it must be attributed to him who uses the money. Similarly, when *lucrum cessans* is claimed by the lender, he is not indemnified for profit forgone on money as such, but rather for the lost opportunity to exercise his own industry. Consequently, proof of intent to actually use his own money as an alternative to lending it was required of the lender before this title to interest could be honored. Some of the most important infighting over scholastic usury doctrine took place over the question of how specific such intent had to be. Odonis, more liberal than most, argued that the lender does not in fact sell the borrower's industry, he sells "the cessation of his own industry," since "both cannot use the money at the same time."[18] However, the moment the general scarcity of money becomes a legitimate title to interest, the doctrine breaks down, since this is tantamount to attributing profit to something different than industry.

In the industry theory of usury the early modern students of medieval doctrine found an analogy to the labor theory of value in commodity exchange. As the labor interpretation tended to be abandoned in favor of a demand interpretation of the just price, a disharmony between the two main areas of doctrine seemed to appear. But it is apparent only; first, because a demand criterion of the just price does not exclude a labor criterion (as shown above); second, because the attribution of profit to industry does not ignore the fact that money is in demand, it just insists that this demand is driving the price of money above a just level, which ought to be zero. *Why* it ought to be zero under normal conditions (extrinsic titles and other, non-acceptable, factors not intervening) is then the crux of usury theory. An explanation in modern terms is perhaps possible. In the scholastics' own words — very strange and suspicious-sounding in modern ears — money can claim no share in profit because it is *sterile*. To try to understand this proposition, we must consider briefly the Aristotelian theory of money.

The most famous economic text to emerge from the Middle Ages is probably Nicole Oresme's (d. 1382) tract on money.[19] In this book the author upbraids the princes who debase the currency for their own gain, thereby causing disturbance to trade and much individual injustice. This practice is likened to fraud and stamped as economic tyranny. Oresme is sometimes said to have established a *commodity theory* of money, according to which money must find its own value in exchange, replacing a *sign theory* according to which money does its job provided the prince states firmly what its value is to be at any time, thus permitting profitable value alterations without much harm to anyone. Such a sign theory is believed to be a product of feudal economic conditions, reinforced by the discovery of Aristotle. More correctly, however, the commodity and sign theories are modern concepts, born of the institution of paper money, and apply badly to scholastic theory. Oresme was, as he states himself, an Aristotelian, and frequently built on the scholastic Aristotelian tradition. Thus a catalogue of required monetary properties, utilized by Oresme, is to be found in a number of earlier commentaries on the *Ethics* and *Politics*, for instance in Henry of Friemar's commentary on the former work. Nor was Oresme the first to brand the debaser a tyrant. Guido Terrena (d. 1342), another *Ethics* commentator, had done that several decades earlier.[20] John Buridan, who may have been Oresme's teacher at Paris, transmitted both these traditions.

According to Oresme, the primary function of money is to serve as a medium of exchange. It is this function which is disrupted by debasement of the currency. We now think of money as having several secondary functions. It can store wealth over time between exchanges. If this is done systematically, money will be sifted off from the exchange process and become capital, an object of borrowing and lending. This is what creates usury. While serving as a medium of exchange, money will also provide a scale of value measurement. This combined function is indicated in *Ethics*, V, where both human need and money are said to be *measures* of goods in exchange. But in *Politics*, I, the main locus of monetary analysis in Aristotle, where he explains the foundations of the State, measurement is hardly mentioned. The units of the State are mutually exchanging households. Money was introduced as a medium of exchange when simple barter between households became cumbersome. It is clear that Aristotle thinks of the exchange medium mainly in a physical sense, and this crude conception strongly influenced the scholastic theory of money and usury. Money is coin, specie.

It is in this connection that the concept of sterility is first introduced. In Greek the word for usury also means *offspring*, and the Latin translator of the *Politics* explained this rather than translating the word. Aristotle could then be read to mean that the usurer tries to make money breed an offspring, of which a lifeless piece of metal is not capable. But this is to misconstrue Aristotle. He actually states a teleological proposition regarding money, to which the scholastics wholeheartedly subscribed, while the most perceptive among them soon discarded the "barren metal" dogma. It is not that usury is wrong because money *cannot* breed; it is rather that money *should not* be made to breed, because this is an unnatural use of money, such as in money-changing, usury, and debasement. Oresme condemned all three. The only natural use of money is to serve as a medium of exchange. This is money's true end. But the end for which a thing is invented is subordinated to man's end, reinterpreted by the scholastics in Christian terms. Making money breed is wrong because it is inspired by cupidity, said Albert the Great.[21] This need not be (though it sometimes is) the motivation if money is used merely as a practical means for the easier exchange of necessaries. Note, however, that some scholastics (such as Henry of Ghent and Guido Terrena) came to acknowledge the usefulness of money-changers,[22] just as Albert the Great and Thomas Aquinas had acknowledged the need for professional merchants. Where merchants of different regions met, it was useful to have someone provide a supply of different coins and currencies. The money-changers might even charge a fee to cover labor and expenses. Similarly, money-*lenders* might ask to have their cost or loss covered under *extrinsic* titles. But any claim above this, based on the fruitfulness of money as such, was inspired by blameworthy cupidity and must be rejected. Thus the teleological argument still rested on the notion that money is sterile, but sterility gradually took on a different meaning.

Other traditions also provided some arguments against usury. Critics have summarized them by stating that the usurer (1) sells something which belongs to the borrower, (2) sells something which does not exist, (3) sells time, which belongs to all. We have already encountered the first of these arguments in the version of Scotus, but it also had a precise legal meaning. In patristic sources the word "usury" is often used quite loosely. Following Roman and canon law, it was restricted in scholastic usage to a particular loan contract in *fungibles*, where repayment was to be made not in the identical objects lent but in equivalent objects of the same identical species. Such contracts were not limited to money but could be made in commodity fungibles as well, such as wine, corn, or the like. Arguments against usury thus defined rely heavily on the physical conception of money. Since other pieces of coin (or bushels of corn or casks of wine) are to be paid back, ownership of the pieces lent must pass to the borrower, hence payment for the use of these pieces (*viz.* usury) is payment for something which already belongs to the borrower. This *ownership argument* was developed in canon law. On it, Aquinas built the *consumptibility argument*: wine and corn are borrowed in order to be consumed. Likewise, money is a consumptible; not because consumptibles are necessarily bought with borrowed money; it is a consumptible even if it is invested in business, since it is exchanged for something else, and in this first exchange the very pieces borrowed are alienated and thus consumed. In other words, in the case of such objects their intended use is the same thing as their substance; hence to pay for the substance (by returning an equal amount or measure) and then also to pay for its use (by an additional amount or measure) is to pay for the same thing twice or to pay for something which does not exist.[23]

Now these aruguments do not sound overly convincing. One rests on the legal definition of a certain type of contract, the other on the somewhat dubious proposition that use *is* substance. In a very influential treatise on usury, Gerardo of Siena (d. before 1336) restated the two arguments in terms of sterility. While rejecting the "barren metal" proposition from Aristotle, Gerardo argued that *all fungibles are sterile*. It is not that their use and their substance are the same thing, but that they are *one value*, since substance and use are consumed together and alienated together, and this composite remains unaltered in value all the while. It does not bear any fruit. Therefore also, referring to the ownership argument, the point is not that the borrower pays for something that is already his, but that he pays for something which has no separate use value.[24] The argument that usury is sinful because it amounts to "selling time" is of patristic origin. It could also be restated in terms of sterility. Many contracts involve a time element without therefore being usurious, since the values of the objects in question would change over time. But in the case of fungibles, said Giles of Lessines (d. after 1304), time is only an "extrinsic measure of duration," through which duration the value of the object, being sterile, remains unaltered.[25] In other words, a charge is made *merely because time passes*, and this can not be permitted.

The sterility of fungibles is a proposition which has engaged critics ever since it was rediscovered in scholastic sources. It is usually referred to as the "Andrean argument," after the canonist Joannes Andreae (d. 1348), who copied it,[26] as did Bernardino of Siena, both being very influential authors. The argument cannot be completely countered by showing that fungibles do change in value over time, just as the general price level (i.e., the value of the fungible money) changes. Gerardo explicitly conceded that they do. But although the level of interest may be influenced by price level changes, they are not its primary determinant. The real point of the argument is the value-permanence of money in terms of itself, not in terms of other things. Nor can the argument be fully met, as has often been attempted, by pointing out that money borrowed can be converted into nonfungible, fruit-bearing objects and thus bear fruit indirectly. In most statements of it, this counterargument implicitly pre-supposes the existence of a positive rate of interest, since otherwise the expected fruit would be anticipated in the value of the object bought. Criticism of Gerardo's argument must therefore retreat to the question of the social acceptability of the reasons *why* interest actually exists. This permits a remarkable analogy to be drawn between the scholastic theory of usury and the scholastic theory of just price in commodity exchange.

In modern economics, the fact and rate of interest are partly attributed to technological and growth factors, factors which, though hardly non-existent, may have played a smaller part in the medieval economies both compared to their subsequent importance and compared to other determinants then operative. These other psychological causes of inter-est are thought to be partly the tendency to overvalue present utility as compared to future, expected utility (so-called "intrinsic time pre-ference") and partly the tendency to expect (rightly or wrongly) the future to be more plentiful than the present, thus making a positive payment for anticipating the future profitable owing to different marginal utilities. Now all interest theorists agree that these phenomena are most clearly manifest in the needy and in the thoughtless and immature, i.e., in precisely the type of person the just-price doctrine was designed to protect. It is those who shut their eyes to the day of reckoning, and those in such dire straits that a loan is imperative, who will consent to pay the highest rate of usury, but in the scholastic view of things, such consent is only conditional, induced by fraud and compulsion. Add to this the fact that medieval money markets were highly imperfect and often dominated by usurers with near monopolistic powers, and it becomes less difficult to understand a theory which denies that *any* fruit is due to money as such.

There is no difference in principle between usury and just-price theory. They proceed analogously in so far as the "double rule" is concerned, applying the principles of cost and indemnity and the principle of the irrelevancy of the utility of the opposite party. But usury theory must do without the checks and correctives provided by a common estimate. In the case of money, no resort can be had to a rough guess as to what the market rate of interest would be, since the competitive market (had it existed) would have ruled out all those factors which could make the rate positive. *All* consent to pay usury is necessarily conditional only; all usury is the result of compulsion. In a question to Book IV of the *Ethics*, where Aristotle discusses the virtue of liberality, Gerald Odonis asks whether all usury is evil in itself. His first argument in opposition is that a usurious contract may be voluntary and profitable on the parts of both lender and borrower. Not so, says the commentator. The contract is not voluntary on the latter's part, for necessity forces him to borrow. Nor is it profitable, for he must repay more than he got.[27]

Usury differs little or not at all from robbery, says Raymond of Peñafort (d. 1275) in one of the most influential early *summae* for confessors,[28] thus expressing an idea which can be traced back through canon law to the Church Fathers. Virtually all later scholastics agreed on this, and they frequently employed an Aristotelian simile to explain why: usury is robbery because money, in a certain sense, is barren. Its use, in itself, is worth nothing; all apparent use value is either due to something else or evidence of personal distress or disorientation. In retrospect this can certainly be shown to have been an overstatement. Most likely it must have halted business. Its redeeming merit may be that it also halted a practice which to the scholastic doctors seemed a much more serious evil, namely the exploitation by the resourceful lender of the resourceless borrower unprotected by the justice of the competitive market.

If scarcity and business opportunities persist, human ingenuity will invent subterfuges to bypass moral strictures against lending money or selling goods and services at a profit. With the coming of capitalism, philosophers who addressed themselves to such matters set out to prove that the old strictures were illogical and even immoral in the first place. The long period of scholastic decline, which began to make itself felt already in the fifteenth century, tells the story of this readjustment. Most general histories of economics omit it and start afresh in the eighteenth century with the new conviction that "private vice is public virtue." In this brief chapter I have had to let positive scholastic doctrine (so often misunderstood) take precedence over the broader philosophical issues and the longer historical views. They deserve some brief remarks by way of conclusion.

From an analytical and terminological point of view, there is much of scholastic teaching that can be seen to have survived into modern economics. This is not surprising, since (at least if this observation is limited to our Western civilization) it was in the high Middle Ages that the foundations were first laid for the kind of systematic reasoning about social relationships that has run on continually to the present day. Sometimes, as in the case of the fairness of the market price, it was deemed pertinent above to point out a subtle shift in the moral basis which supported an apparently unaltered doctrine. Elsewhere, where doctrines have changed as radically as in the case of lending at interest, the scholastics can still be credited with posing the terms of an ongoing argument. So it would seem that much of the old vessel remained to receive new content. The question is how completely it was ever emptied of the ferment first prepared for it in the medieval schools. This is a subject which requires a book rather than a few lines. In fact, it has been the subject of many books, some of them provoked or inspired by Max Weber's ideas about religion and capitalism. For simplicity, let us recall that scholastic economic ethics rested on three intellectual traditions. The first support was the tradition of the Bible and the Church Fathers with its emphasis on individual duty. The second was the tradition of the recently rediscovered Roman law with its emphasis on individual rights. The two traditions were made to balance briefly and precariously in the Thomist synthesis by means of a third support in Aristotelian social philosophy. The "spirit of capitalism" with which scholasticism was eventually countered in the sixteenth century was also originally "justified" on the individual level. It is one of the merits of the Weber thesis to have focused on this fact. Social justification came later and transformed the ideology. Initially (to put it simply), it was mainly a question of a secularized natural rights philosophy defeating Christian deontology. "So long as the capitalist spirit remains the 'sin' of the individual," said the Italian economic historian and statesman, Amintore Fanfani, "it is not a force that will organize the world." It can do so only with "the waning of faith...in a Catholic world" or with a denial of "the relation between earthly action and eternal recompense" (as in the Protestant ethic). It would be hard to summarize one aspect of the Weber issue more succinctly than that.[29]

But this particular aspect of it does not directly involve Aristotle, the heathen philosopher, who remained a source of inspiration for Western social philosophy. It is easy to fault the scholastics for trying to rectify the evils of a fundamental maldistribution by meddling with market value instead of going to the root of the problem, which was political rather than economic, and much of this blame can be laid at the door of Aristotle, who sanctioned slavery and extreme material inequality. But this point is not one that modern economists have been any more inclined to argue than were their scholastic predecessors, and it is not difficult to show that the more readily we accept the political framework as it is, the more will our economics stand in need of Aristotelian "checks and correctives" not usually specified in elementary textbooks.

The textbook definition of social optimum is a point of balance between agents and forces each striving toward their separate conflicting extremes, unchecked by any inherent "natural limit" in the Aristotelian sense. To the Aristotelian, limitless quest in whatever direction is vicious because it perverts human nature. A perfect balance is to be sought not in externalities but as a mean of virtue in each man's moral constitution.

This ethic does not neglect the community of men, for individual virtue can attain perfection only in the perfect society. If modern "economic man" has ousted the Aristotelian from the stage of economic analysis, he is still summoned from the wings when ideology is at stake. It is no less than remarkable how the most ardent upholders of the libertarian ethic fall back on individual liberality and magnanimity (if not Christian charity) to counteract the ill effects of suprapersonal market forces running wild. This may be mostly a gesture. Unsupported by the kind of positive legislation that the libertarians deplore, scholastic justice in exchange may well be an unattainable ideal. Nevertheless, the historical fact remains that it was once taught for centuries, evidently not without some modest effect on a barbaric world.

Notes

1. Olivi, critical edition by A. Spicciani, Rome, 1977, p. 261.
2. Henry of Lagenstein, *On Contracts*, I, 11. Ed. Cologne (1484). In John Gerson's *Opera*, vol. 4, f.190v.
3. *Opera*, vol. 8, Paris, 1891, p.108.
4. *Commentary on the Sentences*, IV, 15, 2. In *Opera*, vol. 18, Paris, 1894, p. 283.
5. *Ed.cit.*, p. 256.
6. Strasbourg, 1516, f.75r.
7. Second *Commentary on the Ethics*. In *Opera*, vol. 7, Paris, 1891, p. 353.
8. *Opera*, vol. 47, Rome, 1969, pp. 294–5.
9. *Commentary on the Ethics* (unprinted). Basel: Universitätsbibliothek, cod. F.I.14; economic comments on ff.132r–135v.
10. *Questions on the Ethics*, V,16. Ed. Paris, 1513, at f.106r.
11. Sermon 35,1,1. In *Opera*, vol. 4, Quaracchi, 1956, at p. 191.
12. Siena, Biblioteca Comunale, cod. U.V.6, f.295v; cp. Ed. Spicciani, p. 255.
13. *Ed. cit.*, pp. 258–60.
14. *On Contracts* (unprinted), Siena BC, U.V.8, f.82v; cp. *Commentary on the Ethics*, Brescia (1482), f.X₅r.
15. *Commentary on the Decretals*, III, 17, 1,Venice 1578, f.75v.
16. *Summa theologiae*, II–II, 77, 1.
17. *Op. cit.*, p. 292.
18. *On Contracts*, f.91v.
19. Critical edition by C. Johnson, London, 1956.
20. Paris, Bibliothèque Nationale, cod. 1at. 3228, f.45r.
21. *Comm. Pol.*,p. 61.
22. Henry, *Quodlibeta*, VI, 22, Paris, 1518, f.243r; Guido, *loc. cit.*
23. *Sum. theol.*, II–II, 78, 1; cp. *Quodl.*, III, 19, and elsewhere.
24. *On Usury*, Cesena 1630, pp. 176–80.
25. *On Usury*, Parma 1864. In Aquinas's *Opera*, vol. 17, p. 426.
26. *Quaestiones mercuriales*, Lyon, 1551, ff.261v–62r.

27. *Ed. cit.*, ff.P$_3$v–P$_4$r.
28. Rome, 1603, p. 227.
29. Fanfani [2], pp. 18, 178, 205.

References

Baldwin, John W. "The Medieval Theories of the Just Price." *Transactions of the American Philosophical Society* 49:4, 1959.

Dempsey, Bernard W. *Interest and Usury.* London: 1948.

De Roover, Raymond. *San Bernardino of Siena and Sant' Antonino of Florence. The Two Great Economic Thinkers of the Middle Ages.* Boston: 1967.

Fanfani, Amintore. *Le origini dello spirito capitalistico in Italia.* Milan: 1933.

——————. *Catholicism, Protestantism and Capitalism.* London: 1935.

Gonnard, René: *Histoire des doctrines monétaires*, I–II Paris: 1935–36.

Gordon, Barry. *Economic Analysis before Adam Smith.* London: 1975.

Langholm, Odd. *Price and Value in the Aristotelian Tradition.* Bergen: 1979.

——————. "Economic Freedom in Scholastic Thought." *History of Political Economy* 14:1982, 260–283.

——————. *Wealth and Money in the Aristotelian Tradition.* Bergen: 1983.

——————. *The Aristotelian Analysis of Usury.* Bergen: 1984.

Miller, Constantin. *Studien zur Geschichte der Geldlehre bis auf Oresmius.* Stuttgart: 1925.

Monroe, Arthur Eli. *Monetary Theory before Adam Smith.* Cambridge, MA: 1923.

Nègre, Pierre. *Essais sur les conceptions économiques de Saint Thomas d'Aquin.* Aix-en-Provence: 1927.

Noonan, John T., Jr. *The Scholastic Analysis of Usury.* Cambridge, MA: 1957.

O'Brien, George. *An Essay on Mediaeval Economic Teaching.* London: 1920.

Schlatter, Richard. *Private Property. The History of an Idea.* London: 1951.

Schreiber, Edmund. *Die volkswirtschaftlichen Anschauungen der Scholastic seit Thomas v. Aquin.* Jena: 1913.

Spicciani, Amleto. *La mercatura e la formazione del prezzo nella riflessione teologica medioevale.* Rome: 1977.

Viner, Jacob. "Religious Thought and Economic Society." *History of Political Economy* 10:1978, 1–192.

Weber, Max. *The Protestant Ethic and the Spirit of Capitalism.* London: 1930.

Worland, Stephen T. *Scholasticism and Welfare Economics.* Notre Dame, IN: 1967.

Commentary by Stephen T. Worland
Scholastic Economics *Commentary*

A major factor affecting the spirit and content of scholastic economic thought was the rediscovery of Aristotle and the subsequent effort to synthesize his pagan views into the mainstream of Judeo-Christian revelation. To fully appreciate Langholm's thoughtful and illuminating exposition of scholastic economics, it might be helpful to emphasize two basic factors in the Aristotelian revival. Doing so will clarify both the historical development from patristic to scholastic economic thought and will also bring out a crucial philosophical distinction between the latter and contemporary mainstream neo-classical economics.

For one thing, a critical difference between medieval and patristic thought emerges when scholastic natural law theory takes over and incorporates into its analysis of moral obligation and social relationships the basic structure of Aristotle's ethical system. Thus, in his "Treatise on the Last End" where he lays the foundation for his system of natural law,[1] Aquinas develops a line of analysis which parallels closely Aristotle's sustained effort to identify man's highest good in terms of a characteristic human function — the exercise of reason. Using Gospel images such as the Mary and Martha story, he adopts and makes his own the major and crucial principle of Aristotle's analysis. Man's highest good involves a blending of the contemplative life of the sage with the active life of the man exemplifying moral, cultural, and political excellence. This is not to say, however, that Aquinas merely accepts and restates the Aristotelian doctrine. On the contrary, writing as a Christian theologian, he provides a very significant extension for Aristotle's natural teleology by introducing a differentiation between two levels of human perfection, or between two dimensions of man's highest good. He distinguishes between "perfect happiness" — the cognitive union with God attainable as a divine gift in the afterlife — and that combination of practical activity and rational contemplation which, as Aristotle had shown, constitutes man's highest natural human good, to be attained in this life through the cultivation of wisdom and virtue. To mark the distinction, Aquinas identifies the latter as "imperfect happiness."[2] An accurate appraisal of scholastic economic thought requires that the relationship between these two dimensions of human perfection be carefully understood.

Man is brought to an understanding of the "perfect happiness" attainable in eternity only through revelation and the gift of faith. That condition of human well-being designated "imperfect happiness," on the other hand, is a natural good. Knowledge of its content and conditions for realization is acquired, not from supernatural sources, but through the kind of systematic enquiry exemplified in the philosophy of Aristotle. Now, to note an absolutely crucial point, the relationship between these two levels of perfection is conceived in the scholastic system as complementary. The fact that perfect happiness transcends natural happiness does not imply that the latter is to be sacrificed for the sake of the former. On the contrary, the adoption of Aristotle's psychology as the base for the natural law system of ethics, incorporation of his conception of happiness into the Christian tradition, involved recognition of the crucial fact that each level of happiness — perfect and imperfect — carries its own intrinsic value and dignity. This means that, although the ultimate fulfillment of human desire comes only with the attainment of a supernatural good — the cognitive union with the Divine Essence — scholastic moral philosophy also requires that the kind of "imperfect happiness" exemplified in the exercise of wisdom and virtuous activity be considered the appropriate teleological objective for worldly human conduct. The implication for human history and institutional development is crucial. The family of mankind is to move through history toward ultimate perfect happiness over a mundane route — by pursuing the path of personal and cultural development that, as Aristotle had shown, leads to the exemplification of those intellectual, practical,and cultural excellences which constitute man's natural characteristic good and perfection.[3]

At an earlier stage in the development of Judeo-Christian culture — when the social system could offer nothing better than the fractured security of feudalism to counter the anarchy of barbarism, when withdrawal into the isolation of monasticism offered the only plausible way to live a life exemplifying Christian values — dedication to man's transcendent and supernatural good may have required an ascetic rejection of those natural and psychological social drives which, so the study of Aristotle was eventually to show, serve to locate and identify authentic human perfection. But such a conception of the relationship between natural and supernatural values could not survive in principle — though the older view maintained a continuing impact on practice — the rediscovery and systematic adaptation of Aristotle's moral philosophy. Henceforth, those natural, worldly goods the value of which could be vindicated by rational enquiry were to be accepted as morally obligatory objects of pursuit,their attainment being considered as preparatory and contributory to those transcendent joys promised the faithful believer by Judeo-Christian revelation.

Langholm indicates [p. 1] that the development of scholastic economic thought involved a "searching for norms" to be applied to a range of newly discovered social problems.this observation lends emphasis to a second critical aspect of the Aristotelian revival. As a species of ethical naturalism, the Aristotelian system identifies the good as the object of natural desire and assigns to practical reason (as distinguished from theoretical science) the task of discerning, articulating, and rectifying through the moral virtues the pattern of natural inclination. Such a conception of the good and of moral knowledge implies the operation of a progressive social dynamic, a pervasive tendency which — though subject to deflection by accidental factors such as the barbarian invasions — pulls the wagon train of history along the route from barbarism toward civilization.[4] According to such a perspective, the anthropological discovery that social institutions evolve from a primitive stage governed by tribal instinct to a higher level where social relationships are more deliberate and rational — from *gemeinschaft* to *gesellschaft* in Toennies' formulation, or from "*status* to *contract*" as in Sir Henry Maine's classic principle — is an empirical corollary of the Aristotelian-scholastic conception of the way mankind acquires and accumulates insight into the ever-expanding possibilities for human perfection and excellence.[5] Moreover, as Langholm notes, the monumental effort to integrate Aristotle into the Christian world view coincides historically with a series of related developments in the European cultural system — the shift from feudalism toward a more stable social order based upon Roman conceptions of law; the revival and growth of town life; the rise of universities; the emergence of new social classes including masters and students, merchants, lawyers, and a municipal bureaucracy. Medieval society thus represents a culture in transition from a near-anarchic barbarism tenuously stabilized by feudal loyalties toward a more articulate social order where reason and conscious deliberation begin to replace the imperatives of tribal instinct. Development of the medieval social system seems to exemplify the dynamic implied in the scholastic conception of natural law and practical reason.

These considerations suggest a twofold explanatory thesis that might facilitate the understanding of scholastic economics. Such economic reasoning can be understood as an effort to articulate the ethical norms required to regulate economic activity for a culture encountering the tensions of growing rationality — i.e., for a community moving from the primitive stage regulated by biological instinct and tribal loyalties, toward a society wherein social relationships are governed by deliberate reason.[6] Furthermore, the shift toward greater social rationality coincides with the effort to incorporate Aristotle's conception of the good life into the

Christian ethical system. This being the case, the economic norms to be articulated, while true to the belief that man's perfect happiness is not of this world, would have to acknowledge that natural goods and perfections have their own proper claim on human conduct and institutional design.

The dissonance encountered in the transformation of tribal community into political society can be detected in the development of the basic principle of scholastic economics — the just-price doctrine. As Langholm explains it, the scholastics took over the Roman legal principle that "a thing is worth what it can be sold for" [p. 5], but adapted the principle so as to forbid taking advantage of a buyer's special need. Thus they were led to identify the just price as that determined by the *communis aestimatio* as the latter is expressed "unintentionally through the impersonal working of the economy" [p. 11]. Using neoclassical terminology to make his point, Langholm concludes that the price identified by the scholastics as the *just price* coincides with what current textbooks designate as "normal competitive price" [p. 11], equal at equilibrium with long-run average cost [p. 12]. Though invited to do so by Aristotle's discussion of exchange between craftsmen [*Nichomachean Ethics*, Book V], so he also finds, the scholastics never propounded the crude notion that the exchange ratio between commodities is determined by the relative "social status" of the producers. With this critical conclusion, Langholm differs decisively with what was once accepted as the standard interpretation of the medieval just-price doctrine.[7] The difference between his view and that of his predecessors can be reconciled by taking account of how the perception of economic morality shifts and develops in a culture advancing in rationality from tribal community to political society.

A primitive community forced to resort to such crude expedients as the "Truce of God" to mitigate the brutality of feudal warfare, or to trial by ordeal to settle private disputes, might very well adopt as a rule of exchange a principle that, however crude, would minimize the possibility of social instability. Such a stabilizing principle could be found in the proposition that the just price of a commodity must be such as to maintain the producer in his given and customary social position. However, as it evolves into a political society — building towns, setting up universities, learning to use the rational principles of Roman law — such a community would also begin to acquire a deeper, more carefully reasoned understanding of the process of production and exchange. Complemented by the recovery of Aristotle, expanding social rationality would eventually discern the critical distinction between two kinds of justice — *distributive*, governing the relationship between society and the individual, and *commutative* justice, bearing upon the interaction of one private individual and another — and come to recognize that private exchange, where the value of the price of a commodity is crucial, is governed by the second kind of justice. When the developmental process is completed, such a society will have made the rational discovery that exchange ratios are rightly determined by the relative utility of commodities as reflected in prices prevailing on an open and fair market. Requiring exchange at prices determined by producer social position will at this higher stage of social development, be recognized for what Langholm says it is — "economic nonsense." In its economic institutions, such a society will have negotiated the transition identified in Sir Henry Maine's famous thesis [p. 141] as the movement of a "progressive society" from "Status to Contract."

A comparable growing regard for rationality is also reflected in the scholastic teaching concerning usury. In the earlier stages of medieval social development, as a specialized, urbanized economic system first began to take shape within the heretofore rural and feudal community, the prevailing attitude toward money and its role in the social system was characterized by what one commentator [Little, 1978, pp. 177f] has identified as a "notable irrationality." As Langholm's exposition makes clear, the situation had changed decisively by the time Aquinas came to compose Question 78 — "Of the Sin of Usury" — in the *Secunda Secundae* of the *Summa Theologica*. Using a classification borrowed from Roman law, Aquinas concludes that interest taking is unjust on the grounds that money (a cash balance) is *res fungible* — a commodity the use of which cannot be separated from its ownership. To charge for the use of money — to demand return of the ownership of a stock of money, plus a charge for its use — is to take advantage of the special need of the borrower and hence unjust. In place of superstitious vilification of the money-lender, Aquinas offers a reasoned argument, an analysis susceptible of rational exposition, of clarification, and of the logical development required to adapt to changing circumstances. As an instance of the latter, recognizing the legitimacy of charging for the use of *res non fungible* — a category which would include durable producers' goods — seems to imply moral approval of the practice of collecting interest for investment in real capital [Stark, 1956, p. 15]. Pushed to its logical conclusion, such an interpretation of the usury doctrine would disprove the contention that the just price theory presupposes the labor theory of value, and thus provide definitive rejection of R. H. Tawney's grandiloquent conclusion [1947, p. 39] — "The last of the schoolmen was Karl Marx."

In his discussion of the institution of property, Langholm takes note of a significant change of emphasis between the older, patristic and the later scholastic views. As he indicates [p. 3], the Fathers of the Church "explained property as an institution made necessary by man's sinful nature."[8] With the discovery of Aristotle, however, the justification for private property begins to change. Aquinas adopts the key principle that a blend of contemplative and virtuous activity constitutes the highest of natural human goods and goes on to draw a critical Aristotelian inference — "external goods" (material wealth) are good and desirable because they are necessary to maintain the biological life of the body, and also because such goods can be employed as "instruments" in the exercise of virtuous activity — e.g., in the performance of acts of liberality.[9] Since virtuous activity must be self-initiated, the "instruments" of virtue must, as Langholm notes, be controlled by the acting agent — hence, the justification for private property. Thus, the shift in attitudes toward private property derives from the effort to incorporate Aristotle's conception of the good life into the Christian ethic.

The reference to wealth as desirable and good, not only as providing biological subsistence but also as "instruments" required for the exercise of moral and artistic excellence, also points to a critical difference between the perception of economic activity in the tribal community and such perception as operative in political society. In the first, economic goods are perceived mainly as necessary for sustaining the biological life process of individual and tribe. In such a culture, the economic process — the production and distribution of material wealth — is oriented toward, and takes as its end, the satisfaction of biological need. As the community evolves from tribe to political society, and as it is recognized that such society exists to allow men not only to live, but to "live well," as reason replaces tribal instinct in the articulation of ethical norms, the perceived goal or purpose of economic activity shifts — from that of providing mere necessary sustenance, to that of providing the material instruments needed for exemplification of the full, complementary panoply of human excellence. To note the contrast with classical economics, Adam Smith's famous dictum [1937, p. 625] — "consumption is the sole end and purpose of all production" — involves a crucial and valid moral insight, one of immense importance for discerning the moral disorientation characteristic of the mercantile system. However, with the reference to "consumption," Smith's statement seems to take subsistence, rather than the exemplification of excellence, as the end and goal of economic activity. In doing so, he adopts a point of view appropriate for a tribal community, not for a rational political society, and in the process, so the scholastic conception indicates, understates the cosmic significance involved in mankind's production, distribution, and exchange of material goods.

Langholm points out [p. 4] that since the exercise of liberality is intended to contribute to the common use of property, the case for liberality as adopted in scholastic economics would be restated in terms of "such Christian virtues as compassion, charity, and mercy." His point is well taken but must be carefully understood. The distinction between charity as required by the Christian view and the classical conception of liberality as a natural perfection would appear to be critical. Acts of charity (almsgiving) are ordinarily intended to provide for the relief of those in need. Thus, if the common use of wealth is to be achieved *only* through charity (and not also through the exemplification of such natural excellences as *liberality* or *magnificence*) then production is oriented exclusively toward biological consumption — including that of both the original wealth-owner of him who benefits from the act of charity. A society which so conceives of economic activity is in danger of lapsing into the archaic, tribal perception of the production of wealth and into a similar perception of the social relationships associated with production. Moreover, according to the relationship between nature and grace implied in scholastic natural law theory, such a society has institutionalized a misperception of the relationship between *perfect* and *imperfect* happiness, failing to observe the crucial principle that the latter, with all the natural perfections that it implies, has its own intrinsic value and is a "participation" in and preparation for the former.

To come to a final interesting point raised by Langholm, as he notes there is a "sense of contradiction" inherent in the scholastics' analysis of economic activity. Forced to acknowledge that such activity is apparently motivated by the desire to maximize individual economic benefit, they nevertheless adhered to the belief that the "Gospel message" requires one to "shun worldly riches" and to "love one's neighbor as one's self" [p. 2]. It is indeed the case that such an ambivalence is often encountered in scholastic works on economics. In a set of policy recommendations formulated for the King of Cyprus, Aquinas [1949, sections 76, 78] at one point roundly denounces trade because such profit-seeking activity "awakens greed in the hearts of the citizens" and induces "each one to seek his own profit, despising the public good." In a subsequent passage, however, he also acknowledges that trade provides the natural mechanism for redistributing local surpluses, forestalling the waste of resources, and therefore concludes that professional traders have an essential role to play in "the perfect city."

The scholastics were master logicians and great systematizers. This being the case, the "sense of contradiction" displayed in their discussion of economic matters is puzzling — how could a body of analysis typically expressed in tight syllogistic form fall into what appears to be a patent inconsistency? Anglo-Saxon folk memory — e.g., as reflected in Shakespeare (*MacBeth*, Act II, Scene 3) — suggests one rather unedifying explanation for the "contradiction." The scholastics, like their post-Reformation Jesuit successors, were great "equivocators." They knew how to bend a moral principle when doing so would suit their own, and especially the papacy's, financial purposes. However, the distinction between community and society also suggests an alternative, perhaps more fruitful, explanation for the apparent incoherence. The sense of contradiction referred to by Langholm reflects the difficulties encountered by a culture negotiating the transition from archaic, feudal community to rational political society while trying to articulate an evaluation of economic practices based on Aristotle's conception of the good life.

Following Aristotle, Aquinas holds that the production of economic goods serves a twofold purpose — assuring biological subsistence for the population, but also providing those material "instruments" needed for the exemplification of moral and cultural excellences (e.g., in the practice of liberality, magnificence, and the fine arts).[10] Now as previously suggested, it seems plausible to assume that the perception of the first purpose might predominate in a tribal community while recognition of the second would emerge in the transition to political society. While the first perception endures, economic expansion beyond that needed to satisfy basic needs would seem to have no moral justification. The gains from economic growth could go only to feed the wanton desire for consumer luxuries by a tribal elite. Moreover, in a feudal community obsessed with the necessity of achieving an end to violence and private warfare, the kind of innovative rationalizing conduct required to achieve economic expansion would be perceived as destabilizing, a threat both to public order and received tribal values. Commentators trying to give formal expression to such moral instincts could find plenty of textual justification in the Gospel message and in Aristotle for denouncing such profit maximizing as selfish — as the old vice of *avarice* appearing in new form amid emerging market relationships.

However, as universities and towns develop, as the cultural level rises, as the regard for artistic grandeur emerges into collective consciousness — in short, as the community-to-society transition gets underway — the perception of economic activity shifts and deepens. Production no longer serves mere biological subsistence; rather, the purpose of economic activity is elevated and enhanced toward providing the instruments needed to exemplify cultural and artistic excellence. Economic expansion thus acquires a moral justification not apparent in the tribal community. Moreover, as the community grows in collective rationality — e.g., adopting Roman legal forms and procedures as a supplement and corrective for tribal custom — the regard for rationality would spread to the evaluation of economic practices and institutions. If such is the case, profit-oriented trade and market relationships might come to be perceived, not as devices permitting free play for destructive private egoism, but as social mechanisms needed to release economic incentive so as to build the material base for a flowering culture.[11]

An accurate understanding of the historical significance of scholastic economics requires that this latter inference be carefully understood. Langholm indicates that progress in economic analysis requires a "new philosophical outlook" which, unlike scholastic practice, accepts human-nature "for what it is and seeks to guide it towards socially useful ends" [p. 2]. Such a shift in philosophic outlook — e.g., as reflected in the work of Hobbes or Bentham — has indeed occurred since the scholastics wrote and has no doubt contributed a great deal to the advance of formal economic analysis. However, from the modern perspective, rational profit maximization as assumed in neo-classical analysis appears as a special case of generalized egoism. Economic agents including traders and entre-preneurs are selfish because all men are selfish and successful public policy will have to recognize the fact.[12] Careful consideration of the natural law explanation for social development, on the other hand, indicates that the historical connection between egoism as exemplified in Hobbes' theory, institutional reliance on the profit motive, and progress in economic analysis is accidental. Recognition of the cultural justification for economic expansion, adoption of rational procedures in law and other institutions — emerging in the transition from tribe to society — provide a moral justification for profit maximization that does not depend on the assumption that economic behavior is naturally egoistic. According to this latter view, the goal of economic policy is not to channel native selfish-ness toward socially beneficial objectives. Rather, economic institutions must inculcate those moral virtues — primarily *justice*, but also the practice of *liberality* and *magnificence* — that give moral direction to the natural human inclination to search out opportunities for economic gain.

Notes

1. *Summa Theologica*, I–II, Q. 1–Q.5.
2. *Ibid.*, Q. 3, a. 2, ad 4; Q. 3. a. 5; Q. 4. a. 5. Cf. Troeltsch [1931, pp. 264ff].
3. Thus, according to Troeltsch [1931, p. 405], Aquinas is said to have incorporated

"into the...Christian end of...the Vision of God, the Aristotelian end of social welfare
...the full development of intellectual and physical...capacities, subordinating them as
an intermediate end, the attainment of which disposes and prepares the soul for the *finis
ultimus.*" Cf. Christopher Dawson's assertion [1958, p. 176] that integration of "Aristotelian
ethical and sociological principles...into the structure of Christian thought" led to emphasis
on the "concordance and harmonization" between secular, natural values, and Christian
ideals rather than, as in patristic thought, on their opposition.

4. Cf. Etienne Gilson [1936, p. 389]. Cf. *Summa Theologica*, I–II, Q. 97, a. 1.

5. Cf. the explanation of how, in the Aristotelian natural-law model, the social system is
conceived as evolving from tribal *community* to political *society* discovering and exemplifying more rational, higher cultural norms along the way, in Gilby [1953].

6. Cf. Little [1978, chapter 2, "Adopting to the Profit Economy"].

7. Cf. Worland [1977, esp.p. 505].

8. For similar statements of the Church's Fathers' views on property, cf. Little [1978,
p. 176]; Gilby [1953, p. 23].

9. *Summa Theologica*, I–II, Q. 4, a. 7. "...it is lawful to desire temporal
things...insofar as they are the means of supporting life, and are of service to us as
instruments in performing acts of virtue...." Cf. *Ibid.*, II–II, Q. 83, a. 6.

10. For an example of a commentator who singularly underestimates Aquinas as to the
twofold purpose of economic goods and thereby comes to a quite inaccurate interpretation
of the relationship between scholastic economic ethics and capitalism, cf. A. Fanfani's
classic work [1984, esp. p. 127].

11. Cf. Gilby's observation [1953, p. 188] that, according to the social dialectic of
Aquinas, "the best political system...can allow for the incentive of private profit without
apology...."

12. For a recent restatement of the connection between Hobbes' philosophy and the
legitimation of economic self interest, cf. M. L. Myers [1983, esp. pp.29–34].

References

Aquinas, Thomas. *Summa Theologica*. Literally translated by Fathers of the
    English Dominican Province. New York: Benziger Brothers, 1947.
Aquinas, Thomas. *On Kingship*. Done into English by Gerald B. Phelan.
    Toronto: The Pontifical Institute of Medieval Studies, 1949.
Dawson, Christopher. *Religion and the Rise of Western Culture*. Image Books
    edition. New York: Sheed & Ward, 1958.
Fanfani, A. *Catholicism, Protestantism, and Capitalism*. First published in 1935.
    Notre Dame, IN: University of Notre Dame Press, 1984.
Gilby, Thomas. *Between Community and Society*. London: Longmans, Green,
    1953.
Gilson, Etienne. *The Spirit of Medieval Philosophy*. New York: Charles
    Scribners' Sons, 1936.
Little, Lester K. *Religious Poverty and the Profit Economy*. Ithaca, NY: Cornell
    University Press, 1978.
Maine, Sir Henry. *Ancient Law*. First published in 1861; reissued with an
    introduction by Sir Carleton Allen. London: Oxford University Press, 1931.

Smith, Adam. *The Wealth of Nations*. Modern Library Edition. New York: Random House, 1937.

Stark, W. *The Contained Economy*. Aquinas Paper No. 26. London: Aquinas Press, 1956.

Tawney, R. H. *Religion and the Rise of Capitalism*. Mentor Book edition. New York: The American Library of World Literature, 1947.

Troeltsch, Ernst. *The Social Teaching of the Christian Churches*. Trans. by Olive Wyon. New York: The Macmillan Co., 1931.

Worland, Stephen T. *"Justum Pretium*: One More Round in an 'Endless Series.'" *History of Political Economy* 9:1977, 504–22.

6 THE DEVELOPMENT OF MERCANTILIST ECONOMIC THOUGHT

Richard C. Wiles

I

Eli Heckscher, prominent interpreter of mercantilism both as a system of thought and as a body of policy-oriented proscriptions, made a valiant but desperate effort to place his topic in the sweep of Western economic thought and development. Heckscher suggested that mercantilism flourished from the end of the Middle Ages until the advent of laissez-faire. If one today were convinced of the accuracy of such an elastic definition — assuming agreement could be reached on the beginning and ending dates — it would be thought remarkable that any body of economic doctrine would have been able to retain consistency over some six to seven centuries. It is even less likely that an advocate of mercantilist approaches to the economy and society at the beginning of Heckscher's time period would bear any close resemblance to an economic writer in mid-eighteenth century [Heckscher, 1954].

Without belaboring this point and becoming enmeshed in the rather unproductive task of defining and delimiting mercantilism, it is best to accept a time period less ambitious than Heckscher's which most analysts agree could be characterized as the "heyday" of mercantilist thought and

147

practice. This view would suggest that European economic development from approximately the sixteenth to the eighteenth centuries provides the proper backdrop for the economic analysis, practical policy suggestions, and legal applications that have been rather loosely judged to be mercantilist.

Thus Heckscher's ending date — the advent of laissez-faire — may be accepted as the end of the mercantilist paradigm. If paradigm it was. This is especially the case with eighteenth century English economic writing. Such a demarcation, however, is not meant to suggest that mercantilist-like ideas did not precede this period, nor that remnants of such thought departed from the economic scene forever with the publication of the *Wealth of Nations*. As Alexander Gray noted years ago, the economic thought of any period is a "fricassee" of the ages [Gray, 1959].

With this new time limitation for the period of mercantilism, a warning: the consistency of a mercantilist body of thought and analysis that one would not expect over Heckscher's lengthy period is by no means a foregone conclusion from the sixteenth to the eighteenth centuries. Realizing this does not necessarily argue for the charge often made in the critical literature that the mercantilists were unsystematic, ad hoc, and merely special pleaders in their economic writings who rushed to suggestions for state policy in a haphazard manner to enrich the sovereign. For there is more continuity and cohesiveness in mercantilist literature than such a view allows. Interpreters have been led to such conclusions by the fact that there are indeed many "mercantilisms" over our time period. The differences may be partly national and partly due to the state of economic doctrine and institutions at the time one takes a snapshot of their work. It is certainly true that one does not find the consistency in analytical approach and policy proscriptions in mercantilism that one discerns, for example, in scholastic analysis. Yet consistency there is, in subsectors of their economic thought. At times their economic and political goals, their economic analyses, and their socio-economic policies did have more cohesiveness than is often admitted, even though such cohesiveness may not be present across national boundaries or sub-time periods.

To attempt to generalize too broadly about mercantilist economic thought is to lose its richness and variety as well as its changing mode of analysis over time. Standard interpretations have often missed this aspect in a too facile attempt to fit mercantilism into either a "school" or "stream" pattern in the long sweep of economic doctrine and its development. Mercantilist ideas, like most periods and schools of economic thought, did change and develop. Yet a continuity remained. To conclude, as many have, that all we see in reading mercantilist literature over our period are hasty policy promulgations devoid of analysis, is to read their work superficially and to ignore the institutional and systematic structure within which they worked. As an example, Eli Heckscher maintained that although his research did not include works after 1710, one was likely to find from that point until Adam Smith's great contribution appeared some amalgam of laissez-faire ideas with more "typical" mercantilist analyses. As will be argued below, his guess was an accurate one, especially in the British context. Yet such an amalgam is not necessarily a hybrid body of economic thought but simply yet another variant of mercantilist analysis and one that can be considered the fullest flowering of mercantilism in general. Edgar Furniss has referred to this period and its writers in England as "later English mercantilists" [Furniss, 1957].

One final aspect of the term "mercantilism" should be mentioned. In this context, the economic *doctrine* of such writers is of prime concern and not policy in an applied form. Many disagreements as to the systematic or unsystematic character of mercantilism or the question whether it constitutes a "school" arise from the critics' concentration on actual economic *policiés* of France, Germany, England, and others in this period. For example, the most interesting recent work of Ekelund and Tollison [1981] interprets mercantilist policy as a search after economic rents via regulation. This is a most provocative view which reinterprets the economic history of the period by broadening policy goals beyond bullionist aims. Yet the mercantilist *ideas* that one finds in the literature do not necessarily fit such a pattern of analysis. In short, policy and doctrine deserve separate treatment. Such a demarcation between policy and doctrine — though they obviously overlap at times — is crucial in this analysis [Coleman 1969, p.100]. Yet even if one concentrates on the thought aspects of such writers, consistency has been denied. As Philip W. Buck [1942, p. 2] concludes in his *The Politics of Mercantilism*: "There is no coherent body of theory developed by one writer; there is not even the relatively consistent viewpoint of a group of allied thinkers." On the other hand, as mentioned above, is there such solidarity of doctrine in any period of economic thought of equal time span? One of the few who recognized this problem was S. J. Brandenburg in his work on British mercantilism. In 1931 he maintained that one should not expect consistency from any group writing over at least a two-century span [Brandenburg, 1931, p. 282]. Yet, having noted this, he, like many other critics, charged mercantilism with being "system-less" even though comprehensive. Such writers, in his view, had little connection with one another and, with few exceptions, worked independently [Brandenburg,

1931; Buck, 1942, p. 2]. Spengler agrees, holding that the mercantilists, unlike the scholastics, physiocrats, or the classical economists, built no system [Spengler, 1960, p. 17; Schumpeter, 1954, p. 39]. It is extremely difficult to substantiate such charges, especially among the later English mercantilists, as will be shown. The contacts among them and the internal evidence in their writings show extensive awareness of each other's work. Yet even such criticism does not prevent this same group of critics from discovering overall aims and themes among the very same writers they see as haphazard and even disjointed in their approach to economic phenomena. Two examples will point this out. William Cunningham stresses the overall aim of mercantilist thought as that of seeking power for the nation. In his mind this was true of all "publicists" in our period until Adam Smith's work:

> Till his [Adam Smith's] time the main object, which publicists who dealt with economic topics had had before their minds, was the power of the country; they set themselves to discuss the particular aspects of industry and commerce which would conduce to this end, according to the circumstances of different countries. The requirements of the State had been the first consideration of seventeenth century writers, and they had worked back to the funds in the possession of the people from which these requirements could be supplied [Cunningham, 1912, II, p. 593].

Others have commonly picked up on the power goal — some tempering it a bit with the addition of complementary aims of national economic welfare or wealth of the nation. The national power aim is most forcefully and prominently stated in Heckscher's great work on mercantilism. In stressing the mercantilists' concern with *external* power of the state, Heckscher turns the table slightly in admitting that such singlemindedness in this body of thought required a uniform body of doctrine [Heckscher, 1954, I, p. 22]. In fact, the second part of his famous study is entitled "Mercantilism as a System of Power." For Heckscher this power goal appeared under two guises: power per se, especially in a military sense, as well as the power to be achieved via national economic prosperity [Heckscher, 1954, II, ch. II]. Thus a welfare ideal would be merely auxiliary to an ulterior goal. As mentioned above, Heckscher's work includes few eighteenth century sources, so that his isolation of goals might have been altered had he extended his research. In fact, in an article published after his book had appeared, he admitted the mercantilist aim to be more inclusive than he first thought to be the case. He now perceived a dual aim, opulence as well as power. Yet he still clung to his earlier contention that although the aims were dual, power held the more prominent place in mercantilist thought [Heckscher, 1936, p. 48].

A more recent piece continues the debate. Robert K. Schaeffer, writing of the "entelechies" of mercantilism, interprets the goals of mercantilist economic thought in philosophical terms, arguing that during the seventeenth and eighteenth centuries the words *nation* and *state* were not interchangeable and that Heckscher and, before him, Gustav Schmoller used the state as both subject and object of mercantilism, Schmoller emphasizing that "state-making" and "national economy-making" occurred at the same time. Schaeffer contrasts this view with that of Adam Smith and J. M. Keynes, who saw the "nation" as the aim of mercantilism. Such a discussion moves the search for "mercantilism" to another plane, and one is almost led back to the suggestion of E. A. J. Johnson that the term "mercantilism" is a "positive nuisance" [Schaeffer, 1981; Wilson, 1957, p. 62]. Perhaps this confusion in the ferreting out of goals — especially the non-economic ones — was simply a way to organize what seemed hopelessly variegated materials. Indeed, even mercantilist writers themselves noted the disarray and the lack of integrated material. For example, John Bennet wrote in 1736, arguing for some collation, yet not despairing of its possibility:

> Most certainly it would be of singular Use and Benefit to the Publick, if the Science of Trade were brought to some certainty, by an established Set of Principles and Maxims, which might assist and direct our Conclusions. All other Arts and Sciences almost, by the Care and Industry of Men, have their Postulata, and fixed Principles methodized; why then should not the Science of Trade be cultivated and Improved, and be brought to some kind of Perfection? Is it not for want of some certain Rule to guide us, that private Interest has so often got the better of publick Good in Deliberations of so much Concern and Importance, as are Matters of Trade and Commerce, upon which the Happiness and Glory of Great Britain, in the Highest Degree, are known to depend?

Bennet then calls for a synthesizer:

> Scarce any Architect has yet appeared in this Science: Indeed there have been some good Workmen, and some very good designers; but where is the regular, useful, and magnificent Structure, which they have built? Almost every one has laid down Propositions suited to the End he had in view; and Men differ not more in anything than they do in items of Trade [Bennet, 1736, pp. 4, 32].

Joseph Massie saw the same array of disjointed tracts on commerce which needed to be worked up into some systematic order [Massie, 1760, pp. 1, 17–18]. This was required in order to gain understanding of trade as a "national concern."

Yet in such a search, for the mercantilists themselves as well as for later critics, the area of concern was too circumscribed and too much coherence was expected of different time periods and differing national views. It certainly is true that Heckscher's spectre looms over the dispute, with his enormous prestige the starting point for any such discussion. Under his influence the connecting tissue between mercantilist writers with respect to goals has been their non-economic aims — state-building, power, and military might. When the economic realm is stressed, as in Adam Smith's interpretation, the central tenet is seen as a bullionist outlook with a favorable balance of trade the touchstone for success. Though Smith's mercantilist was a straw man to a large degree, his interpretation has been a popular one with lengthy staying power. Of course, one should be aware of the close affinity between bullionism and the power aims. One could speak of short-run and longer-run concerns, the former the mechanism by which the long-run power goals were achieved.

But is it enough to credit these thinkers with an understanding of economic mechanisms and the operations of economic institutions? To label all of mercantilist thought as seeking national hoards of bullion for the ulterior goals of "sinews of war" and national power is to miss the richness, originality, and the complex economic interrelationships these writers considered. These concerns grew far more sophisticated and complex over our lengthy time period and did differ, at times, between nations. Yet if we abstract the thinking from the policies suggested or applied, there is firm evidence of an amalgam. It is further the case that such an amalgam, in a doctrinal sense, reached its fullest development in the very period in which Heckscher expected a mix of laissez-faire and mercantilism. Variously defined, one could isolate this period from approximately 1650 to 1776 in England. Joseph Schumpeter finds in this phase a critical revision of previous work, a revision "which constitutes the main analytical effort of the mercantilist writers" [Schumpeter, 1954, p. 362]. A sketch will be attempted of the major developments of the economic thinking of such writers over this time period as well as a summary of the changing goals of their economic analyses.

II

To begin with an ancient intellectual device, it is useful to attempt to ferret out the economic reasoning of an "ideal type" mercantilist, bearing in mind the variations that such a device would allow. First, a word about the literature. To construct or reconstruct the mercantilist doctrine one must review a vast and variegated series of pamphlets, broadsides, monographs, and proposals of schemes. Such a body of writing, difficult to collate, extends throughout the eighteenth century. Monographs of an overall analytic nature are rare, though far more frequent in the century before the *Wealth of Nations*. What must be done is to take a synthetic approach to extract the commonality from such pamphleteers and schemers as well as from the more technical economic tracts. Herein lies one of the major reasons for the long-standing debate over the lack of systematization in mercantilism. The literature has been read as fragmented, ad hoc in nature, and its authors segregated from each other. The commonality has been denied along with serious doctrinal changes in economic viewpoint over the centuries.

Much has been made of the national differences between mercantilists: that is, that the German context produced works dealing more with public finance and the sources of public revenues, often referred to as Cameralism. There is no question that different national settings and policies affected the *stress* and *emphases* of these writers. The lack of unity in Germany called for analysis of state finance and perhaps gave Schmoller the basis for his famous interpretation of mercantilism:

> Only he who thus conceives of mercantilism will understand it; in its innermost kernal it is nothing but state making — not state making in a narrow sense, but state making and national-economy making at the same time; state making in the modern sense, which creates out of the political community an economic community, and so gives it a heightened meaning [Schmoller (1884), 1931, pp. 50–1].

His context — political as well as economic — perhaps called for Cameralism more so than in other European regions. In any case, the public finance orientation is there. It is exemplified by Johann Von Justi's famous *System des Finanzwesens* which appeared in 1766. The work is a clear and precise analysis of sources of revenues, level of expenditures, and the principles of taxation. One excerpt from Von Justi will typify the approach of the Cameralists: "Taxes and contributions are the payments by the subjects from their private property, which they have to make for the necessary expenses of the state in a certain proportion to their property and earnings when the revenues from the domain and prerogatives are inadequate" [Monroe, 1945, pp. 388–89].

A similar type of interpretation has been drawn from the French "brand" of mercantilism, especially during the years of Colbert. His name is attached to this national version known as "Colbertism" which consisted of a series of government supported schemes of an import-substitution type, as well as an array of tax levies and industrial regulations aimed at control of the industrial sector. Yet much of the French writing of this period is concerned with administration of such policies. The theoretical underpinnings came from other corners: for example, from the work of Jean Bodin, Antoine de Montchretien, and Barthelemy de Laffemas [Cole, 1931].

Other national orientations have also been stressed. The Spanish version has been seen as a preoccupation with the desirability of obtaining and retaining stores of precious metals with the allied aspect of the favorable balance of trade with emphasis on the prohibition of the export of bullion. This, again, was a policy proscription and the analyses of it tend to stress antibullionist arguments. This was true of English writers who pointed to the inflationary impacts of such policies and the futility of such an export restriction. If one characterized the Spanish variant of mercantilism it would certainly have to be a judgment that is levied, often unfairly, at mercantilist analysis in general: that is, the identification of money with wealth and with bullionism the final goal of policy.

British and Dutch writings of the period are not so easily characterized. If one needed a single theme from them, the analysis of trade and its domestic impact would fit as well as any. Yet as one recent writer has pointed out, Holland has not been studied by economic historians as mercantilist since she had already achieved the mercantilist goals of the other European nations [Shaeffer, 1981, p. 93]. Whether this can be argued in a doctrinal sense is, perhaps, an open question. Yet at the same time it is certainly true that French and British mercantilist thinkers throughout the seventeenth and eighteenth centuries used the Dutch economic success as a touchstone for their economic analyses and, in the case of British mercantilist theory, made substantial changes in their chains of analysis about the economic system.

However, transcending all such national differences is a body of thinking that, more than in broad outline, argues for a more cohesive model than many critics in economic thought have allowed. In distilling such a vast literature one must simplify and abstract, a process which has the strength of isolation of the major themes and analytic concepts, as well as the weakness of covering over individual idiosyncrasies. Yet an ideal type mercantilist can be constructed.

The reason why this process has been seen as an impossible task is that the goals and aims of mercantilist *economic thought* have been wrongly assessed. As mentioned above, the power goal has been the overwhelming choice of critics over the years. This is an especially important point in the case of Eli Heckscher whose work has been so influential in interpretations of mercantilist thought ever since. Even though he qualified his initial position a bit and suggested a dual aim — power as well as opulence — Heckscher and most other critics do not become *economic* enough in their reading of mercantilist works. It would seem that a different goal, almost as broad but much more meaningful in terms of the ingredients of this literature, exists. It can be argued that the all encompassing aim and goal was economic development or "progress" if one reads it in terms of the seventeenth and eighteenth century setting. Such a notion of economic progress or the prosperous development of an economy creates a unifying characteristic from which to view what have been seen in the past as short-run goals and ad hoc schemes without any connecting principle [Wiles, 1974]. In short, the problem has been the viewing of these writings as a series of short-run objectives without a standard by which to judge them. The longer-run objectives of economic development or growth provide such a standard.

If this were the case then one should find an optimism for economic progress; that is, that the domestic economy is capable of economic development and that the mechanisms these writers will isolate can coalesce to bring about this long-run goal. In the later centuries of the mercantilist period this view is far more discernible than earlier — probably accompanying the growth of an international vision. The optimism of the eighteenth century writers is apparent. Nicholas Barbon, writing in 1690, held that the prospects of an economy were limitless. The stock of a nation is infinite, both in its natural and artificial forms. This stock can never be totally consumed: "For what is Infinite, can never receive Addition by Parsimony, nor suffer Dimunition, by Prodigality" [Barbon, 1903, p. 11]. Some years later the same theme is expanded in the work of Josiah Tucker, one of the most sophisticated of English writers. Tucker stressed the importance to the economy of developing skills and knowledge for the growth of both invention and production: "The Importance of this will appear the greater, when we consider, that no Man can pretend to set Bounds to the Progress that may yet be made both in Agriculture and Manufactures..." [Tucker, 1774, p. 31]. More optimistic than Barbon, Tucker saw a limitless horizon for development: "And is it not much more natural and reasonable to suppose, that we are rather at the Beginning only, and just got within the Threshold, than that we are arriv'd at the *ne plus ultra* of useful Discoveries?" [Tucker, 1774, p. 31]. Without further citation, it may be concluded that a review of the literature reveals scarcely a tract or work of the time that does not contain in its title or contents the idea of the possibility of an "increase," "improvement," or "advancement" of trade in general or of certain sectors of the economic system in particular. Or as a corollary, the work will attempt an explanation of the reason or reasons for the decay, decline, or stagnation of trade.

If the aim of development is seen as the overriding goal of our ideal mercantilist, all the other mechanisms in his analytical tool kit do not automatically fit. For one could obviously aim at economic progress via a series of beggar-my-neighbor policies or economic warfare in general which have been seen as characterizing the mercantilist body of doctrine for years. Heckscher, for example, called their vision "static" as opposed to a "dynamic" view. He maintained that this static approach did not enable the mercantilists to recognize the possibility of domestic economic improvement without a rather war-like raid upon, or selfish policy toward, other nations; in short, by taking away the gain of the other nation through successful competition abroad [Heckscher, 1954, II, pp. 24–7; Buck, 1942, pp. 28–30]. One can see, therefore, that if Heckscher's assessment is accepted, a whole host of related ideas and analyses stem from it, especially charges of economic nationalism as well as the power goal so often linked to mercantilism. It also leads to the view of much of the critical literature that the *external* economic relationships of an economy were of more importance to the mercantilists than the mechanisms of the domestic economic system.

What has been unstated or understated in these views, however, is the notion of mutuality that exists in the thinking of these writers. Such mutuality was recognized both at home and internationally. This allowed them to envision advancement and progress without a mere shifting of chessmen on the same sized international board. There was the crucial recognition of the chance of a bigger board. Growth was not a one-sided process.

There is no question, however, that there are examples that support Heckscher's "static" charge, especially earlier in the period. One example is the often-cited work of Philipp Wilhelm Von Hornick, *Austria Over All if She Only Will* [1684]; the very title supports Heckscher's interpretation. Hornick's analysis, though quite sophisticated in other respects, argued for development independent of others and is aimed at the increase of an economic surplus at home [Monroe, 1945, ch. X]. But such crude analyses were fast fading even at the time of Hornick's work. The mercantilist literature began to note the importance and potential of domestic development and its linkages with international commerce. Sir Dudley North saw the two as one closely intertwined entity and addressed the thinking that Heckscher viewed as basic to mercantilist doctrine — that wealth stemmed from the international sector:

> It will be objected, that the Home Trade signifies nothing to the enriching of a Nation, and that the Increase of Wealth comes out of Foreign Trade.
>
> I answer, That what is commonly understood by Wealth, *viz.* Plenty, Bravery, Gallantry etc. cannot be maintained without Forreign Trade. Nor in

Truth, can Forreign Trade subsist without the Home Trade, both being connected together [North, 1907, pp. 27–8].

Charles Davenant, in his 1698 *Discourses on the Public Revenues and On Trade*, noted the same interrelationship, asserting that gold and silver are mere measures of foreign trade. He maintained that the origin of such trade was "the natural or artificial product of the Country, that is to say, what their land, or what their labor and industry produces." In the same work, Davenant, like North and others, saw that both domestic and foreign trade were sources of wealth: "By annual income, we mean the whole that arises in any country, from land and its product, from foreign trade and domestic business..." [Davenant, 1698, I, pp. 251, 354]. Daniel Defoe, in a rather remarkable work in 1745, lucidly stated the same theme of interaction: "The inland trade of England is a thing not easily described.... It is the foundation of our wealth and greatness; it is the support of all our foreign trade, and of our manufacturing" [Defoe, 1745, p. 332].

Thus an ideal mercantilist could be said to view international and domestic trade as both major ingredients of economic progress and development. Even so, the charges of international economic warfare could still be accurate. To use a "counterfactual" hypothesis, if Heckscher and others are wrong in their claims, one could isolate in mercantilist doctrine a notion of mutual gain from international commerce.

There certainly was change over the period in this area — from the favorable balance of trade in a bilateral sense to a more multilateral vision of the international trade mechanism. In the often-quoted tract from mercantilist writer Thomas Mun, *England's Treasure by Forraign Trade* [1630], the notion of multilateralism appeared though the favorable balance of trade aspect is still dominant. As Mun put it: "The ordinary means therefore to encrease our wealth and treasure is by Forraign Trade, wherein we must ever observe this rule, to sell more to strangers yearly than we consume of theirs in value" [Monroe, 1945, p. 171]. Yet this "rule" was becoming more flexible among mercantilist writers who believed in the development contribution of domestic trade as well. The notion of mutual gain from commerce was seen earlier than has usually been recognized — some 50 years at least before David Hume's essays on trade. For example, a reader of Simon Clement in 1695 would have been introduced to this "liberal" notion of mutuality. For Clement maintained, first, that profits from trade are not to be computed, as earlier thinkers had thought, from considering particular trade balances, but that a nation's balance of trade in general should be taken into account. He brought the mutuality idea home by comparing domestic with international commerce. The foreign trader should be aware that "neither may he expect to drive a Publick Trade in the World without some such seeming Disadvantages, with more Reason, than that a Private Man should refuse to Buy of his Neighbour what his Necessity Requires, and he cannot so conveniently procure from another, because that Neighbour had no Occasion to lay out any of his Money with him" [Clement, 1695, p. 15]. Though the first, early acceptances of this notion were slow and grudging, Daniel Defoe in 1713 showed it to be a rather well-thought-out position — even if special pleading were the occasion for his argument:

> Trading Nations, the Christian, ought to maintain Commerce with all the people they can get by. Gain is the Design of Merchandize. 'Tis a Commutation of Merchantable Commodities between one Country and another, and for the mutual Profit of the Traders. The Language of Nations one to another is, I let Thee gain by me, that I may gain by Thee [Defoe, 1713, No. 27].

While space will not permit the extension of such quotations, they should not be read as isolated examples of an as yet unaccepted vision. As Jacob Vanderlint wrote in 1734: "All Nations of the World, therefore, should be regarded as one Body of Tradesmen, exercising their various Occupations for the Mutual Benefit and Advantage of each other" [Vanderlint, 1914, p. 47]. In the original version of this important tract in the collection of the Kress Library of Business and Economics of Harvard University, H. Somerton Foxwell has noted that Vanderlint's work is "a characteristic mercantilist tract."

Coupled with the notion of mutually advantageous trade, there was growing awareness by the mercantilists over the period that factor endowments in some way were connected and closely associated with mutual gains. It has been argued that mercantilism avoided such analysis [Spengler, 1960, pp. 40–54]. Indeed it seems that international specialization was recognized by these writers and the earlier, crude self-sufficiency model left behind. For mutual dependence was noted: "The Divine Providence hath not been more conspicuous in anything, than in endowing different Countries with particular Productions, some in a less, others in a greater Degree, whereby they might be mutually dependent upon each other" [Haynes, 1715, p. 1]. Such thoughts also pointed to the inadvisability of a policy of import substitution so often identified with mercantilism. Henry Martyn saw this in 1701 in his defense of the East India Company: "Manufactures made in England, the like of which may be imported from the East-Indies, by the Labour of fewer Hands, are not profitable, they are a Loss to the Kingdom; The Publick therefore loses nothing by the Loss of such Manufactures" [Martyn, 1954, p. 583]. Arthur Dobbs applied the same notion to his analysis of trade between England and Ireland in 1729. Division of labor "makes in effect every Nation, that is possess'd of an extended Commerce, enjoy the benefit of the best Soils and Climates; tho perhaps, from their situation, they might otherwise be in the worst. Trade makes the People of the whole Earth as one great Family supplying each other's wants." Although a bit of Heckscher's static charge remains in Dobbs' analysis of Ireland's and England's gains stemming from displacement of some third nation, the latter is convinced of their ability to aid each other. Note the Hume-like phrasing in the following:

> I would willingly hope therefore, that from a just Representation and view of our Trade, they will see that our Prosperity and Wealth contribute vastly to the Prosperity and welfare of Britain; And that as long as a Harmony is promoted between us, our mutual Happiness and riches will increase; and whatever we do in promoting each other's welfare, contributes in a great degree to the Prosperity of both [Dobbs, 1729, p. 146].

It is clear that by the time of the appearance of David Hume's essay "Of the Jealousy of Trade" in the mid-eighteenth century, the ideas of mutuality and international division of labor were in the wind. In fact, the ideas were occasionally seen as having a "natural" explanation, as in Matthew Decker's work in 1744:

> ...for Nature has given various Products to various Countries, and thereby knit Mankind in an Intercourse to supply each other's Wants: To attempt to sell our Products, but to buy little or none from Foreigners, is attempting an Impossibility, acting contrary to the Intent of Nature, cynically and absurdly; and, as ours is a populous manufacturing Country, highly prejudicial to our own Interests: For could we raise all Necessaries and Varieties within ourselves, this Intercourse designed by Nature would be destroyed...[Decker, 1744, p. 67].

Such analyses are also related to the development of colonies, for so long accepted as one of the two major characteristics of the "ideal" mercantilist, the second being the accumulation of bullion via a favorable balance of trade. Yet the discussions of the relationship of domestic and foreign trade and the mutual advantages arising from international commerce would seem to present a different analytic structure within which to deal with the role of colonies. There is probably no more commonly met definition of a mercantilist than one who envisions the use of a colony for the benefit of the mother country. The character of this use is usually seen to be an exploitative relationship — a sort of seven-

teenth and eighteenth century version of the "dependency" thesis. However, no matter what form British, French, and other European nations'
policies took to their colonies, the economic thinking of mercantilists
showed a consistency deriving from the ideas stressed above. Domestic
economic development, they argued, was consistent with economic
progress in the colonies, even if sales growth was the indicator they used.
The expansion of markets in general was emphasized and the colonies
fitted into such a pattern. In short, the ideal of income growth abroad was
tied into their domestic development aims. Daniel Defoe, Malachy
Postlethwayt, Joseph Massie, and others in the first half of the eighteenth
century may be included as examples of this interrelationship [Defoe,
1728, pp. viii–x, 53; Defoe, 1713, No. 124; Postlethwayt, 1757, II, pp.
218–219; Massie, 1760, p. 23]. Thus we can see that mercantilist doctrine
presented an integrated outlook on national and international development, an expansive view that would seem to render Heckscher's charge of
"static" inapplicable, at least for the latter part of the period, and
suggests a more "dynamic" reading in his use of that term.

   With this interaction of domestic and foreign sectors in mind, the
"ideal" mercantilist would most naturally have considered some analysis
of circulation in the economic system. This, along with the bullionist
epithet, is an aspect often integrated with the static charges levied at
mercantilism. But the connections between them are not clearly seen. For
if accumulation of bullion were the major intent of a favorable balance of
trade, one must then allow for one of the most commonplace emphases
of these writers — the circulation of money through the economy.
Indeed, if bullionism — the identification of wealth with precious metals
— was a trademark of mercantilism, did the emphasis upon circulation
involve any real contribution to economic development or was it simply
what Heckscher terms a "fear of goods" syndrome? In fact, Heckscher
makes the totally unsupportable statement for the later period of his topic
and for English evidence that: "I know of no mercantilist analysis which
opposed [influx of treasure] or attempted to replace it by another"
[Heckscher, 1954, II, pp. 177, 195]. In fact, he concludes: "With the
exception of the period of laissez-faire no age has been free of those
ideas."

   Without surveying the myriad definitions of wealth among mercantilist
writings, let it suffice to say that bullion alone was not typically interpreted as wealth per se, even though the *Wealth of Nations* asserts that
such was the case. Nor was the discouragement of the export of bullion
commonplace. Real variables, such as bullion's relation to commodities,
the gross produce of an economy, and the skilled labor force are more

commonly studied. It is virtually impossible to level a bullionist charge against writers from 1650 to Adam Smith and, as Bishop Berkeley asked in his *Querist* in 1735–37, "Whether there can be a greater mistake in Politics, than to measure the Wealth of a Nation by its Gold and Silver?" [Berkeley, 1910, p. 110]. When one reviews the literature, the mercantilists are seen as having asked a correlative question as they cast their eyes to Spanish policy forbidding the export of bullion, a policy they considered ineffective and counterproductive for development of a national economy. In fact, the analysis moves from those who saw free export of bullion leading to an increase in its inflow in the future, as did Thomas Mun, through those who began to interpret bullion flows as international capital movements and as important balancing items when the foreign exchanges moved against an economy. The French writer Jean Francois Melon argued in 1739 that if policy were to forbid the export of bullion, imbalances would continue to the nation's disadvantage until its debts were paid [Melon, 1739, pp. 312–13; Law, 1705, pp. 25–6].

Since the mercantilist writers were keenly aware of price movements and their impact on trade and development, it is only logical that inflows of bullion — even if desirable — would be seen as having domestic price effects. That is, in some measure, the recognition of the quantity theory's international application. The quantity theory of money, of course, has a long history of evolution, beginning with the scholastic economic writers' struggle with the role of money and its relation to price differentials. Jean Bodin, in the last half of the sixteenth century, analyzed the impact of American mines on European price levels. Yet early writers of the mercantilist type did not make the connection between a favorable balance of trade, resulting inflows, and a rising price level at home. However, this connection — often credited to David Hume in his price-specie-flow mechanism — had been recognized before Hume's essays, "Of the Balance of Trade" and "Of Money," published in the 1750s [Hume, 1955].

Roger Coke in a 1675 work commented on the domestic price impact of a policy of encouraging imports of bullion [Coke, 1675, pp. 44, 47–8]. A fuller and more sophisticated analysis of these linkages appeared in 1734 in an important tract by Jacob Vanderlint:

> But no Inconvenience can arise by an unrestrained Trade, but very great Advantage; since if the Cash of the Nation be decreased by it, which Prohibitions are designed to prevent, those nations that get the Cash will certainly find everything advanced in Price, as the Cash increases amongst them. And if we, who part with the Money, make our Plenty great enough to make Labour sufficiently cheap. . . . , our Manufactures, and everything else, will soon become

so moderate as to turn the Balance of Trade in our Favour and thereby fetch the Money back again [Vanderlint, 1734, pp. 48–9].

And, in an anonymous tract of 1748, the accumulation of bullion was pilloried much as Adam Smith would do 30 years later. Shall the nations accumulating treasure, the author asked, make "pots and utensils" from it, or bury it? For unless the nation does these things, the circulation of the bullion will cause prices to rise and exports to be hindered [*Two Letters...*, 1748, p. 1]. Thus Hume worked toward his price-specie-flow analysis with earlier recognitions of the linkages between bullion and prices, although he had doubts about whether the conclusions of his essays were adequate. His discussions — mainly via correspondence — with Josiah Tucker raised important questions in Hume's mind as to whether the balance of trade would continue to reverse itself as bullion flows were allowed and prices were responsive. Tucker maintained that the wealthier and more progressive of two trading nations could never be overtaken by the poorer and more backward trading partner, even though bullion flows took place between them. In fact, Tucker was pleased to note that after their debate, Hume acknowledged the correctness of his position.

The doubts that mercantilist writers had from at least the early seventeenth century onward point to the fact that circulation in its real aspects was foremost in their minds. This was probably put in its most sophisticated form by Sir James Steuart in 1767 who saw circulation of income and its impact on consumer demand influencing prices and supply more than the circulation of bullion [Steuart, 1805, II, pp. 86–7]. Yet one does not have to await Steuart's work on the eve of the *Wealth of Nations* to note this emphasis on circulation; it appears early in mercantilist writing and seems to flow logically from their recognition of the interaction of domestic and foreign sectors, as well as from their goal of economic development. In fact, writers such as Tucker included the circulation of labor under this head, not simply money as is usually charged. The "mass of metals" is no longer important; its circulation and real impact are the points stressed. As Postlethwayt put it in 1757: "It cannot be too often repeated, that a great Mass of Metals is in itself indifferent to a State, considered abstractly, from other States. It is in the Circulation of its Commodities, either at home or abroad, that constitutes the People's Happiness; And that Circulation requires a proportional Distribution of the general Mass of Money in all the Provinces, by which Commodities are furnished" [Postlethwayt, 1757, p. 80].

In short, what was beginning to be more clearly seen was the overall integration of the subelements stressed by the "ideal" mercantilist. This recognition involved a shift from the earlier stress on single factors such as bullion accumulation and a favorable balance of trade to the domestic and international implications of such mechanisms for economic development. Yet in the search for a mercantilist model it is clear that such an overall vision did not lead to unanimity among such thinkers any more than contemporary economists agree on interactions in a policy-oriented system. Nowhere was this more clearly shown than in the seventeenth and eighteenth century mercantilist writings concerning the role of domestic prices, particularly wages and interest rates in furthering economic progress at home. If the usual vision of mercantilist policy is that of a low-wage, low-price suggestion for furthering international sales, the latter two centuries of our period present some fascinating debates over this goal. Thus the interrelationships seen thus far begin to be analyzed as links in a longer and more complex economic chain.

In the area of wages, such discussions are particularly noticeable and exemplify the evolution of mercantilist thinking. As the emphasis upon circulation moved away from simple flow of money through the system to a discussion of income movements and their development potential, it is only to be expected that a wage-income connection would have been recognized. And indeed it was. Here there was a basic split between mercantilists: that is, between those authors espousing high wages and those favoring a low and more competitive wage level. The differing positions are based on disparate outlooks upon the economic process. The two viewpoints, if one can oversimplify, can be termed the Keynesian and the classical. The former group of writers looked to the income and consumption effects of wages on the economic system and favored relatively high wage rates. The latter, or classical view, saw wages as a cost of production and therefore defended a low wage level as beneficial to trade.

There is one interconnection between the two groups. The high wage advocates, in some cases, argued for the impact of productivity on price levels, the obvious bridge needed to reconcile the two wage positions. John Cary, as an example, defended high wage rates as not causing high prices of goods and provisions. It is clear that his case rested upon a view, imperfect though it was, of technological progress. He saw falling prices "proceeding from the Ingenuity of the Manufacturer, and the Improvements he makes in his ways of working...., all which save the labour of many Hands, so the Wages of those employed need not be lessened" [Cary, 1695, pp. 145–46; Cary, 1719, pp. 96–8]. Henry Martyn in 1701 treated the same relationship with the notice of the possibility of competitive prices without reductions in wages. There is no question, however, that the roles of productivity and money wages were imperfectly understood. Their interrelationships were grappled with throughout the seventeenth and eighteenth centuries. Perhaps the clearest statement on the matter — approaching a unit cost analysis — was that of Josiah Tucker later in the eighteenth century. In his discussion with David Hume, Tucker developed his argument in terms of the division of labor enabling an economy to afford higher wages while still retaining its competitive edge via productivity gains. Thus Tucker concluded that the lower cost nation would not lose its place to a poorer nation whose wages and prices were expected to be low. "In such a Case, Is it not much cheaper to give 2s.6d. a Day in the rich Country to the nimble and adroit Artist, than it is to give only 6d. in the poorer one to the tedious, awkward Bungler?" Thus development allows a higher wage to be paid [Tucker, 1774, p. 34; Anderson, 1777, pp. 350–1].

Yet this productivity-price-wage connection was slow in coming. Most of the emphasis in opposition to the traditional low wage arguments fell in the income flow area, a logical appendage to the stress on circulation in the domestic economy. In fact, in the Hume-Tucker debate, Josiah Tucker saw that the price-specie-flow analysis did not allow income effects to affect the balance of trade. This discussion is important as a representation of the shifts in mercantilist attention from a low wage economy to the ability of a "rich" country to be progressive and competitive. Such interchanges had been common for some time before Hume and Tucker debated the issue. The major thrust on the high wage side was a Keynesian-like emphasis upon income and consumption. Daniel Defoe's work is prominent in espousing this view. He warned against lowering wages; such a policy would require a fall in the prices of provisions. Land values would also likely decline and "so you wound the Capital at once; for the Poor cannot earn little and spend much...." Further, as Tucker was to do 30 or 40 years later, Defoe identified high wages with successful development of an economy and a source of consumption:

> ...'tis by the Largeness of their Gettings, that they are supported, and by the Largeness of their Number the whole Country is supported; by their Wages they are able to live plentifully, and it is by their expensive, generous, free way of living, that the Home Consumption is raised to such a Bulk, as well of our own, as of Foreign Production: If their Wages were low and despicable, so would be their Living; If they got little, they could spend but little, and Trade would presently feel it; as their Gain is more or less, the Wealth and Strength of the whole Kingdom would rise or fall: For as I said above, upon their Wages it all depends [Defoe, 1728, pp. 60, 102].

Notions of this nature are far more common in the mercantilist literature than has been stated and far earlier than the scant references to such views have allowed. High wages, even with a glance at a more equitable distribution of income, were major strains of thought over the period. Thus circulation for the mercantilists is not as crude a mechanism as the critical literature would have it [cf. Barbon, 1903, p. 23; Gardner, 1696, pp. 16–17; Johnson, 1726, pp. 9, 14; Braddon, 1717, p. 18].

If there is one variant of mercantilist thought that has been understated or unrecognized in the secondary literature, it is the impact of income flows on growth and development. While any reader of mercantilist writing must note the emphasis on circulation in the analyses, the interpretation is simply that it was a way of disposing of the desired influx of bullion. This was the view of Eli Heckscher. In searching for motives for such an outlook, Heckscher maintained that their vision centered upon an increase in employment via a greater "diffusion of exchange" as well as the desirability of rising prices at home and a preoccupation with prices in other countries [Heckscher, 1954, II, Part II, ch.iii]. Yet income movements, which in the mercantilists' minds created employment, growth in consumption, and economic progress, are not part of his analysis.

Just as the wage level and high versus low wages were continuing concerns of the mercantilists over the period, so too the treatment of the interest rate also led to two different positions. Here, again, the debate turns on the relationship of interest to economic development. Keynes, in his *General Theory*, summarizes the mercantilist view as stressing "low" interest rates for economic progress and wealth. Yet he admits his interpretation is largely drawn from the work of Heckscher [Keynes, 1936, p. 341]. The literature on this topic is more complex. As. G. S. L. Tucker, in his work *Progress and Profits in British Economic Thought, 1660–1850*, put it: "The notion that 'interest is the barometer of the state, and its lowness is a sign almost infallible of the flourishing condition of a people' had by this time [eighteenth century] become an axiom of political economy. But there remained the problem of explaining this phenomenon" [Tucker, 1960, p. 33]. The explanations, like those for wages, do show disagreement in mercantilist thought; one group of writers from the late seventeenth century argued that low interest is the *effect* of economic development, as pointed out by Sir Dudley North, John Pollexfen, and Joseph Massie. This view stressed the differences in the rates of interest between "less developed" areas such as America and other colonies and the European economies. David Hume's famous essay, "Of Interest," picked up this variant of thought [North, 1934, pp. 18–19; Pollexfen, 1697, p. 64; Massie, 1912, p. 53].

On the other hand, approximately during the same period, a second group of writers — also supporting low rates of interest — reversed the above analysis and placed interest in a causal role. That is, they envisioned interest as a forerunner and sine qua non of economic progress. John Cary, Josiah Child, Arthur Dobbs, and William Mildmay may be mentioned as examples of those supportive of this position [Child, 1693, pp. 16, 36, 164; Dobbs, 1729, pp. 21–22; Mildmay, 1765, p. 121]. Cary summed up this view in 1695: "By falling the interest of Money, this would very much quicken Trade, and indeed is the true Measure of it, the Merchant would be better able to cope with Competitors abroad in the Manufactures when his Interest did not last so deep as now it doth, and the Maker would be enabled to sell them cheaper at home" [Cary, 1695, p. 31]. Though disagreement remained, both groups were certain that low interest and economic development were closely related. The goal was clear.

III

Though one, in constructing an "ideal type" mercantilist, has to allow for changes in certain parts of the mercantilist doctrine, it is difficult to see serious disagreement with respect to the overall aim of economic development. What is more, this development potential was approached not in a static framework but within one which allowed for mutual growth in the international arena.

Yet development, of necessity, is a long-run aim. A question thus arises: was there a shorter-run goal, or an intermediate touchstone, that would allow judgment on the effectiveness or ineffectiveness of specific economic policies as the mercantilists, at least in theory, planned for development? An answer here is given in the important and perceptive work of William D. Grampp, who supports full employment as the economic goal of policy proscriptions. He separates this goal from the older interpretations of the aims of national power and strength. Grampp holds that these writers, as the classicals, were ready to sacrifice efficiency and justice for greater national power. The difference between the two groups is the mercantilists' belief that national interest required a prosperous, fully employed, and growing economy [Grampp, 1960, pp. 63–4]. Had this idea been worked into an analysis of a shorter time period than Grampp's 1500–1750, the mix of goals would change, the prosperous economy becoming the final end while full employment fits as a success indicator en route.

There is very little question of the presence of the full employment goal in the mercantilist structure. The literature abounds with examples of it, not just employment growth but often explicit references to "full employment." They write of this as the end of schemes and policies and as the guide to the policy-maker, planner, or statesman as to the efficacy of his programs. As Nathaniel Forster put it in 1767: "There cannot therefore be a nobler object of government, than the keeping all its hands employed." Mildmay agreed: "Numbers of people being the strength of a nation and their skill and industry the foundation of its riches; to promote their Encrease, and procure means for their Employment, must be the chief maxim of every government" [Forster, 1767, p. 12; Mildmay, 1765, p. 5]. At about the same time, in what is unquestionably the most synthetic statement of the variegated ideas treated in this essay, Sir James Steuart wrote of the economic balance the statesman must keep in mind in his policies: "That number of husbandmen is best, which can provide food for all that state; and that number of inhabitants is the best, which is compatible with the full employment of every one of them" [Steuart, 1767, I, p. 117].

Thus it would seem that the mercantilist construction is complete. Goals, both short- and long-run, argue for more cohesiveness to their policy suggestions and the linkages established in their writings. Yet there is one more barrier that critics have erected which argues that the mercantilists worked themselves into an analytical "cul-de-sac." This is the fact that as the mercantilists were interested in economic progress and supported innovations on the way to their longer run goal, the full employment end was unreachable. As Heckscher put it: "Clearly, then, it had become psychologically impossible to oppose the new labor-saving methods. In other words, through its general social outlook mercantilism had already decided in favor of technical innovations." This, in his view, was inconsistent with a policy of creating employment [Heckscher, 1954, II, pp. 127–28].

Yet the sophistication of the mercantilist analyses at least proposes an answer to Heckscher. Here his lack of work in the eighteenth century precludes his notice of this aspect of the literature. For the awareness is there. Earlier writers as John Cary and Henry Martyn noted the probable labor displacement and concluded that better wages could be paid to those still employed after the application of the innovation. Yet later in the century, Heckscher's dilemma is faced head on with long- versus short-run effects explained. Postlethwayt explicitly noted this in 1757:

Such discoveries are not, as may be thought at first sight, contrary to the object and first intent of manufactories, which is to employ the greatest number of men possible. They will, on the contrary, be found, with very little reflection, to tend to that end, by multiplying works, and increasing the produce of the balance, which never ceases to increase home consumption [Postlethwayt, 1757, II, p. 417].

Tucker also saw that growth would offset the short-run dislocation effects with greater employment opportunities generated:

And surely enough has been said, to convince any reasonable man, though even the great author of *L'Esprit des Loix* should be of a different Mind, that that System of Machines, which so greatly reduces the Price of Labour, as to enable the Generality of a People to become Purchasers of the Goods, will in the End, though not immediately, employ more Hands in the Manufacture, than could possibly have found Employment, had no such Machines been invented [Tucker, 1757, p. 242].

The opinion of James Steuart can be added as the culmination of a long heritage of mercantilist thought. Machines, for Steuart, were a necessity for economic development though, as the others cited above, he also noted the disemployment possibility. He concluded:

And if they [machines] have the effect of taking bread from hundreds, formerly employed in performing their simple operations; they have that also of giving bread to thousands, by extending numberless branches of ingenuity, which, without the machines, would have remained circumscribed within very narrow limits [Steuart, 1767, I, p. 391].

Even if Heckscher's dilemma took a long time for the mercantilists to resolve, it is clear that their development and employment goals were high priorities. The dilemma was hardly endemic to mercantilism.

A final and, in some ways, crucial dilemma in the mercantilist body of doctrine lies in their nascent ideas on economic planning; that is, some sort of policy mechanism to achieve their economic goals. This is not the same as suggesting that these writers merely produced a myriad of schemes that often conflicted with one another and which were not based on economic analysis. Yet as we began stressing mercantilist economic thought so we end with a similar policy emphasis — here on their policy ideas and their position on the role of the state in economic development. Why, first, did they see a need for planning? The answer seems to be clear in their work. Many critics, including Grampp and Heckscher, have noted "liberal" ideas creeping into mercantilist writings, especially in the seventeenth and eighteenth centuries. Yet as this took the form of more discussion of private interest and its economic implications, the mercantilists saw a conflict between public and private interests. The aim of national economic development is not guaranteed by a pre-Adam Smith invisible hand. Josiah Child, for example, warns us not to identify the profit of the merchant with the gain of the nation, while James Donaldson in 1700 pessimistically wrote of the same conflict: "That every Man should imploy himself not only for advancing of his own Interest, but likewise that he may propogate the Welfare of others, will, I suppose be sooner granted than practiced" [Donaldson, 1700, p. 5]. Many of the writers examined above picked up on this conflict as the period wore on. Most saw it as another dilemma — a possible thwarting of the long- and short-run goals without some policy program to resolve the conflict. As Nathaniel Forster wrote in 1767: "For surely it often happens, that a branch of trade is by no means advantageous to the public in the same proportion in which it is profitable to the private adventurer. These two circumstances are rather in an inverse ratio to each other" [Forster, 1767, p. 20].

What was the solution? There is no question, especially later in the period, that private gain was thought to be an effective and appropriate driving force for economic progress; yet it must be tempered by economic policy and an overseer. In a policy conclusion reminiscent of Adam Smith, George Lowe summed up the need to resolve the conflict:

> ...there is no intention to represent the selfish passions as either unuseful or pernicious, because they certainly are the great springs to all action; but still there are distinctions to be made: a labourer, an artisan, or a merchant in licit trade cannot, for example, benefit himself without at the same time doing service to his country; but a landlord or corn-jobber, who seeks to promote his own interest by means that ruin our manufactures and diminish our national commerce, (which are its best sources of strength and wealth) does therein indulge a selfish passion that is highly pernicious to the state, and therefore deserving to be curbed and discountenanced. In short, the welfare of the state as well as of individuals depends on the right operations of the selfish passions, under the steady guidance of such social policy as insensibly establishes a perfect coincidence between individual and general welfare [Lowe, 1768, pp. 63–64].

J. M. Low has maintained that the basic ideal of planning and the role for government, given this conflict, was to correlate, as Lowe pointed out, individual and national interests [Low, 1953, p. 75]. The mercantilists did this, it would seem from what has been shown above, through their emphasis on economic development which makes the merchants' and the nation's interests one. As Tucker put it, the problem in planning was whether self-interest and "social happiness" could both be achieved.

Most of these writers thought this merging of interests was possible via some form of intelligent planning; they were no more consistent in this than are contemporary discussions of the desirability and appropriate directions for policy. Guidelines, only, were suggested — the short-run panaceas of earlier mercantilist writers are not part of this discussion. It was a more coordinated and cohesive planning structure they sought. It would seem appropriate to conclude with the suggestions of Sir James Steuart for his policy-maker — the "Statesman." It is a perfect blend of what the above analysis has considered to be the major ideas and goals of mercantilism. Further, Steuart, as others, saw the need for coordination of policy to achieve these goals. He argued that the statesman must examine three topics in his planning formulations: "the propensity of the rich to consume, the disposition of the poor to be industrious; and the proportion of circulating money, with respect to the one and the other" [Steuart, 1767, II, p. 53; cf. Hirschman, 1977, part 2]. What a world of ideas in Steuart's charge to his statesman — and that world is the world of mercantilist economic thought.

References

Anderson, James. *Observations on the Means of Exciting a Spirit of National Industry. . . .* Edinburgh: 1777.

Barbon, Nicholas. "A Discourse of Trade (1690)." In *A Reprint of Economic Tracts.* Ed. by J. H. Hollander. Baltimore: Johns Hopkins Press, 1903.

Bennett, John. *The National Merchant or Discourses on Commerce and Colonies.* London: 1736.

Berkeley, George. "The Querist Containing Several Queries Proposed. . . (1735–1737)." In *A Reprint of Economic Tracts.* Ed. by J. H. Hollander. Baltimore: Johns Hopkins Press, 1910.

Braddon, Lawrence. *The Miseries of the Poor. . . .* London: 1717.

Brandenburg, S. J. "The Place of Agriculture in British National Economy Prior to Adam Smith." *Journal of Political Economy* 39:1931, 281–320.

Buck, Philip W. *The Politics of Mercantilism.* New York: Henry Holt & Co., 1942.

Cary, John. *An Essay on the State of England. . . .* Bristol: 1695.

Cary, John. *An Essay Towards Regulating the Trade and Employing the Poor of this Kingdom,* 2nd ed. London: 1719.

Child, Sir Josiah. *A New Discourse of Trade.* London: 1693.

Coats, A. W. "Changing Attitudes to Labour in the Mid-Eighteenth Century." *Economic History Review* 11:1958, 35–51.

Coke, Roger. *England's Improvements.* London: 1675.

Cole, Charles W. *French Mercantilist Doctrines Before Colbert.* New York: Richard R. Smith, 1931.

Coleman, D. C. "Eli Heckscher and the Idea of Mercantilism." In *Revisions in Mercantilism*. Ed. by D. C. Coleman. London: Methuen, 1969, pp. 92–117.

Cunningham, William. *The Growth of English Industry and Commerce*. 2 vols. Cambridge: Cambridge University Press, 1912.

Davenant, Charles. *Discourses on the Public Revenues and on Trade*. London: 1698.

Decker, Matthew. *An Essay on the Causes of the Decline of the Foreign Trade*. London: 1744.

Defoe, Daniel. *The Complete English Tradesman*, 5th ed. 2 vols. London: 1745.

—————. *Mercator: or, Commerce Retrieved*. London: 1713–14.

—————. *A Plan of the English Commerce*. London: 1728.

Dobbs, Arthur. *An Essay on the Trade and Improvement of Ireland*. Dublin: 1729.

Donaldson, James. *The Undoubted Art of Thriving*. Edinburgh: 1700.

Ekelund. Robert B., Jr., and Robert D. Tollison. *Mercantilism as a Rent-Seeking Society*. College Station, TX: Texas A & M University Press, 1981.

Forster, Nathaniel. *An Enquiry into the Causes of the High Price of Provisions*. London: 1767.

Furniss, Edgar S. *The Position of the Laborer in a System of Nationalism*. New York: Kelley and Millman, 1957.

Gardner. *Some Reflections on a Pamphlet Intitled....* London: 1696.

Grampp, William D. "The Liberal Elements in English Mercantilism." In *Essays in Economic Thought: Aristotle to Marshall*. Ed. by Joseph J. Spengler and William R. Allen. Chicago: Rand McNally, 1960, pp. 61–91.

Gray, Alexander. *The Development of Economic Doctrine*. London: Longmans, 1931.

Haynes, John. *Great Britain's Glory....* London: 1715.

Heckscher, Eli. "Mercantilism." *The Economic History Review* 7: 1936, 44–54.

Heckscher, Eli. *Mercantilism*, rev. ed. 2 vols. New York: Macmillan, 1954.

Hirschman, Albert O. *The Passions and the Interests*. Princeton: Princeton University Press, 1977.

Hume, David. *Writings on Economics*. Ed. by Eugene Rotwein. Madison, WI: University of Wisconsin Press, 1955.

Johnson, E. A. J. *Predecessors of Adam Smith*. New York: Prentice Hall, 1937.

Johnson, Samuel. *The Advantage of Employing the Poor in Useful Labor*, 2nd ed. London: 1726.

Keynes, John M. *The General Theory of Employment, Interest and Money*. London: Macmillan, 1936.

Law, John. *Money and Trade Considered....* Edinburgh: 1705.

Low, J. M. "A Regional Example of the Mercantilist Theory of Economic Policy." *Manchester School of Economic and Social Studies* 21: 1953, 62–84.

Lowe, George. *Considerations on the Effects....* London: 1768.

Martyn, Henry. "Considerations on the East-India Trade (1701)." In *A Select Collection of Early English Tracts on Commerce*. Ed. by J. R. McCulloch.

Cambridge: Cambridge University Press, 1954.

Massie, Joseph. "An Essay on the Governing Causes of the Natural Rate of Interest (1750)." in *A Reprint of Economic Tracts*. Ed. by J. H. Hollander. Baltimore: Johns Hopkins Press, 1912.

——————. *A Representation Concerning the Knowledge of Commerce as a National Concern*. London: 1760.

Melon, Jean F. *A Political Essay Upon Commerce*. London: 1739.

Mildmay, William. *The Laws and Policy of England, Relating to Trade*. London: 1765.

Monroe, A. E. *Early Economic Thought*. Cambridge: Harvard University Press, 1945.

Mun, Thomas. "England's Treasure by Forraign Trade (1630)." in *Early Economic Thought*. Ed. by A. E. Monroe. Cambridge: Harvard University Press, 1945, pp. 169–98.

North, Sir Dudley. "Discourses upon Trade (1691)." in *A Reprint of Economic Tracts*. Ed. by J. H. Hollander. Baltimore: Johns Hopkins Press, 1934.

Pollexfen, John. *A Discourse of Trade and Coyn*. London: 1697.

Postlethwayt, Malachy. *Britain's Commercial Interest Explained and Improved* (1757a). London: 1757.

——————. *Great Britain's True System* (1757b). London: 1757.

Schmoller, Gustav. *The Mercantile System and its Historical Significance*. New York: Peter Smith, 1931.

Schumpeter, Joseph A. *History of Economic Analysis*. New York: Oxford University Press, 1954.

Shaeffer, Robert K. "The Entelechies of Mercantilism." *Scandanavian Economic History Review* 29:1981, 81–98.

Spengler, Joseph J. "Mercantilist and Physiocratic Growth Theory." In *Theories of Economic Growth*. Ed. by Bert Hoselitz, Glencoe, IL: Free Press, 1960.

Steuart, Sir James. *The Works, Political, Metaphysical and Chronological*, 6 vols. London: 1805.

Suviranta, Br. *The Theory of the Balance of Trade in England*. New York: Augustus M. Kelley, 1967.

Tucker, G. S. L. *Progress and Profits in British Economic Thought 1650–1850*. Cambridge: Cambridge University Press, 1960.

Tucker, Josiah. *Four Tracts on Political and Commercial Subjects*, 2nd ed. Gloucester: 1774.

——————. "Instructions for Travellers (1757)." In *Josiah Tucker, A Selection from his Economic and Political Writings*. Ed. by Robert L. Schuyler. New York: Columbia University Press, 1931.

Two Letters on Trade. Dublin: 1748.

Vanderlint, Jacob. "Money Answers All Things (1734)." In *A Reprint of Economic Tracts*. Ed. by J. H. Hollander. Baltimore: Johns Hopkins Press, 1914.

Wiles, Richard C. "Mercantilism and the Idea of Progress." *Eighteenth Century Studies* 8: 1974, 56–74.

—————. "The Theory of Wages in Later English Mercantilism." *The Economic History Review* 21:1968, 113–26.

Wilson, Charles. "'Mercantilism': Some Vicissitudes of an Idea." In *Economic History and the Historian*. Ed. by Charles Wilson. London: Weidenfield and Nicolson, 1969, pp. 62–72.

Commentary by Lars Magnusson
The Language of Mercantilism $\lfloor$ p/47 $\rfloor$.

I

Mercantilism is one of those concepts that always seem to stir up controversy and initiate bitter academic disputes. Ever since it first was used by Count de Mirabeau in 1763 as the "mercantile system" (*systéme mercantile*), its appropriateness as a definition of a certain phase in the history of economic thought has been discussed. During the last decades, the debate has been especially intense and has increasingly become an excuse for discussing more general questions, as, for example, the relationship between economic ideas and reality and between such ideas and policy, thus transcending the older and more narrow debate about the historical appropriateness of the concept and its historical interpretation. This is probably also the reason why the question of mercantilism still is in the forefront of discussion. Another important reason why it still arouses controversy is, of course, its political connotations. It must be remembered that Mirabeau and Smith created the concept "mercantile system" to define a certain policy which they strongly opposed, while Schmoller and Cunningham on the contrary hailed "Merkantilismus" as a policy of forced industrialization that should be utilized by backward nations striving for economic modernization. Heckscher's ambition in *Mercantilism* was to oppose this view and to defend laissez-faire against the kind of economic nationalism he saw emerge during the interwar period.

In his chapter on the development of mercantilistic thought, Wiles pays hardly any attention to this debate.[1] At least to some extent, this is a wise decision because of its extensive character. On the other hand, it means that he avoids some difficult questions that perhaps should be taken into account in this context. As far as I can see, Wiles puts forward two major points in his discussion. First, that mercantilism can — and indeed should — be seen as a coherent system of thought, and, secondly, that its goal was to serve economic development and progress. Generally, mercantilism in Wiles' interpretation is more "modern" than in Heckscher's or Schmoller's version and much more related to the Enlightenment than to the theories of the schoolmen and the Renaissance. While I in principle agree with both these points, there are several qualifying remarks that must be made, and my general aim here is to point out directions in which these questions might be further explored.

II

A controversial question which Wiles quickly passes over is whether or not mercantilism can be regarded as a "system of thought." He simply seems to state that it contains "at least a handful of settled principles," which is enough to define it as a system [Judges, 1939, p. 35]. Most certainly he would disagree with, for example, D. C. Coleman's dictum that mercantilism is a "non-existent identity" [Coleman, 1980, p. 791]. This is sound, I think, as far as it goes. Without doubt the "mercanti-listic" literature of the seventeenth and eighteenth centuries shares some common themes and tends to interpret some aspects of "reality" along similar lines; whether that is enough to make it a system is a question of definition that hardly would be worth the effort of much further elabora-tion here. Wiles would probably also disagree with Coleman's further proposition that the mercantilistic literature mainly contains practical suggestions for practical political problems or with Schumpeter's without doubt exaggerated statement regarding the mercantilists that "they did not analyze at all" [Coleman, 1956, 1969, 1980; Schumpeter, 1972, p. 343]. Obviously this leads to a mistaken view about policy and the political process. Politicians are clearly guided by certain general ideas and principles — or prejudices — when they try to solve what they perhaps themselves perceive as simple "practical" problems. After Kuhn, such a position would not be easy to defend, to say the least.

However, even if we can trace some common ideas in mercantilist discourse, let's say from the beginning of the seventeenth to the middle of the eighteenth century, there are still some important problems left. In my view perhaps the most difficult is this: In what *sense* can we speak of mercantilism as a system of thought? Was it a system in the same sense as the classical or neo-classical system, and was it developed to answer the same kind of questions? Shall we regard a "theory" like the famous theory of the favorable balance of trade or statements pointing out that only foreign trade can enrich a country as propositions of the same order as, for example, the labor theory of value in the systems of Smith and Ricardo? These seem to me to be important questions that we must come to grips with before we are able to interpret mercantilism or define its position in the history of economic thought. This also implies that we must learn to avoid an anachronistic perspective. Unfortunately Keith

Tribe is quite accurate when he describes much of mainstream history of political economy in the following way:

> The primary device which the history of economics employs for the demarcation of the economic archive is the structure of contemporary economic theory. A simple teleology makes possible the construction of a history of economics as the process of rational growth of the analysis of the economy [Tribe, 1978, p. 7].

Instead, we must explore methods and procedures for interpreting mercantilistic texts with the standards of their own period and seeing them as a form of specific discourse in which concepts were used in certain ways and in which arguments were contextually shaped in definite forms. For this purpose some kind of semiotical approach might be useful, and it could perhaps help us to avoid at least some of the more obvious anachronistical fallacies. That the study of mercantilism really is in need of such a new perspective was recently noted by A. W. Coats:

> ...to apply a conceptual apparatus developed under one set of conditions to those of very different time and place involves a kind of "translation" process, which, as linguistic philosophers have shown, involves compromises which necessarily affect the communications of meanings. There is no literary neutral language by which the concepts and terms of one theoretical system can be translated into those of another.... Indeed, one of the reasons for the sharp conflicts of opinion about mercantilism among economists past and present is that they have been starting out from incompatible or even "incommensurable" paradigms...[Coats, 1985, pp. 32 ff.; and also Coats, 1973, pp. 489 ff.].

One of the few scholars who have tried to deal with this problem of "translation" regarding mercantilistic texts is Bruno Suviranta. In his suggestive but rather neglected 1923 study,[2] he emphasised that the mercantilists should be read from the point of view of the seventeenth and eighteenth centuries and not as some sort of "premature" version of classical economics. In his book he set out to study the theory of the favorable balance of trade and how it ought to be interpreted. Suviranta pointed out that propositions such as that domestic trade was sterile and that only foreign trade could make a nation rich should *not* be interpreted — which is so often the case — as comparable to Smith's discussion about the "original sources of value." In fact, they were never utilized by the mercantilists for that purpose. The mercantilists knew very well, he argued, that production played a leading role in the creation of "wealth," as well as that the different factors of production contributed to that end. They also knew the connection between the growth of domestic trade and the wealth of a nation and, against this background, he summarizes his position:

It is thus beyond doubt that mercantilists possessed a fundamentally right idea of production. But that being so, it is also evident that the numerous passages where home trade was expressly stigmatized as sterile and foreign trade alone thought productive, must not be taken at their face value. We have rather to do with the same kind of generalizations as in the case of the balance of trade v. the balance of indebtness. One factor regarded as the most important among several different factors, is more or less consciously abstracted and to it alone attributes the character common to them all...the home trade as sterile, not in an absolute, but in a relative sense [Suviranta, 1923, p. 135].

Suviranta also states that it would be wrong to say that the mercantilists were only emphasizing the advantages brought about by the surplus originating from a positive balance of trade. They also knew that a large foreign trade in itself — the "big balance" in Child's words — was advantageous for a nation. Sometimes they only used the existence of a positive trade (or payment) balance as an indicator of how successful a nation was in its foreign trade [Suviranta, 1923, p. 140].

Suviranta's discussion is, of course, impressionistic and not totally convincing in all its details. However, as a point of departure for further investigation I think his approach is both fruitful and valid. A close reading of how mercantilistic texts are structured, how concepts are used and arguments put forward, can perhaps also make us better equipped to understand some of the paradoxes and contradictions which are so apparent in mercantilistic treatises. That mercantilists used arguments in a slightly different fashion than for example nineteenth century economists was also noticed by a keen observer, Edwin Cannan:

It is quite possible to quote from those [mercantilistic] writers passages in which bullion and wealth are identified, and the riches or poverty of a nation made to depend upon the quantity of bullion it possesses. But whether this is absurd or not entirely depends on the meaning given to the words wealth, riches and poverty. A writer may use a word in a sense which is not given to it in ordinary conversation without being ridiculous. It would be ridiculous, indeed, to contend that a nation could be well fed and comfortably clothed and housed by gold alone; but there is no reason to suppose that the wildest mercantilists ever suffered from that delusion. The mere existence of the fable of Midas was a sufficient safeguard. The mercantilists may be justly accused of exaggerating the importance of having a hoard of bullion...but none of them ever imagined gold and silver to be the only economic good [Cannan, 1903, pp. 2 ff.].

All this might seem trivial, but I think it in fact is highly relevant with regard to Wiles' discussion about the "modern" character of early eighteenth century mercantilism. It is apparent that most mercantilistic writers, at least from the end of the seventeenth century, recognized that economic life in general was influenced by and even governed by some principles and "laws": the law of supply and demand, etc. However, in the same treatise where they used the quantity theory of money to show that an inflow of money only led to rising prices, they could still argue that a positive balance of trade increased the wealth of a nation. Wiles never discusses how such paradoxes should be interpreted, but this seems to me to be both a crucial and urgent task which must be done with tools developed in the context of a "close reading."

However, this would not only imply a rereading of the texts themselves; we also have to pay more attention to the circumstances in which they were written and for what purposes. This also includes a better understanding of how the discourse of economics slowly evolved in the seventeenth and eighteenth centuries. It is clear that most of what we would define as economics proper would have been dealt with, if at all, within some branch of natural science or in the old tradition of Aristotelian "*Haushaltungswissenschaft.*" It was only in the eighteenth century that economics emerged as an academic subject in its own right with the establishment of chairs in "Oekonomie-, Polizie-, und Kameralwissenschaft" in Germany and Sweden in the 1720s and 1730s [Dittrich, 1974; Magnusson, 1985]. Only gradually did this new subject become a place where general "economic" principles which could apply to all human societies were distilled. This shift of emphasis and the objectives behind it have still not been studied in detail.[3] However, this is a field which must be further explored, in that it makes us aware of the fact that the mercantilists were adressing a quite different set of questions than later economists and used different methods and concepts. Increasingly, we must take this into account when we define a certain system of mercantilism within a general history of "economic" thought.

III

Wiles argues that economic growth was the overriding goal of the mercantilists and that proposals for a favorable balance of trade should be seen in this context. Such an approach was also developed by W. D. Grampp in an important paper [1952], and on the whole it seems to me that Wiles shares the views of that author, although, of course, the two also differ. Grampp, for example, argued that the mercantilists' goal was full employment. At the same time, however, he made it clear that this goal was emphasized by mercantilist writers merely because they defined labor as the most important factor of production — and hence to maximize the utilization of that factor was to maximize growth. Nonetheless, the general approach is the same in both papers.

Very much in accordance with Wiles, Grampp points out that "there was nothing primitive about their [the mercantilists'] ideas." On the contrary, they in fact even "anticipated the ideas of the classical economists" [Grampp, 1952, pp. 499, 491]. Thus, for example, they agreed with Smith regarding the dangers of restrictions and monopoly, and to some extent openly opposed the prohibitive governmental policies of the age.

However, by stressing the "modern" features of mercantilism, there is a danger that we forget that still in the beginning of the eighteenth century mercantilist writings contained viewpoints and ways of arguing that indeed seemed absurd from the standpoint of a later age. It is true that the doctrine of the favorable balance of trade was in "a dying state" in the beginning of the nineteenth century, but most mercantilists still thought that foreign trade was of special value to a nation [Suvrianta, 1923, pp. 142 ff]. At least outside Britain, economic thinkers and policy-makers were still obsessed with the balance of trade and with how to find measures for the achievement of an export surplus. In the name of a favorable balance of trade the establishment of manufactures became a major policy question in continental Europe and in Scandinavia [Glamann-Oxenböll, 1983; Magnusson, 1985; Dittrich, 1974; Schmoller, 1931]. And in the beginning of the eighteenth century, most mercantilists still feared free trade and regarded "polypoly" — to use the concept of the seventeenth century Austrian mercantilist Becher — as at least as harmful as monopoly.

This is not the only difficulty that is apparent in Grampp's article. Grampp tends to explain such "strange" features of mercantilistic thought that do not fit into a slowly evolving Smithian paradigm by pointing to certain institutional factors working within the framework of the pre-industrial economy *or* by the argument that the mercantilists were analytically unsophisticated. It is not clear whether Wiles would agree with this at all, but it seems most likely that he — inferring from the way he presents his case — at least to some degree considers the second explanation to be true. But then, of course, the Smithian paradigm teleologically slips in again as an objective measuring stick with which to compare other "systems" of thought. It can also be argued regarding both these explanations that they tend to play down the importance of ideology in mercantilistic thought, which I believe can lead to serious mistakes.

It was, of course, Heckscher more than perhaps anybody else who especially stressed this ideological element or "vision" within the discourse of mercantilism. For polemical purposes he could even go so far as to state: "There are no grounds whatsoever for supposing that mercantilistic writers constructed their system...out of any knowledge of reality whatsoever" [Heckscher, 1955, II, p. 347]. This is, of course, an extreme standpoint, as so many have pointed out, but I do not think it does justice to Heckscher's views on these matters. Above all it should be remembered that it only appears in the second edition of *Mercantilism* in a context where he discusses some of the critical points brought up by his reviewers. However, what he was stressing here, I believe, was this ideologic aspect of the mercantilist system of thought.

Without doubt Heckscher would have agreed with the view that the mercantilists' overriding goal was economic growth or improvement. It is probably because he does not use eighteenth century texts at all in his study that he (as Wiles notes) never emphasizes this explicitly anywhere in *Mercantilism*. In other contexts, however, he acknowledges this goal in many mercantilistic texts, especially when he discusses Swedish and German mercantilism in the eighteenth century [Heckscher, 1949, II, pp. 812 ff.; also 1935/36]. However, in his view, what justifies our talking of a mercantilist *system* of thought is not so much its goal — which it shares with other systems of economic thought, for example, the classical — as its means to achieve that goal; it was here that the ideological influence was most apparent. This is, by the way, never really taken into account by Wiles, who seems to think that a common goal — that of economic growth — is sufficient in order to be able to speak of a specific "mercantilistic" economic thought. But is its special character really defined mainly by this thought, or should we rather, with Heckscher, look to some other perhaps more important features shared by most mercantilists? A problem with Wiles' approach is that it is difficult to understand why the promotion of economic growth in one system could lead to such different proposals for policy (regulation) than when the same goal was pursued in quite another system (the invisible hand).

In Hechscher's view the most important feature of mercantilistic thought was its fear of too much freedom and its reliance on the state to plan and regulate economic life. Basically, he explained this in terms of the transition from a barter to a money economy and the confusion that arose: "...the connection between purchasing and sales disappear, being concealed by the cloak of money" which resulted in that peculiar "fear of goods" that was such a typical feature of the mercantilist doctrine according to Heckscher [1936/37, p. 37]. However, to explain these ideological elements within mercantilism he also emphasised the influence of a broader "general conception of society," to which I shall return in a moment.

From his discussion regarding the "conflict between public and private interest" within mercantilistic discourse, it is apparent that Wiles is aware of such ideological influences here. Although he seems to regard this conflict as crucial, he unfortunately does not say anything about its origins or the intellectual background to such a view. I propose to end by giving some clues that may serve as a point of departure for further investigation regarding the intellectual and ideological framework of mercantilist thinking.

While discussing the "paradox" that the mercantilists shared, a "conception of society" that to a great extent resembled the conception held by the classical economists, Heckscher himself pointed out in which direction a possible solution might be found:

> ...mercantilism has a side which has until now been mostly overlooked. That may be called its general conception of society. The remarkable feature of this conception was its fundamental concord with that of laissez-faire; so that, while mercantilism and laissez-faire were each other's opposites in practical application and economic theory proper, they were largely based upon a common conception of society.... From other points of view the existence of ideas common to mercantilism and its successor ought to be less surprising for they were in harmony with the general trend of thought dominating Europe since the Renaissance. Philosophically, their basis was the concept of natural law...[Heckscher, 1936/37, p. 31].

I think it can be argued that this is both right and wrong. When Heckscher emphasizes that the economic debate in the seventeenth and eighteenth centuries was heavily influenced by the tradition of natural rights discourse, he is without doubt highly accurate. This was also pointed out in the older literature on this topic, and the most ambitious attempt to find general connections between natural rights speculations and mercantilism is still Louise Sommer's extensive treatise in two volumes [1920, 1925] on the central European Cameralistic and mercantilistic tradition. Sommer argues that within the natural rights discourse of Grotius, Hobbes, and Pufendorf, speculations about the state held a central position. The highly influential Pufendorf argued, for example, that both natural and human societies were governed by law. But as men were free they could choose to act against the moral dictum prescribed by God which was an argument for having a strong state that with the help of the stick and the carrot could prevent this from happening. Furthermore, in the primitive state, men were weak and lonely and for that reason they created the state for protection and shelter. However, by signing a social contract, they turned over some of their original rights (but not all of them) to the ruler, who was seen as the keeper of the common good [Krieger, 1965; Medick, 1981]. In Pufendorf's view the state was a moral person and creator of civilized society, and this had a tremendous impact, says Sommer, on mercantilist and Cameralist thinkers from Beecher to Justi and Sonnenfels [Sommer, 1925, p. 161].

The extent to which the cameralistic tradition was impregnated with natural rights ideas has, of course, also been pointed out by several other scholars [Brückner, 1977; Dittrich, 1974; Preu, 1983]. Moreover, this general influence has also been noticed outside the specific German form of mercantilist thought. In an important study, Hont and Ignatieff [1983] emphasized the impact of natural rights ideas on the Scottish philosophers in the eighteenth century and its role in the formation of the new Smithian paradigm: "Natural jurisprudence...provided Smith with the language in which his theory of the functions of government in a market society took shape" [Hont — Ignatieff, 1983, p. 43].

It may then be argued that Heckscher was perfectly right when he pointed out that both mercantilists, Cameralists, and the followers of the model of the invisible hand were influenced by the discourse on natural rights. This seemed to furnish the mercantilists with a view of the state as a moral person that served the cause of civilization and the Scottish philosophers with a model of a law-governed society where the common good was ensured by some mysterious, invisible hand.

On the other hand, Heckscher was clearly wrong when he saw this as a paradox. Natural rights discourse was clearly not a coherent and unchanging system "dominating Europe since the Renaissance." Like everything else, it changed over time, and it is clear that it implied something quite different in the middle of the eighteenth century than it had a century before. In this process Pufendorf has often been regarded as a major turning-point [Tuck, 1979, pp. 156 ff.; Hont-Ignatieff, 1983, pp. 31 ff.]. First, the role of the state tended to become generally less pronounced in the eighteenth century debates. Secondly, Hont and Ignatieff have pointed out that Pufendorf's attack on the notion of primary natural rights was extremly important in this context. By reducing "the range of preceptive natural law to a minimum," Pufendorf upset the old paternalist vision that previously had been utilized to defend a system of rights and obligations that shaped the relationship between master and servant and between rich and poor. This in turn opened the way for the kind of "market" solution propagated later by Smith [Hont-Ignatieff, 1983, p. 32] and Bentham [Tuck, 1979, p. 161].

Thus, the development of mercantilism — as well as its downfall —

was accompanied by certain shifts in the tradition of natural rights, and it is highly plausible that these two phenomena were interconnected. We can, of course, differ in our interpretation of how far this general change in the "conception of society" influenced thinkers putting forward proposals for economic modernization and growth and also how far — admittedly an even more difficult task — it influenced "practical" policy in the seventeenth and eighteenth centuries. Probably there is also much more to be said about the natural rights tradition in itself and how it should be interpreted. However, by asking fundamental questions about the ideological elements within mercantilist thinking, we at least admit that there are aspects of mercantilism that cannot be easily explained by institutional factors without taking into account how they were interpreted and intellectually constructed. The natural rights tradition provides one important framework in this respect, but there are probably others to discover.

Notes

1. For a review of the debate see, for example, Coleman [1969] and Coats [1985].
2. See, for example, Heckscher's unfair judgment of it [1955, II, p. 266].
3. In the near future some results from the international project "The Institutionalization of Political Economy" with contributions from a great range of European and non-European countries will be published and might provide some fresh information.

References

Brückner, J. *Staatswissenschaften, Kameralismus und Naturrecht.* München: Verlag CH Beck, 1977.

Cannan, E. *A History of the Theories of Production and Distribution in English Political Economy From 1776 to 1848.* London: P.S. King & Son, 1903.

Coats, A. W. "The Interpretation of Mercantilist Economics: Some Historiographical Problems." *History of Political Economy* 5: 1973.

——————. "Mercantilism, Yet Again!." In *Gli economisti e la politica economica.* Ed. by P. Roggi. Naples: Edizione Scientifiche Italiane, 1985.

Coleman, D. C. "Labour in the English Economy of the Seventeenth Century." *Economic History Review*, Sec. ser. 11: 1956.

——————. "Editor's introduction." In *Revisions in Mercantilism.* Ed. by D. C. Coleman. London: Methuen, 1969.

——————. "Mercantilism Revisted." *Historical Journal*: 23 1980.

Dittrich, E. *Die Deutschen und Österreichischen Kameralisten.* Darmstadt: Wissenschaftliche Buchgesellschaft, 1974.

Glamann, K.-Oxenböll, E. *Studier i dansk merkantilisme.* Köbenhavn: Akademiskt Förlag, 1983.

Grampp, W. D. "The Liberal Elements in English Mercantilism." *Quarterly Journal of Economics* LXVI: 1952.

Heckscher, E. F. *Mercantilism,* 2 vols. London: George Allen & Unwin, 1955.

————. "Mercantilism." *Economic History Review* 7:1936–37, Cit. from the reprint in *Revisions in Mercantilism.* Ed. by D. C. Coleman. London: Methuen, 1969.

————. *Sveriges ekonomiska historia sedan Gustav Vasa,* vol. II:2. Stockholm: Bonniers, 1949.

Hont, I., and Ignatieff, M. "Needs and Justice in the Wealth of Nations." In *Wealth and Virtue: The Shaping of Political Economy in the Scottish Enlightment.* Ed. by I. Hont and M. Ignatieff. Cambridge: Cambridge University Press, 1983.

Judges, V. A. "The Idea of a Mercantile State." *Transactions of the Royal Historical Society,"* fourth ser., 1939. Cit. from the reprint in *Revisions in Mercantilism.* Ed. by D. C. Coleman. London: Methuen, 1969.

Krieger, L. *The Politics of Discretion: Pufendorf and the Acceptance of Natural Law.* Chicago & London: University of Chicago Press, 1965.

Magnusson, L. "Anders Berch and Early Political Economy in Sweden." paper presented for the volume *The Institutionalization of Political Economy* (forthcoming).

Medick, H. *Naturzustand und Naturgeschichte der bürgerlichen Gesellschaft: Die ürsprünge der bürgerlichen Sozialtheorie als Gesichtsphilosophie und Sozialwissenschaft bei Samuel Pufendorf, John Locke und Adam Smith.* Göttingen: Wandenhoek und Ruprecht, 1981.

Preu, P. *Poliziebegriff und Staatszwecklehre.* Göttingen: Verlag Otto Schwartz, 1983.

Schmoller, G. *The Mercantile System and its Historical Significance.* New York: Peter Smith, 1931.

Schumpeter, J. *A History of Economic Analysis.* London: Allen & Unwin, 1972.

Suviranta, B. "The Theory of the Balance of Trade in England." Diss., Helsinki, 1923.

Tribe, K. *Land, Labour and Economic Discourse.* London: Routledge & Kegan Paul, 1978.

Tuck, R. *Natural Rights Theories.* Cambridge: Cambridge University Press, 1979.

7 IN SEARCH OF ECONOMIC ORDER: FRENCH PREDECESSORS OF ADAM SMITH

Robert F. Hébert

One may say, if one disregards the influence of Stoic conceptions of a world order (revived during the Renaissance), that the eighteenth century conceptualized the economic (or social) universe. It made the hidden processes of the social order visible even as the seventeenth had become aware of those of the physical order and made them visible....

— J.J. Spengler [1984, p. 3]

Introduction

The field of eighteenth century economic thought is far more fertile than commonly believed. Even before Adam Smith's monumental contribution in the last quarter of the century, peak performances in economic analysis had emerged in France (Boisguilbert, Vauban, Cantillon, Quesnay, Turgot), Italy (Galiani, Verri, Beccaria), Germany (Justi,

---

Unless otherwise noted, all translations of French into English are my own. I would like to thank R. B. Eckelund, Jr., and P. D. Groenewegen for helpful comments on an earlier draft. Any errors that remain are stubbornly my own.

Sonnenfels), and Spain (Campomanes, Jovellanos). A complete investigation of these and other contributions would convince even the most reluctant skeptic that economics was anything but a product of exclusively British manufacture.

This chapter does not attempt to survey the full range of continental economics before Adam Smith. Space constraints limit the exposition to major French contributions of the period. This is, however, defensible on two grounds: (1) the French tradition was (arguably) the most robust of the continental contributions; and (2) there is a demonstrably close connection between French writers, particularly the physiocrats, and Adam Smith.

In his critical remarks that follow this essay, Professor Groenewegen expresses the view, shared by many, that the most important conceptual achievement of French economic thought in the eighteenth century was "the development of the surplus model of economic growth, where at least part of the argument is focused on the disposal of the surplus through taxation and government spending." There can be little doubt that economic growth was a major concern of eighteenth century writers on economic topics. I would, in fact, judge Adam Smith's monumental economic treatise as the greatest of all time on the subject of economic growth. But there is another side to the issue of growth that typically receives less attention. Smith argued that limited government is an efficient way to organize an economy. This was a revolutionary view, whose acceptance required a thorough understanding and detailed explanation of an alternative social order.

How could anything fill the vacuum created by the diminution of government authority? Smith found the answer in the economic marketplace. By economic order, then, I mean the form and function of a system of markets that operates, in the absence of a central authority (be he monarch, dictator, or parliament), to achieve the production and distribution of goods in a way that promotes economic welfare. Smith's economics is not merely growth economics; it is also welfare economics. And the linchpin of Smith's welfare economics is the unfettered operation of the market. How did Smith come to understand and appreciate this market view? A complete answer cannot be given here, but it is clear that much of the groundwork for our understanding of the economic order was laid in advance of Smith, a large measure emanating from France. This essay attempts to probe those French contributions, concentrating only on peak performances, and including one writer who, though not French by birth, made his mark on economics by that language and, at least partly, by its culture.[1]

Formal Beginnings: Boisguilbert and Vauban

The leading economists of France in the closing years of the seventeenth century and the early years of the eighteenth century were Boisguilbert and Vauban, the former a magistrate, the latter a brilliant military engineer and national hero. The economic thought of each was strongly conditioned by events that strained the military, political, and economic power of the country. The previous century belonged to Louis XIV, longest reigning of the French monarchs, who held the throne until his demise in 1715. At the turn of the century, however, French hegemony was already seriously threatened by three major circumstances. First, as early as 1667, France embarked upon a series of wars which lasted more or less continuously until the end of Louis XIV's reign. These wars placed a tremendous burden on the French treasury, ultimately producing large deficits, debasement of the currency, and oppressive taxation. Second, the revocation of the Edict of Nantes, urged on the king by his mercurial mistress, Madame de Maintenon, extracted a terrible toll in wealth and human capital by the ensuing persecution and emigration. Third, though not the outcome of policy decisions, the famines of 1693 and 1694 conspired to exacerbate the aforementioned ills.

Pierre le Pesant de Boisguilbert (1646–1714)

Boisguilbert was an inveterate reformer and projector who accumulated wealth in agriculture and trade after an unsuccessful attempt at a literary career. According to a common practice, he subsequently purchased positions in the magistracy of Rouen, his native town. In various ranks, he exercised authority over peasants, gentry, and clergymen, supervising law and order, health and sanitation, economic justice, and public morality, including censorship of the press. As one of the officials responsible for food supply, Boisguilbert focused much of his attention on the price of wheat.

According to Hamilton [1969, pp. 127 ff.], Boisguilbert conceived value in terms of supply and demand, recognized inelasticity in the demand for wheat, and made a tentative approach toward marginal analysis. Spengler [1984, p. 77] also attributes to Boisguilbert at least glimpses of the following economic concepts: division of labor, circular flow, velocity of money, the multiplier, diminishing utility, diminishing returns, economic equilibrium, and the cobweb-price model. McDonald [1954] credits Boisguilbert with the earliest theory of national income based on aggregate demand. Most contemporary writers agree, however, that Boisguilbert was much more a practitioner than a theorist. He was interested, above all, in analyzing what constitutes the true wealth of a nation and in identifying those factors that account for its growth. This concern, above all others, places him in a direct line of economic thought leading to Adam Smith.

Boisguilbert wrote at a time when mercantilist doctrines were the conventional wisdom, yet he rejected mercantilist views of money and wealth. The first modern aspect of his thought was the fact that he based his economic analysis on aggregate consumption rather than on money. Almost two and a half centuries before Keynes, Boisguilbert developed a theory of national income based on aggregate demand. The chief, almost the only, component of his aggregate demand function was consumption. "It can be set forth as a *principle*," said Boisguilbert (1695, 602) "that *consumption and* [national] *revenue are one and the same thing,* [emphasis added] and that the ruination of consumption is the ruination of [national] revenue." At the base of this statement is the recognition of what later came to be known as Say's Identity (after another French economist, J. B. Say), namely, that the aggregate costs of annual output are identical to the aggregate revenues derived from annual production [Bast 1966, p. 37; McDonald 1966, p. 105].

In addition to recognizing its key role in economic activity, Boisguilbert also attempted to analyze the determinants of aggregate consumption. His conclusion, less sophisticated than Keynes', nevertheless fits the conditions of his day. According to Boisguilbert [1707c, p. 1006], aggregate consumption is a function of the division of income between classes. Specifically, aggregate consumption will be greater the more income is in the hands of the masses (*le menu peuple*) because, as we would say today, they have a higher propensity to consume. This last fact is dictated by their station in life, which implies that all or nearly all of their incomes are spent on necessities.

Investment played a minor role in Boisguilbert's aggregate demand theory, not because he did not recognize it as a legitimate outlet for savings but because he was less concerned with the elaboration of a general theory than he was with explaining the observed unemployment of land and labor. His observations on the subject seemed to depend less on the role of investment as an active determinant of national income and more on its role as a stopgap, should the level of consumption fall below its optimum. Despite some recognition of the role of expectations and the rate of interest on investment decisions, Boisguilbert did not add to economic theory along these lines.

He did, however, ably analyze the process of economic decline that had beset eighteenth century France. His persistent appeals for tax reform in order to raise the level of aggregate consumption heralded later theories of business cycles keyed to the level of aggregate demand. France was facing secular stagnation as a result of an oppressive and uneven tax system that directly and indirectly restricted aggregate consumption. The fact that the court, clergy, and landed aristocracy were exempt from paying taxes exacerbated the situation because of the lower propensity to consume of these groups. Boisguilbert [1707a, p. 876] called for major fiscal reform to more evenly distribute the tax burden and to stabilize agricultural income (i.e., the price of grain) at a level that would allow full employment of land and labor.

Boisguilbert developed a concept of economic order that incorporated notions of exchange, utility, movement, and price. He considered *equilibrium* synonomous with a state of opulence, while *disequilibrium* meant stagnation, decline, and/or misery. Price is a significant aspect of Boisguilbert's economic order because it signals the mutuality of interest potentially present in each exchange. Unlike the mercantilists, who viewed exchange as a zero-sum game, Boisguilbert stressed reciprocity. For every good sold there is a "utility gain" to the buyer and a "revenue benefit" to the seller. Thus those prices are efficient (*prix proportionnels*) which simultaneously convey this benefit to each buyer and cover each seller's costs. In terms of the macroeconomy, moreover, Boisguilbert asserted that the persistence of prosperity is dependent upon *continuity* of expenditure. Thus it is important that the income-flow patterns of an economy are not interrupted by oppressive taxation, by hoarding, or by depression.

Boisguilbert did not develop a theory of individual price formation, merely an analysis of the general relationship of prices to the goal of economic growth. His concept of proportional prices describes an actual price structure consistent with a stable economic order. Faccarello [1984, p. 49] likens Boisguilbert's price structure to that which exists in a general equilibrium system where supply is equal to demand in every market simultaneously, but he does not recognize the potential conflict between a Walrasian static equilibrium and Boisguilbert's identification of equilibrium with incessant movement (i.e., progress). Roberts [1935, pp. 241–42] equates Boisguilbert's notion of proportional price to Adam Smith's conception of natural price. But whereas Smith's natural price is a theoretical statement of central tendency, Boisguilbert's proportional price structure is a practical necessity for the maintenance of general prosperity. In Boisguilbert's economy, a fall in the price of one product below its costs of production reduces the consumption of those dependent on this industry, initiating a disorder that quickly spreads throughout the economy. Thus he recognized the general interdependence of a market system, even if he did not formalize its mathematical properties.

The notion that there is a pattern of prices and incomes consistent with economic prosperity implies the formulation of economic policy to achieve this end. Boisguilbert's position on the role of the state in economic policy was remarkably liberal for its time, so much so that he is considered an important forerunner of Adam Smith [Daire, 1843; Horn, 1867; Cadet, 1870; Roberts, 1935]. He argued that optimal policy consisted not so much in positive action as in the prevention of artificial conditions which induce maldistribution of goods and incomes. Thus he advocated a limited role for government, insisting merely that appropriate tax and fiscal policies be followed, that markets (especially grain) be open, that products be allowed to freely move about, and that the price system be allowed to adjust to adverse price movements (due to natural causes) before a permanent or major decline in consumption could set in. More than once, Boisguilbert [1707a, p. 873] affirmed that it was nature, not the state, that must perform the regulation of economic activity. Given the rudimentary nature of his analysis, however, he was unable to describe in satisfactory detail the adjustive mechanisms included under the heading of "nature."

Boisguilbert was one of the first writers to employ the phrase *laissez-faire* in his economic writings. But more importantly, he gave force to the principle by demonstrating how disequilibrating forces in the political order impacted on the economic system. He called attention to the income-contracting effects of government policy in general, including tax, fiscal, trade, and miscellaneous policies. He singled out tax policy more than any other, however. He insisted that taxes must be certain, not arbitrary; that they be easily and cheaply collected, proportional to ability-to-pay, and not restrictive of agriculture and commerce. Each of these ideas has subsequently become important canons of modern public finance, albeit more through the influence of other writers. One by one, Boisguilbert assessed the various tax measures of the monarchy against these standards, and he found each one lacking. He condemned the existing excise taxes (the *aides* and the *douanes*) on the grounds that they raised prices sufficiently high enough to seriously curb consumption and that they discouraged enterprise. Surprisingly, he ignored the hated salt tax (the *gabelle*), saving his most trenchant criticism for the *tailles*, a kind of income tax. He condemned the latter as expensive to collect, uncertain, arbitrary, regressive, and destructive of capital formation.

Another revenue measure, the sale of offices by the crown, entailed additional burdens for much of the population. Tax farming and related practices, added Boisguilbert [1707c, p. 982], intensified the uncertainty and arbitrariness of the taxes and interfered with the all-important continuity of consumption.

Several of Boisguilbert's contemporaries also recognized the need for tax reform and the removal of restrictions on commerce. Fenelon (1651–1715), Boulainvilliers (1658–1722), and Sainte-Pierre (1658–1743) all sounded similar themes in their writings. But it was Vauban's proposal that commanded the most attention.

Sebastien le Prestre, Seigneur de Vauban (1633–1707)

Vauban, of whom Fontenelle [1821] said, "He brought mathematics down from the heavens to meet the needs of men," was widely reputed to be the greatest military engineer of the seventeenth century. Besides his many military victories on behalf of Louis XIV's armies, Vauban was more responsible than any other single person for the professionalization of French engineers, a legacy that proved especially rich for the development of economics a century or so later, when the best minds in French economics turned out to be engineers from the professional cadre Vauban had helped to establish [Ekelund and Hébert, 1978].

Although Boisguilbert holds priority as the founder of an analytical tradition, two things about Vauban are especially noteworthy.

1. He had a personal penchant for statistics. He never tired of collecting them or of making drastic reform proposals based upon them. Indeed, he employed others to gather statistics for him, paying them out of his own pocket. He also observed with his own eyes the values of land, trade, industry, and the nature of taxes and their levy, as he crisscrossed the kingdom on one military campaign after another. With a single-mindedness undeterred by such distractions, Vauban devoted himself to these researches the last two decades of his life.

2. He had the mind-set of the economist, despite his military orientation and training. In one of his earliest writings on economic subjects, Vauban attacked the revocation of the Edict of Nantes, citing the consequent loss of human capital and financial wealth that followed. What is especially noteworthy is that Vauban approached this subject — ostensibly one of religious toleration — from the perspective of political economy, bolstering his argument with statistics on population.

Vauban's famous proposal on tax reform, *Dîme Royale*, was not published until the year of his death (1707), even though Blomfield [1938, p. 95] reports that he may have transmitted the same idea to Louvois, the Finance Minister, 20 years earlier. In the meantime, he had read and met Boisguilbert, with whom he was in general agreement on tax matters, although he did not share Boisguilbert's näive optimism that France's economic problems would disappear within mere weeks of the enactment of a few simple reforms.

Vauban's proposal for tax reform took the form of an income tax, without exemption, ranging from 5 to 10 percent of the gross yield of agriculture and a similar levy on income from any other form of property, pension, salary, or wage. His guiding principles of taxation were simplicity and equity, and he was far more adamant (courageous?) than Boisguilbert in his insistence that no exemptions be allowed. Neither king, court, nor clergy were to be exempt; he denounced favoritism in assessment, and pleaded for taxation based solely and fairly on ability to pay. Like Boisguilbert, Vauban saw the revenue of the state as being dependent on the prosperity of its citizens. Above all he wished to moderate the tax burden, to spread it in accordance with the capacity of taxpayers to provide revenue, and to make the system adjustable to the king's needs. Unlike Boisguilbert, however, he pushed for gradual introduction of reforms, expecting the restoration of prosperity to take about 15 years.

Although the income tax was the cornerstone of his tax reform program, Vauban was not a single-tax advocate. He did not reject external customs duties and certain minor taxes. Even the hated *gabelle* was to be retained, albeit in a greatly modified form, shorn of its most objectionable features. As always, he adorned his economic arguments with statistics. Vauban [1707, pp. 34–35] estimated that approximately 10 percent of the French people lived in penury and depended on alms for a living, that a full 50 percent of the populace were too close to poverty to give alms, that 30 percent of the people were burdened by debts and/or lawsuits, and that only 10 percent of the nation was well off. This last 10 percent, however, numbered no more than 100,000 families, of which not even 10,000 were completely comfortable. Other statistics from the period reveal how expensive foreign wars and court extravagances brought France to the brink of economic ruin. When Colbert died in 1683, the net revenue of France was 93 million *livres* and its expenditure, 109 million. In 1715, the year Louis XIV died, receipts had fallen to 74 million while expenditures climbed to 119 million (pushing the deficit from 16 million to 45 million). France tried all manner of revenue measures to mitigate the problem: loans at high interest, conversions of interest, debasement of the coinage, the sale of monopoly privileges, offices, and rank.[2] In spite of it all, however, the deficits continued.

Outside of France, Vauban has attracted little attention from historians of economic thought. Most textbooks on the subject do not include him. Nevertheless, he added a second prominent voice to Boisguilbert's against France's ruinous fiscal policies. Modern intellectual historians disagree as to the extent of Vauban's liberalism in economic matters. Hamilton [1969, p. 139] declared him "mercantilist to the core." Yet Hecksher [1934, II, p. 264] judged Vauban free of mercantilist leanings. Spengler [1984, p. 86] took a more eclectic approach, citing both aspects of Vauban's thought. Bast [1966, p. 31] linked Vauban with Boisguilbert, treating both as early antimercantilists. Yet there are appreciable differences. Although he endorsed the idea of freer trade, Vauban did not believe that public and private interests were harmonious. His own loyalty undeniable, Vauban held that individuals should be subordinate to the state. He favored colonies financed and regulated by the government, and he also championed an ambitious public works program. His profound dislike of financiers and monopolists gave his writings something of an anticapitalist tone. In the end, he remains an odd mixture of idealist and realist, always ready to prescribe solutions worked out in minutest detail.

The First Economic Treatise: Cantillon[3]

In an important, but nonexclusive sense, the history of economic thought is the story of how individuals came to recognize, refine, and progressively understand the concept of economic order. In this regard, Boisguilbert is an important early contributor. But his early glimpses of economic order were superseded in a few short decades by Richard Cantillon (d. 1734), called "the first of the moderns" by Spengler [1954]. Jevons [1881, p. 342], in the rush of scientific discovery, declared Cantillon's *Essai sur la nature du commerce en général* [1755] the first treatise in economics.

What transforms Jevons' claim from mere puffery is the fact that no writer before Cantillon so successfully analyzed the economy as an organization nor so completely understood its components. While economics was yet in its infancy, his *Essai* gave force to the proposition championed two centuries later by Frank Knight [1933, p. 6], namely, that because economics deals with the social organization of economic activity, the structure and working of the system of free enterprise constitutes the main topic of discussion in a treatise on economics. Like Knight, Cantillon understood that every organization requires a directing authority, and he was one of the earliest writers to recognize that in an economic society, the *market* is one form that this authority can take.

Also, like Smith, and even more than Boisguilbert, Cantillon was fully aware of the self-regulating nature of the market.

Other writers have cited Cantillon's multiform contributions to modern economics. Hayek [1931] lauded Cantillon's theory of money and its effect on relative prices. Spengler [1942, 1954], Tarascio [1981], and Brems [1983] analyzed Cantillon's population theory. Huq [1954] attributed the concept of the multiplier to Cantillon, although priority of discovery should perhaps go to Boisguilbert. Sekine [1973] credits Cantillon with the independent (though incomplete) discovery of international monetary equilibrium. Any one of these contributions would probably have assured Cantillon lasting fame in the history of economic thought. But for the present purpose, the concept of economic order that he so skillfully explicated requires elaboration.

Cantillon wrote the *Essai* in the decade before his death in 1734; in it he described the society that he knew. The French Revolution was more than 50 years away; the property rights of a privileged aristocracy were both respected and accepted as the natural consequences of society. Yet trade had become so general that the farmer already produced for the market. The interconnected markets through which trade was conducted had become the organizing principle of the entire complex of economic activities stretching beyond the estates of the landowners to the cities and even beyond national boundaries. This is what Cantillon perceived and described.

The originality of Cantillon's treatise consists of its complete orientation to the economic functions of the members of society. His experience (from which he shrewdly profited) with John Law's disastrous paper money experiment convinced Cantillon that land alone held its value against the ravages of inflation. Insofar as land in his day was concentrated in the hands of a few, two distinct economic classes existed: those who were financially independent by virtue of land ownership; and everyone else who was dependent on the landed proprietors in one way or another. The second class, although united in their dependency on the first, is nevertheless heterogeneous insofar as some of its members enjoy certain incomes whereas others (the entrepreneurs) do not. Cantillon [1931, p. 56] concluded: "I will therefore lay it down as a principle that the proprietors of land alone are naturally independent in a State; that all the other classes are dependent, whether they be entrepreneurs or hirelings, and that all the exchange and circulation of the State is conducted by the intercession of these entrepreneurs." This pivotal role of the entrepreneur will be discussed in more detail below.

On this division of society, Cantillon erected an economic model utilizing a "great estate" as the basic unit. In the first version of this model, Cantillon [1931, pp. 58 ff.] assumed that there was only one great estate and that the owner managed it himself, making all the decisions with respect to resource use and output selection. This enabled him to expose the basic elements and relationships that comprise economic activity in what amounted to a scaled-down version of a centrally planned economy. The conclusion Cantillon [1931, p. 64] reached was that the pattern of production depends on demand; or as he put it, "The fancies or fashions of the landowners determine the use of the land and bring about the variations of demand which cause the variations of market prices."

Next Cantillon modified the simple model, making it more realistic. He assumed that in order "to avoid so much care and trouble" the owner makes a deal with the overseers of his land so that they become entre-preneurs, who now make the decisions regarding what and how to produce. The question then arises: how will this introduction of market-directed activity change the order of production? Cantillon [1931, p. 60] answered that it doesn't change at all, because the demand of the pro-prietor hasn't changed. If anything did change, if for example, the farmers produced more grain than usual, a corrective (market) process would come into play to reestablish the former pattern of things. Only if the owner changed his mode of living would the pattern of output change to reflect the new pattern of demand. All other causes of a change in demand were dismissed by Cantillon's [1931, pp. 62–64] claim that: "Artisans and workers who live from day to day change their mode of living only from necessity. If a few, well-off farmers, master craftsmen or other entrepreneurs vary their expenditure and consumption, they always imitate the lords and landed proprietors." Following Petty, he ignored unsystematic factors on which theory had little to offer, specifically excluding bad weather, foreign invasion, or other accidents, which might unnecessarily complicate the analysis.

In this way, Cantillon exposed the fact that demand is the driving force of economic activity. A number of implications are suggested by Cantillon's analysis. Thus, it emerges that the centralized direction of the estate is abandoned because of the "care and trouble involved" — a kind of economic evolution, perhaps. It becomes obvious that exchange and competition subsequently arise and that these, in turn, require the use of money, both as a measure of value and as a medium of exchange. It also becomes evident that production does not adjust to demand of its own accord. The centralized decision-making of the proprietor must be replaced by a different decision apparatus so as to ensure that supply is in fact adjusted to demand. This last function is taken up by the entrepreneur, who figured so prominently in Cantillon's system.

To Cantillon, the entrepreneur is an integral component of the competitive market system, and given his many references to the entrepreneur there can be little doubt of that figure's prominence in Cantillon's system.[4] The essence of entrepreneurship is the accommodation of uncertainty, which is the consequence of things unknown and unknowable. The entrepreneur is the economic agent who finds willing buyers and sellers, moves goods and resources to where they are desired, and stores goods until they are wanted. But he does all this at considerable risk to himself. Not knowing the future, the entrepreneur must stake his chips on his judgment. If he errs in judgment, he loses his profit, and possibly his capital. If he judges correctly, he reaps the reward of his diligence and acumen, preserving his capital and even adding to it.

Cantillon developed this theme in considerable detail in Chapter XIII, part 1 of his *Essai*, entitled "The Circulation and Exchange of Goods and Merchandise, as Well as Their Production, Are Conducted in Europe by Entrepreneurs, and at Risk." There he repeatedly made the point that whether they be farmers, merchants, wholesalers, retailers, drapers, hatters, shopkeepers, miners, carpenters, sailors, cooks, inkeepers, artisans, shoemakers, needle-women, chimney-sweeps, water-carriers, wigmakers, painters, physicians, lawyers, beggars, or robbers, the chief characteristic of the entrepreneur is that he lives at uncertainty. In what is merely the most obvious case, that of the merchant, Cantillon [1931, p. 50] noted that he "gives a certain price at the time and place of purchase in order to resell [later] wholesale or retail at an uncertain price."

The second version of Cantillon's model presents in embryonic form the basis of Hayek's [1948] idea that the market is a mechanism for the dissemination of information. In the market economy, as compared to the command economy, the demand of the proprietors and of those who emulate them remains paramount, but is now transmitted *indirectly* via the prices they are willing to offer in the market. These prices cannot be foreseen with certainty, so the overseers, now become entrepreneurs, have to guess which products will pay best. Thus, the uncertainty which confronts entrepreneurs is more than a consequence of nature or chance; it is inherent in the nature of the market.

The essence of the market is decentralized decision-making. The basis for such decisions by the entrepreneurs is the information conveyed through price signals that emerge as consumers buy goods. If the proprietor ceases to make all the decisions himself and confines himself only to indicating his demands through the prices he is prepared to pay, some way has to emerge by which the appropriate supply decisions are made. The entrepreneur takes on this function by continuously adjusting to the changes that occur. These changes are the source of the uncertainty and risk that surround the entrepreneur and which distinguish him from the proprietor on the one hand and from those who are hired on the other.

The following passage from Cantillon [1931, pp. 60–62], which portrays the farmer as an entrepreneur, is rich in suggestions of self-interest as a motive force, of relative prices as signals to adjust resource use, of opportunity costs as a basis of decision-making, and of the economic coordination achieved by entrepreneurial activity.

> ...[I]f some...farmers sowed more grain than usual on their land they would have to graze a smaller number of sheep and would therefore have less wool and mutton to sell. Consequently there will be too much grain and too little wool for the consumption of the inhabitants. Wool will therefore be dear and this will force the inhabitants to wear their clothes longer than usual; and there will be too much grain and a surplus for the following years.... [T]he farmers...will take care the following year to have less grain and more wool, for farmers always seek to use their land for the production of those things that they think will bring the highest market price. But if the next year they have too much wool and too little grain for the demand, they will not fail to change from year to year the use of the land until they have adjusted their production more or less to the consumption of the inhabitants. So a farmer who has adjusted more-or-less his output to the demand, will have part of his farm in grass, for hay, another part in grain, another in wool, and so on, and he will not change his plan unless he sees some considerable change in demand.

No writer of Cantillon's era offered a clearer or more elaborate exposition than he did of the pervasiveness of entrepreneurship and its necessity for the efficient operation of the market. Moreover, not until Frank Knight [1921] took up the topics of risk, uncertainty, and profit anew two centuries later did anyone advance the subject much beyond Cantillon's early treatment. This fact alone would seem to justify a high place for Cantillon in the history of economic thought because the British tradition of political economy that descended from Adam Smith did not give pride of place to the entrepreneur. Although the concept survived in the French tradition, numerous subsequent modifications eventually blurred its economic meaning [cf. Hébert and Link, 1982]. Modern writers such as Israel Kirzner [1973, 1979] are attempting to restore the entrepreneur to a place of central importance in the theory of competitive markets.

As alluded to at the beginning of this section, there is much more of interest in the *Essai* than what can be surveyed here. Cantillon's discussion of value and of what we now call "equilibrium wage differences" are reminiscent of Smith's later treatment. His quantity theory of money was an improvement over Locke's, especially in its handling of velocity and in its sectoral analysis. His analysis of interest and credit filled a specific void in Boisguilbert's theory. His early contribution to spatial economics was also of considerable sophistication [Hébert, 1981]. Moreover, Cantillon was indebted to Boisguilbert on certain aspects of the circular flow, on the general interdependence of markets, the importance of the landlords as major determinants of demand, and on the necessity of prices that cover costs in order to sustain production. Like Boisguilbert, he stressed the importance of agriculture and the value of land; the role of consumption; the flow of money and goods; the velocity or "turnover" of money; the origins of property distribution; and the concept of economic reciprocity. The one issue he ignored was the issue of taxation. Higgs [1892, p. 450] attributes this omission to Cantillon's desire to separate politics from economics, although he gives no evidence in support of his assertion.

The Physiocrats and Turgot

The idea that forms the most tangible link between Cantillon and the physiocrats is the concept of the circular flow. In chapter III of part 2 of the *Essai*, entitled "Of the Circulation of Money," Cantillon identified three "incomes" earned by the English farmer.[5] The first of these is paid to the landlord as payment for the use of land; the second devoted to the maintenance of the men (labor) and horses (capital) employed in cultivation; and the third retained by the farmer as the profit of his enterprise. This chapter set the pattern for Francois Quesnay's famous *Tableau Économique*.

The title *physiocrats* was applied by Dupont de Nemours in his 1767 edition of Quesnay's selected writings, but it did not attain widespread use until the middle of the nineteenth century. The group of disciples who rallied around Francois Quesnay (court physician to Louis XV and his mistress, Madame de Pompadour) in the eighteenth century called themselves simply, *Les Économistes*, the economists.

In the heyday of physiocracy (the term means rule of nature), France's economy was in a transition between the old economic order (feudalism) and the new (capitalism). In many areas of France, agricultural production was carried on under share-cropping arrangements by small-scale, labor-intensive methods (*petite culture*). But in some regions of the country, where a class of landowner-farmers had emerged, large doses of capital had been applied successfully to the land (*grande culture*). One of the most enduring contributions that Quesnay made to economic theory was to recognize the primacy of capital in the production process, and its importance in economic development [Eagly, 1974, p. 10].

François Quesnay (1694–1774)

By the time Quesnay published anything on political economy, he was almost 60 years old, having already achieved eminence as a surgeon and a physician. Agriculture had been a lifelong interest of his since the family gardener had taught him to read, using *Agriculture et maison rustique* as his primer. The beginnings of his interest in economics are less certain, but they must have been stimulated in some measure by Quesnay's eventual awareness of the works of Vauban, Boisguilbert, Cantillon, Melon, Forbonnais, and other French writers.

In 1757–58, the first elements of what was to become the physiocratic school gathered around Quesnay and Mirabeau. By 1763, Mercier de la Rivière, a member of the Paris parliament, and Pierre-Samuel DuPont de Nemours, secretary to the Intendant of Soissons, had joined the founding fathers. During the next four years, the membership ranks swelled to include Louis-Paul Abeille, Pierre Roubaud, Guillaume-François LeTrosne, Jean-Nicolas Saint-Péravy, and Nicolas Baudeau. Turgot, who is sometimes considered a physiocrat, was not a member of the inner circle and warrants separate treatment. Insofar as most members of this sect were imitators and elaborators, it is valid to concentrate on Quesnay in an assessment of their doctrine. Fox-Genovese [1976] assigns almost co-equal status to Mirabeau in the formation of physiocracy, but hers is still a minority view.

The gestation period of physiocratic thought (1756–1763) exactly spanned the Seven Years War, which accelerated the fiscal pressures on France. Thus, the fundamental problem faced by the physiocrats was how to increase the national income from a low level to a high one. Theirs was an inquiry into sound economic policy, but it is to their everlasting credit that they recognized the importance of having a theoretical model as a prerequisite. Fortunately, Quesnay had a rich French tradition to build upon. Following Vauban and Boisguilbert, he saw the connection between the state of agriculture and the royal treasury. Like Vauban, he concluded that a healthy agricultural sector required a rational system of taxation. Like Boisguilbert, he insisted that a healthy economy required freedom of circulation. And like Cantillon, he assigned a major economic role to the proprietors of land.

The following thumbnail sketch, provided by Eltis [1984, p. 4], sets the stage for the discussion that follows. The fundamental propositions of physiocracy are: that (1) only agriculture produces a surplus or "net product" over costs (where these arguably include a "normal profit"), the size of the surplus depending on the capital intensity of production; (2) the economy's effective demand for marketable output depends on the expenditure of the agricultural surplus by its recipients, the landlords, which has a multiplier effect on demand; and (3) the relative size of the agricultural and industrial sectors of the economy depends upon how demand is distributed between them. From these primary assertions, a second set of propositions derive, namely, that agriculture, which alone produces a "net product," must be the ultimate source of all tax revenue; that the economy cannot grow without agricultural growth; and that the industrial sector is wholly dependent on the agricultural, since the demand for manufactures depends on the size of the net product, which is derived entirely from agriculture.

All of this is embodied in the chief analytical novelty of physiocracy, Quesnay's *Tableau Économique*. Upon sending a copy of the work to Mirabeau for his inspection, Quesnay [1758, p. 108] wrote: "I have tried to construct a fundamental *Tableau* of the economic order for the purpose of displaying expenditure and products in a way which is easy to grasp, and for the purpose of forming a clear opinion about the organization or disorganization which the government can bring about." Unfortunately, the simplicity of illustration sought by Quesnay proved more than fleetingly illusive. Mirabeau had a difficult time understanding the original, and the vast literature devoted to physiocracy by modern economists testifies to its subtlety and complexity. A major difficulty rests with the central element of the model: the exclusive productivity of agriculture. On this principle hinges a number of constituent elements: the classification of social groups by economic function, the mechanism underlying the circular flow, the concept of net product, and the single tax.

Ronald Meek [1963, pp. 379 ff.] was one of the first to cogently argue that if one keeps in mind that the physiocrats were describing a *value* surplus in agriculture, the central assertion of exclusive productivity stands in reasonable accord with the facts of the day. The physiocrats took the existence of land rent as evidence of a value surplus, whereas they held that the prices of manufactures produced under competitive (and small-scale) conditions could be no more than the average costs of production. By introducing artificial restrictions, mercantilist policies obviously overturned this last result. But the physiocrats recognized this fact; indeed, they identified all observable surpluses in manufacturing with artificial monopolies, and therefore considered them "unnatural." In contradistinction to Meek, Herlitz [1961a, p. 12] concluded that the physiocratic doctrine of sterility is theoretically self-contradictory.

By most accounts, the physiocrats were guilty of several logical errors.

1. They not only argued that manufacturing *did not*, under competitive conditions, produce a surplus but also that it naturally and inherently *could not* do so.

2. They failed to explain why competition would not produce the same result in agriculture as it did in manufacturing (i.e., zero pure profit).

3. They neither understood nor admitted the role and productivity of capital in manufacturing, even as they extolled its virtues in agriculture. This last paradox was the obvious provocation of Smith's [1937, p. 628] criticism in the *Wealth of Nations:*

> If the rod be bent too much one way, says the proverb, in order to make it straight you must bend it as much the other. The French philosophers, who have proposed the system which represents agriculture as the sole source of the revenue and wealth of every country, seem to have adopted this proverbial maxim; and as in the plan of Mr. Colbert the industry of the towns was certainly over-valued in comparison with that of the country; so in their system it seems to be as certainly under-valued.

The most durable legacy of physiocracy, however, was not their well-reasoned set of policy prescriptions; it was their analytical method. Quesnay's economic method is calculated to expose the nature of the economic order. "The whole magic of a well-ordered society," according to the *Rural Philosophy* [1763], "is that each man works for others, while believing that he is working for himself." The process by which this occurs is market exchange. Quesnay understood that products must have utility if they are to be exchanged, and that exchange presupposes a mutual gain in utility to both buyer and seller. He also recognized that the exchange relationships between contracting parties were governed by prices that were subject to objective laws, which can be ascertained by the study of political economy. Political economy tells us that men normally behave in a regular way when confronted by prices: they seek to buy in the cheapest market and sell in the dearest. The desire for "the greatest possible reduction in disagreeable labor with the greatest possible enjoyment," adds Quesnay [1766, p. 212], "is general among men." These passages are, of course, compatible with Adam Smith's doctrine of self-interest, explicated in great detail a decade later.

According to physiocratic doctrine, the regularities of economic behavior are not arbitrary; they are subject to laws. The substance of these laws takes the form of the "natural order," an unfortunate phrase of physiocracy, because of its metaphysical connotation. By "natural" in the above context the physiocrats meant not only necessary regularities derived from actual economic circumstances but also a sort of God-given absolute toward which men should properly aim. Meek [1963, p. 373] rejects the notion that such formulations were mere verbal camouflage, even as he insists that the physiocrats reasoned from the physical to the moral, rather than the reverse. This last claim is corroborated by Weurlesse [1910, p. 117] and by Fox-Genovese [1976, pp. 47–48], who compares the materialist preconceptions of the physiocrats to those of Marx. Schumpeter [1954a, pp. 49–50] added his authority to this view by asserting that the physiocrats merely expressed the results of their economic analysis in theological or naturalist form *after* they had established them.

Following Boisguilbert and Cantillon, the physiocrats conceived the "general system of expenditure, work, gain, and consumption" as a circular flow, and the economy as a system of interconnected markets. Quesnay likened the economy to the human body, an extremely complex and delicate organism in which a disturbance to any one part eventually communicates itself to all other parts through a complicated process of reciprocal action and interaction. Changes in production, for example, induce changes in demand and vice versa because of the mutual inter-dependence that exists between sectors of the economy. The best way to conceive of this process, argued Quesnay [1766, p. 209], is to link the interdependent sectors of the economy by means of a circle. Thus, any economic policy could be examined by analyzing its effects over time on the dimensions of the circle. Eltis [1984, pp. 42 ff.] has shown how Quesnay used the *Tableau* to analyze the effects on economic growth and/or decline of such factors as the propensity to consume agricultural products, taxation's impact on the supply of agricultural capital, and the profitability of agriculture.

Quesnay was highly critical of those who saw only the immediate effects on particular groups or markets of certain policies (e.g., restrictions on grain export). His *Tableau* was an attempt to cast light on the ultimate, long-run effects of such policies. But he did not stop at the mere recognition that everything economic depends on everything else. His method involved isolating a *key factor* to serve as a kind of analytical prism through which the effects of government policies on the rest of the economy can be ascertained. The key factor chosen for this purpose was the exclusive productivity of agriculture. The fact that it was subject to severe limitations ultimately dulled Quesnay's policy prescriptions, but it did not invalidate his methodological innovation, which was readily assimilated into economic theory.[6]

Although Quesnay's recognition of capital as the major ingredient in a theory of economic development set the tone of economic inquiry for the next century, he did not work out a complete theory of capital accumulation. Some of his followers expanded on the concept of industrial profit as a second form of surplus in the economy. Of these, Turgot was clearly the most illustrious and the most able.

Anne-Robert Jacques Turgot (1727–1781)

Following a family pattern, Turgot spent most of his short, adult life in administration. In preparation, he entered the Sorbonne in 1749. The following year he wrote a critique of a book by Maupertuis which Meek [1973, p. 5] judged of seminal importance in the formulation of the stadial theory of history. At 25, Turgot entered the Paris Parliament as Counciller. Nine years later, at a modest 34 years of age, he was appointed Intendant of Limoges, whereupon he wrote to Voltaire: "A change has taken place for me and I have the misfortune to be intendant. I say misfortune, because in this world of strife, the only happiness is in living philosophically, amidst study and one's friends" [Schelle, 1913, II, p. 2]. The modern solutions that Turgot applied to feudal problems in the poorest of France's provinces spawned the whirlwind that swept him into the Cabinet when Louis XVI ascended to the throne in 1774. Until his enemies got the best of him in 1776, Turgot held the most responsible position in the government, that of Finance Minister.

Sometime around 1758, Turgot attached himself, as near as his independent spirit would permit, to the physiocrats. He was on good terms with Quesnay and Mirabeau. DuPont served as his faithful secretary for many years, although he did not always do right by Turgot when publishing the latter's works in his journal, *Ephémérides*. Having accepted the main lines of physiocracy, Turgot emphasized his difference and his independence on numerous points of detail, and always considered himself an outsider. "I am not an encyclopedist," he once confided to DuPont, "for I believe in God," and "I am not an *économiste*, for I should wish to have no king" (quoted in Higgs [1897, p. 75].)

Practically all of Turgot's economic contributions were written in the rush of administrative duty. With the exception of his *Reflections on the*

Formation and Distribution of Wealth [1766], which he intended as a kind of guidebook on political economy for two visiting Chinese students, Turgot's economic tracts were brief and intermittent. Taken together, however, their high quality amplifies the praise heaped by Schumpeter [1954b, p. 249] upon the *Reflections* alone: "It is not too much to say that analytic economics took a century to get where it could have got in twenty years after the publication of Turgot's treatise had its content been properly understood and absorbed by an alert profession."

Modern economists have learned the details of Turgot's contributions mainly through the interpretations of P. D. Groenewegen [1970, 1971, 1983], the compiler and translator of Turgot's lesser-known papers on economic questions. Insofar as certain ideas of Turgot on money, value, exchange, government regulation, international trade, and taxation have been treated adequately elsewhere, we exclude them here in order to concentrate on his relationship to Cantillon and to the physiocrats regarding the nature of the economic structure of society.

Turgot forged ahead of Cantillon in the theory of production, but less so in the theory of distribution, with the exception of interest theory. To the former, he added the principle of diminishing returns and the law of variable proportions. To the latter he contributed a theory of capital and interest that was the best of its time, incorporating elements of both time-preference and loanable funds, thereby anticipating "most of the nineteenth century work" [Schumpeter, 1954b, p. 249]. His theories of wages and rent were unoriginal, however: the former enunciated a subsistence theory; the latter rested on the physiocratic concept of net product. Finally, in his overall treatment of income distribution he walked much closer to Cantillon than to Quesnay, a fact not generally emphasized by students of Turgot or of physiocracy.

Turgot was concerned with the transformation of society from agricultural feudalism to *modern* capitalism, in which, for the first time in history, the tenant-farmer provided all the advances of cultivation, thereby becoming a capitalist-entrepreneur. We saw earlier that Cantillon divided the economic structure into landed proprietors (independents) and everyone else (dependents). Inasmuch as Cantillon subdivided the dependent class into workers (who contract their labor at a "fixed" wage) and entrepreneurs (who live by their wits), let it also be noted that Turgot later subdivided his "stipendiary" class into two. Turgot's entrepreneurs were, however, capitalists, exclusively so, whereas Cantillon's entrepreneurs were not necessarily capitalists. (Nor did Cantillon confine profit to agriculture, even though he held land to be the primary source of wealth.) After discussing examples of people who live on fixed stipends or wages, Cantillon [1931, p. 54] concluded: "All the others are entrepreneurs, whether they establish themselves with a capital to conduct their enterprise, or are entrepreneurs of their own labor without any capital, and they may be regarded as living at uncertainty; even beggars and robbers are entrepreneurs who belong to this class."

Contrariwise, the physiocrats' tripartite schema partitioned the economic classes into (agricultural) entrepreneur/capitalists, (sterile) artisans and merchants, and landed proprietors. By maintaining the exclusive productivity of agriculture, this pattern placed an obstacle in the way of Turgot's efforts to expand the role of capital, particularly with reference to manufacturing. In retrospect, Turgot should have found it easier to build upon Cantillon's schema rather than upon the physiocrats'. That he did not do so is something of a surprise, and possibly a detour in the history of economic thought.

Turgot [1766, p. 85] recognized five different ways of employing capital: the purchase of land, the leasing of land for purposes of cultivation, investment in industry, investment in commerce, and making loans at interest. He [1766, p. 87] also recognized a sort of equilibrium between these different uses, insofar as capital naturally flows to the area of highest return. Meek [1963, p. 310] correctly observed that this analysis made substantial inroads into the physiocratic doctrine of the exclusive productivity of agriculture. Yet it does not appear that Turgot fully appreciated this fact, for he concluded the work that unveiled the above analysis of capital by reaffirming that the only true, disposable surplus in a society comes from land. His argument appears to be that since the first profits in every society originally derived from land, therefore all profits (in whatever sector) that issue from subsequent expenditure of this original capital must also come from land [Turgot, 1766, p. 93]. This proposition, seemingly a way to have your analytical cake and eat it too, does not require any extended comment. Meek [1973, p. 33] was clearly on target in his judgment that "Turgot was unable completely to transcend the limitations of the 'agricultural' framework within which the analysis of the first part of the *Reflections* was set."

As for the issue of the symmetry of economic structure between Cantillon and Turgot, although they shared the same basic distributional schema, there is a major difference in the way each writer treated the entrepreneur. Both writers made the entrepreneur a key figure in the market economy, the agent who stimulates economic activity. But though important, the entrepreneur is not the all-pervasive character in Turgot's *Reflections* that he is in Cantillon's *Essai*. Partly this is because Turgot did not emphasize the role of the entrepreneur as a coordinating agent during periods of market disequilibrium. But there are more fundamental differences. As noted above, Turgot's entrepreneur is a capitalist, whereas Cantillon's is not exclusively so. The distinguishing feature of Turgot's [1766, pp. 72–74] entrepreneur is that he makes advances in production or in trade, which must be returned to him at a profit. This "profit" is divided by Turgot [1766, p. 87] into pure interest, depreciation, wages of superintendence plus a risk premium, and opportunity costs. By contrast, the hallmark of Cantillon's [1931, pp. 48–54] entrepreneur is simply that he bears uncertainty. His return, *qua* entrepreneur, is a risk premium associated with this uncertainty.

Alfred Marshall [1926, p. 356] subsequently described profits in much the same manner as Turgot, and defended the latter's position against the opposition of Bohm-Bawerk. Nevertheless, there is much to recommend the Austrian theory of profit, which traces the notion directly and exclusively to the entrepreneur, and thus strives to make the theory less ambiguous. On this point there seems to be a kinship between Cantillon, Bohm-Bawerk, and Knight (1921), who tried to disentangle the hodge-podge of payments that Turgot and Marshall called "profit," in order to arrive at a "pure" notion of the concept. Among modern economists, Kirzner [1973, 1979] is laboring to keep alive this non-Marshallian tradition.

Conclusion

From Boisguilbert to Turgot, a period that spanned the eight decades prior to the appearance of Adam Smith's *Wealth of Nations*, French economists made steady, if not spectacular, progress in uncovering the nature and operation of the emergent economic order. Most of these writers were concerned primarily with economic policy, but sensing, perhaps, the ghost of Newton from the previous century, they each recognized, with seemingly progressive intensity, the need for sound economic theory as a prerequisite.

Their proximity in time and the documented meetings between Turgot and Smith inevitably have spawned speculations about their conjunction of ideas. But the truth is that Turgot had an extensive French intellectual tradition behind him even as Smith drew from a wellspring of Scottish and British sources. That these separate, but roughly equal, traditions should be drawing together near the end of the eighteenth century is not so surprising as the fact that the British variant of the new science so quickly became the dominant force in directing future inquiries. There is a certain appeal, perhaps even a small advantage, to identifying the birth of economics with the publication of that masterful work from Smith's pen. This should not, however, overshadow our appreciation for the earlier conception and gestation of the new offspring.

Notes

1. The reference here is to Richard Cantillon, who was born in Ireland, lived in Paris and London, traveled throughout Europe, and had business interests in almost as many places as he visited.
2. For a detailed discussion of both the tax collection and rent-seeking measures instituted by Colbert, see Ekelund and Tollison [1981].
3. This section follows rather closely the ideas developed by David O'Mahony [1985] and myself [1985] in separate papers of the same issue of the *Journal of Libertarian Studies*.
4. In a treatise of barely more than 150 pages, Cantillon refers to the entrepreneur more than 100 times!
5. Commonly referred to as Cantillon's "three-rents theory," which derives from a too-literal translation of the word *rentes*. Insofar as only one of these amounts is a rent in the usual sense of payment for the use of land, it seems more appropriate to employ the term "income" in this context.
6. Wassily Leontieff [1941, p. 9] has said that he was following Quesnay when he formulated his input-output table of the U.S. economy in 1941.

References

Bast, J. H. "Boisguilbert et le mercantilisme." In *Pierre de Boisguilbert ou la naissance de l'économie politique*, I. Paris: Institut National d'Études Démographiques, 1966, pp. 27–40.

Blomfield, R. T. *Sebastien le Prestre de Vauban 1633–1707*. London: Methuen, 1938.

Boisguilbert, P. P. *Le détail de la France* [1695]. Reprinted in *Pierre de Boisguilbert*, II. Paris: I.N.E.D., 1966, pp. 581–662.

————. "Letter to the Contrôleur-Général," November 26, 1705. Reprinted in *Pierre de Boisguilbert*, I. Paris: I.N.E.D., 1966, pp. 414–15.

————. *Traité de la nature, culture, commerce et intérêt des grains* [1707a]. Reprinted in *Pierre de Boisguilbert*, II. Paris: I.N.E.D., 1966, pp. 827–78.

————. *Factum de la France* [1707b]. Reprinted in *Pierre de Boisguilbert*, II. Paris: I.N.E.D., 1966, pp. 879–956.

————. *Dissertation de la nature des richesses, de l'argent et des tributs* [1707c]. Reprinted in *Pierre de Boisguilbert*, II. Paris: I.N.E.D., 1966, pp. 973–1012.

Brems, H. J. "Richard Cantillon: Resources and Population." *Economie Appliqué* 36: 1983, 277–86.

Cantillon, Richard. *Essai sur la nature du commerce en général.* Ed. by H. Higgs. London: Macmillan, 1931.

Cadet, Felix. *Pierre de Boisguilbert, Précurseur des Économistes* [1870]. New York: Burt Franklin, 1967.

Daire, Eugene (ed.). *Économistes financiers du 18e siècle.* Paris: Guillaumin, 1843.

Eagly, R. V. *The Structure of Classical Economic Theory.* New York: Oxford University Press, 1974.

Ekelund, R. B., and R. F. Hébert. "French Engineers, Welfare Economics and Public Finance in the Nineteenth Century." *History of Political Economy* 10:1978, 636–68.

Ekelund, R. B., and R. D. Tollison. *Mercantilism as a Rent-Seeking Society.* College Station, TX: Texas A&M University Press, 1981.

Eltis, Walter. *The Classical Theory of Economic Growth.* New York: Oxford University Press, 1984.

Faccarello, Gilbert. "Quelques réflexions sur l'équilibre économique chez P. de Boisguilbert." *Economies et Sociétés* 18:1984, 35–62.

Fontenelle, Bernard Le Bovier de. *Éloge du maréchal de Vauban.* Paris, 1821.

Fox-Genovese, Elizabeth. *The Origins of Physiocracy: Economic Revolution and Social Order in Eighteenth-Century France.* Ithaca, NY: Cornell University Press, 1976.

Groenewegen, P. D. "A Reappraisal of Turgot's Theory of Value, Exchange, and Price Determination." *History of Political Economy* 2:1970, 177–96.

—————. "A Reinterpretation of Turgot's Theory of Capital and Interest." *Economic Journal* 81:1971, 327–40.

—————. *The Economics of A.R.J. Turgot.* The Hague: Martinus Nijhoff, 1977.

—————. "Turgot's Place in the History of Economic Thought: A Bicentenary Estimate." *History of Political Economy* 15:1983, 585–616.

Hamilton, E. J. "The Political Economy of France at the Time of John Law." *History of Political Economy* 1:1969, 123–49.

Hayek, F. A. *Prices and Production.* London: Routledge & Sons, 1931.

—————. "The Meaning of Competition." In *Individualism and Economic Order.* Chicago: University of Chicago Press, 1948.

Hébert, R. F. "Richard Cantillon's Early Contributions to Spatial Economics." *Economica* 48:1981, 71–77.

—————. "Was Richard Cantillon an Austrian Economist?" *Journal of Libertarian Studies* 7:1985, 269–79.

—————, and A. N. Link. *The Entrepreneur.* New York: Praeger, 1982.

Heckscher, Eli. *Mercantilism.* 2 vols. London: George Allen & Unwin, 1934.

Herlitz, Las. "The Tableau Economique and the Doctrine of Sterility." *Scandinavian Economic History Review* 9:1961a, 3–55.

—————. "Trends in the Development of Physiocratc Doctrine." *Scandinavian Economic History Review* 9:1961b, 107–51.

Higgs, Henry. "Cantillon's Place in Economics." *Quarterly Journal of Economics* 6:1892, 436–56.

—————. *The Physiocrats: Six Lectures on the French Economy of the Eighteenth Century* (1897). New York: Augustus M. Kelley, 1968.

Horn, I. E. *L'Économie politique avant les physiocrats*. Paris: Guillaumin, 1867.

Huq, A. M. "Richard Cantillon and the Multiplier Analysis." *Indian Journal of Economics* 39:1959, 423–25.

Jevons, W. S. "Richard Cantillon and the Nationality of Political Economy." *Contemporary Review* (1881). Reprinted in Cantillon, *op. cit.*, pp. 333–60.

Kirzner, I. M. *Competition and Entrepreneurship*. Chicago: University of Chicago Press, 1973.

—————. *Perception, Opportunity and Profit*. Chicago: University of Chicago Press, 1979.

Knight, F. H. *Risk, Uncertainty and Profit*. New York: Houghton-Mifflin, 1921.

—————. *The Economic Organization* (1933). New York: Augustus M. Kelley, 1951.

Leontieff, W. W. *The Structure of the American Economy, 1919–39*. New York: Oxford University Press, 1941.

Marshall, Alfred. *Official Papers*. London: Macmillan, 1926.

McDonald, S. L. "Boisguilbert: A Neglected Precursor of Aggregate Demand Theorists." *Quarterly Journal of Economics* 68:1954, 401–14.

—————. "Aspects modernes des theories économiques de Boisguilbert." In *Pierre de Boisguilbert*, I. Paris: I.N.E.D., 1966, pp. 101–20.

Meek, R. L. *The Economics of Physiocracy*. Cambridge, MA: Harvard University Press, 1963.

—————. *Turgot on Progress, Sociology and Economics*. Cambridge: Cambridge University Press, 1973.

O'Mahony, David. "Richard Cantillon — A Man of His Time: A Comment on Tarascio." *Journal of Libertarian Studies* 7:1985, 259–67.

Quesnay, François. "Letter from Quesnay to Mirabeau (1758)." Translated and reprinted in Meek, *op. cit.*, p. 108.

—————. *Dialogue on the Work of Artisans* [1766]. Translated and reprinted in Meek, *op. cit.*, pp. 203–30.

Roberts, H. V. *Boisguilbert, Economist of the Reign of Louis XIV*. New York: Columbia University Press, 1935.

Schelle, Gustave. *Oeuvres de Turgot et documents le concernant*. 5 vols. Paris: Felix Alcan, 1913–23.

Schumpeter, J. A. *Economic Doctrine and Method*. Trans. by R. Artis. New York: Oxford University Press, 1954a.

—————. *History of Economic Analysis*. Ed. by E. B. Schumpeter. New York: Oxford University Press, 1954b.

Sekine, T. T. "The Discovery of International Monetary Equilibrium by Vanderlint, Cantillon, Gervaise and Hume." *Economia Internazionale* 26:1973, 262–82.

Smith, Adam. *An Inquiry Into the Nature and Causes of the Wealth of Nations*. Ed. by E. Cannan. New York: Modern Library, 1937.

Spengler, J. J. *French Predecessors of Malthus*. Durham, NC: Duke University Press, 1942.

—————. "Richard Cantillon: First of the Moderns." *Journal of Political Economy* 62:1954, 281–95; 406–24.

—————. "Boisguilbert's Economic Views Vis-a-Vis Those of Contemporary *Réformateurs.*" *History of Political Economy* 16:1984, 68–88.

Tarascio, V. J. "Cantillon's Theory of Population Size and Distribution." *Atlantic Economic Journal* 9:1981, 12–18.

Turgot, A.R.J. *Reflections on the Formation and the Distribution of Wealth* (1766). Translated and reprinted in P. D. Groenewegen, *The Economics of A.R.J. Turgot.* The Hague: Martinus Nijhoff, 1977.

Vauban, S.P. *Projet d'une dîme royale* [1707]. Reprinted in Daire, *op. cit.*, pp. 31–153.

Weulersse, Georges. *Le Mouvement physiocratique en France.* 2 vols. Paris: Felix Alcan, 1910.

Commentary by Peter D. Groenewegen

The International Foundations of Classical Political Economy in the Eighteenth Century: An Alternative Perspective [185].

In one of his remarkable youthful writings on social progress, Turgot [1751, especially pp. 94–5] produced a schema of intellectual development in which he demonstrated the essential link between the innovating scientist and the work of predecessors. This principle is illustrated in the general argument by a qualified defence of Descartes and a comparison of his achievements with those of Newton, an almost classical comparison in this context, and one also made by Adam Smith on a number of occasions [Smith, 1755, p. 244; 1795, especially pp. 97–8]. Two decades later, Turgot applied this doctrine to the history of economics. This was in the context of criticism of Du Pont's notes on Beccaria's inaugural lecture published in *Ephémérides* which had drawn the anger of Melon's son because of Du Pont's criticism of his father [Melon, 1734].[1] Part of Turgot's argument is worth quoting in commenting on Hébert's vision of the French predecessors of Adam Smith:

> ...despite the errors in his work, I value Melon's mental feat...When I first read his work, its merits in my mind arose from the fact that at that stage no one in France had discussed these subjects, at least in a clear manner. A person coming into the world after Montesquieu, Hume, Cantillon, Quesnay, M. de Gournay, etc. is less struck by the merit arising from Melon's priority, because he does not appreciate it; for him it is no more than a date, and when he read him, he knew already more than his book (Schelle, 1913–23, III, pp. 499–500).

Turgot's remarks have a double significance for Hébert's chapter. In the first place, it endorses Hébert's approach in viewing French developments in economics in the eighteenth century as a gradual development and improvement starting with the work of Boisguillebert and Vauban and ending with Turgot's own substantial contributions. Secondly, Turgot's remarks imply a criticism of the project by drawing attention to the international foundations of development in economics in the eighteenth century because his list of giants includes at least one English writer and probably two.[2] The international transmission of ideas in this period [see Groenewegen, 1983] is one of its more striking characteristics,

211

and it is a pity that Hébert dropped these international aspects in his chapter. Two of my comments are devoted to these implications from Turgot's observations.

Possible Visions of Developments in French Economics During the Eighteenth Century

Hébert confines his discussion of French developments to what he calls its "peak performances," namely, Boisguilbert, Vauban, Cantillon, Quesnay, and Turgot, because these are peak performances on the grand theme of economic order, the development of which he sees as the key feature in the progress of economic science in the eighteenth century. Although Hébert also suggests that "economic thought in France in the eighteenth century was strongly conditioned by events that strained the military, political, and economic power of the country," reflecting the strong interest of French economics at the time in matters of public finance, these subjects are largely ignored in his account. Only his discussion of Boisguilbert and Vauban refers to these crucial fiscal issues at any length; despite the fact that taxation economics and public finance in general greatly concerned the physiocrats and Turgot and engaged the attention of many of the French economists whom Hébert omits from his account. Most surprising in these omissions is Montesquieu. Others include the financial economists of the first half of the century who commented on Law's scheme — for example, Melon and Du Tot — as well as antiphysiocrats like Forbonnais and Condillac. The omission of Law's system itself is rather curious, given its importance in inspiring economic thought [see Hamilton, 1969]. Cantillon is an exception to the French concentration on fiscal matters (but cf. note 2) though even his *Essai* listed benefits from economic prosperity for the revenues of the prince [Cantillon, 1755; for example, p. 191]. An alternative and superior unifying theme in French economic thought of the period is to see it as a gradual development of the surplus model of economic growth where at least part of the argument is focused on the disposal of the surplus through taxation and government spending [Eltis, 1984, pp. 311–2] — one of the major objectives of the emerging science of political economy as Smith [1776, p. 428] reaffirmed at the start of Book IV.

    The superiority of this alternative can be demonstrated after investigating some aspects of Hébert's approach. The concept of "economic order," Hébert's central theme, is defined as "the form and function of a system of markets that operates in the absence of a central authority — to achieve a production and distribution of goods in a way that promotes economic welfare" [p. 186]. Boisguilbert's economic order is said to comprise "notions of exchange, utility movement and price" and is also identified with "a general equilibrium view of the economy" [p. 189].[3] His "liberal" position on the "role of the state in economic policy" suggests that the market is more important for economic order than the state and that much of it is, in fact, induced by "nature" [pp. 190]. The physiocrats — after all, physiocracy "means rule of nature," as Hébert (p. 198) reminds us — greatly developed the notion of natural, social, and economic order, a topic frequently featured in the titles and tables of contents of their major works. Hébert's omission of discussions of the subject in publications like Mercier de la Rivière [1767][4], Baudeau [1771], and Le Trosne [1777] is therefore surprising. His account of physiocracy is not only defective in this respect; it also fails to come to grips with the analytical advances Quesnay produced in his *Tableau économique*, that is, the economic consequences for growth of particular disposals of the net product, which formed the foundation for subsequent classical growth theory [Eltis, 1984, pp. 313–7] and provided the rational foundation for much of their economic policy. The *Tableau's* analytical features were not only fully grasped by Turgot but they formed the basis for Smith's celebrated Book II, chapter 3 (which Hicks [1965, p. 36] has described as the heart of the Smithian system) while Marx developed it into his schemas of simple and expanded reproduction. Although Hébert waxes lyrically [pp. 201–203] on the true "legacy" of "their analytical method," this appears confined by him to their not unusual emphasis on self-interest and their recognition of regularities in economic behavior subject to laws, while Quesnay's more important economic innovations in developing interdependence between production, distribution, and circulation and the role of capital in this process of reproduction are only grudgingly mentioned in an almost derogatory way.[5]

The emphasis on economic order in Hébert's account of the development of French economics in the eighteenth century becomes clearer if its role in his interpretation of Cantillon's work is appreciated. Cantillon's work is seen by Hébert as the peak performance of the period: overshadowing Quesnay's contributions because of Cantillon's superior "laws of price,"[6] and outclassing Turgot on the notion of entrepreneur and his contribution to a theory of profit. Secondly, Hébert presents Cantillon's *Essai* as a demonstration of the superiority of the market in social organization of economic activity by means of a dual modelling procedure in which an initial (and historically prior) model of a "scaled down version of a centrally planned economy" in the form of a landlord-directed estate [p. 195] is unfavorably compared with the model of a competitive market economy with decentralized organization from the entrepreneur guided by a price mechanism [pp. 195–196]. Hébert implicitly presents the displacement of the "command-economy" as a historical process arising from the inconvenience and limitations of such a form of economic organization when exchange, competition, and the introduction of money provide opportunities for introducing a superior alternative [p. 195]. The analytical leap implied in this interpretation is best grasped when it is realized that the only comparisons Hébert makes with other economists' work in this context are references to Knight [pp. 193, 197] and Hayek's "novel" work on the market as an information dissemination system [p. 194]. It is also implied that Cantillon's brilliance was not appreciated by his successors. For example, Quesnay's adaptation of Cantillon on the circular flow model is only partly appreciated [p. 198]. Turgot's profit theory is described as a "hodge podge of payments" in need of disentanglement [p. 206], and Smith is implicitly blamed for omitting the central place of the entrepreneur...in the British tradition of political economy that descended from his work [p. 197]. This interpretation represents a rather startling rethinking of the history of economic thought in the eighteenth century.

Unfortunately, the textual basis for this interpretation of Cantillon is poorly documented. First of all, the dual modelling ascribed to Cantillon does not at all conform to the three parts into which the contents of the *Essai* were divided. Secondly, the stadial theory of development ascribed to Cantillon designed to reinforce the historical connotations of "his" dual model [p. 204] was not found by Meek in his investigation of this subject [Meek, 1976, pp. 29–30; 1977, p. 23], nor can I find any clear evidence of it in Cantillon's text.[7]

Thirdly, Hébert's identification of Cantillon's entrepreneurs with Knight's "uncertainty-bearers" is rather extravagant. In the chapter introducing the entrepreneurial concept, their distinguishing characteristic identified by Cantillon is that they are self-employed and hence include "Beggars even and Robbers" [Cantillon, 1755, p. 55]. Finally, Cantillon's analysis of the competitive framework resembles that of an oriental bazaar and not that of an industrial economy; his "supply and demand" analysis does not even use this terminology, let alone modern demand-and-supply functions; and his emphasis on the role of demand in economic development and the use of resources appears to have more affinity with Boisguilbert than with Knight or Hayek. In short, Hébert's reading of Cantillon seems ahistorical and flawed.

Cantillon's indebtedness to Boisguilbert on aspects of the circular flow, interdependence of producers and consumers, the importance of the landlords' incomes in setting demand, and the need for prices to cover costs to sustain reproduction focuses attention on the more relevant alternative vision of the development of French economic thought in the eighteenth century. Boisguilbert's specific treatment of these subjects is acknowledged by Hébert [pp. 188–189] and needs no further discussion. Cantillon [1755, ch. 16 and cf. 7 on agricultural surplus] enriched Boisguilbert's vision with a surplus analysis derived from Sir William Petty [1662, pp. 30–31, 42–3, 89], and these are then combined in a complex analysis of the circular flow [Cantillon, 1755, Part II, ch. 3]. This was the analytical legacy which Cantillon passed to Quesnay and from which the latter appears to have derived his *Tableau économique* analysis. Its role in stimulating classical growth theory has already been referred to; it informed a substantial part of the coherent analytical framework which formed the basis for classical political economy.

The International Transmission of Ideas in the Development of Eighteenth Century Economic Thought

The previous paragraph has already implicitly referred to this matter by viewing Cantillon in the role of combining aspects of English and French thought by his judicious blending of Sir William Petty's surplus analysis and Boisguilbert's suggestions on interdependence, effective demand, and the circular flow. More widely, Cantillon can be seen as passing on aspects of both British and French tradition in economics insofar as that can be said to have existed at the time because the sources he cites include the leading writers on the subject at that stage: Petty, Locke, and Davenant in England, Vauban and Boisguilbert in France. This is not to diminish Cantillon's status in the history of economic thought: it is rather to enhance it since the form in which he presented these ideas was extremely influential, and Cantillon in the eighteenth century can be very much seen as the economists' economist [Groenewegen, 1983, pp. 50–51]. Cantillon was read and appreciated — though for quite different reasons — in France, in England, and in Italy where the Milanese and Neapolitan schools of economics were then beginning to flower. Irrespective of Cantillon's nationality, and the evidence seems to make him British rather than French, his influence was genuinely international as was that of many other writers of the time.

Some further remarks can be made on these international aspects in the development of economics in the eighteenth century to emphasize institutional factors designed to draw attention to the rapidity of the international transmission of ideas, particularly after 1750. First, the *Encyclopédie* systematically circulated scientific information, including Quesnay's theoretical innovations in economics. Secondly, rarely has translation of important new works been so rapid as during this period. Thirdly, links between Scotland and France during the enlightenment were particularly strong and there was a transmission of people as well as books to and from Paris, carrying special implications for economics with Hume's prolonged residence there and Smith's visit in the mid-1760s. As Turgot mentioned, Hume's contribution to the development of economics in the eighteenth century should not be underrated. Turgot said the same for Montesquieu and his omission from Hébert's chapter is, as noted earlier, therefore surprising. Even though Montesquieu's *Esprit des Lois* contained much economic subject matter, its importance in the history of economics is rather general. It inspired some of the best minds in the social sciences during the second half of the eighteenth century, and liberated history, jurisprudence, politics, and economics from former theological encumbrances. That influence was almost universal and it provided special impetus in the design of Adam Smith's research project. In addition, it directly inspired Turgot's first exercise in economics and was clearly of sufficient importance for Beccaria to include him in the hall of fame in economics in his inaugural lecture as the "immortal Montesquieu" [see Groenewegen, 1983, pp. 48–50]. It cannot be emphasized too often that the emergence of economics during the eighteenth century was an international phenomenon, and the importance this has for explaining the direction of subsequent development in economics overrides "the appeal, perhaps even small advantage, to identifying the birth of economics with the publication of that masterful work from Smith's pen" [p. 207]. The implied division of economics into pre-Adamite and post Adamite is particularly dangerous because it encourages misunderstanding of the meaning of classical political economy for reasons briefly discussed in the final section of this comment.

Classical Political Economy and the Eighteenth Century

Questions are therefore raised by the notion of classical political economy embodied in this project, a matter also not unrelated to Hébert's ahistorical reading of Cantillon's *Essai*. Marx [1859] regarded classical political economy as starting with the economics of Sir William Petty in England and Boisguilbert in France. This is a quite different conception of classical from that viewing Smith's great treatise as the starting point of British classical political economy and consequently seeing the history of economics in pre- and post-Adamite terms. Hébert's unease with the latter and implicit sympathy with the former notion is reflected in his short introductory remarks called "Formal Beginnings" [p. 187] designed to introduce Vauban and Boisguilbert.

In these remarks, Boisguilbert and Vauban are clearly seen as founders in some sense, and economists in the eighteenth century, including Smith, are distinguished from those coming after. Unfortunately, the complexities introduced by such considerations for outlining the major characteristics of classical political economy are too great to permit detailed presentation in the limited space available.

A clue to these characteristics was provided in the final paragraph of the first section where Cantillon's contribution was depicted as a merging of Boisguilbert's circular flow analysis with Petty's surplus analysis and, via the impetus this gave to Quesnay's work, providing a substantial part of the analytical framework of a more complete classical political economy. As Garegnani [1984] has shown, the eighteenth century laid the foundations for the surplus approach to value and distribution theory completed by the work of the nineteenth century classical economists. Surplus itself, once it was identified and determined, provided the foundation for their theories of economic growth and accumulation, of crises and effective demand. The French eighteenth century economists whom Hébert discusses all played a constructive role in this evolution of classical political economy: Boisguilbert, by constructing an analytical framework of interdependence of consumption and production in which prices played some, as yet not clearly specified, role; Cantillon, by building this analysis into a more formal model of the circular flow designed to inform aspects of the circulation of money. In this model, the agricultural surplus, and the landlords' demand its disposal generated, combined with the necessary exchanges between town and country to illustrate the distribution of annual product via the exchanges these aggregated transactions implied. Quesnay developed these arguments further, after enriching them with his theory of production in agriculture which explicitly dwelt on the role of capital in enhancing surplus product, linking that surplus in turn with further capital accumulation, and enhanced demand for final output to permit reproduction on an expanded scale. Turgot placed Quesnay's analysis of reproduction within a wider historical framework obtained from his theory of stadial development, generalized the use of capital to all spheres of production, showing the interconnectedness of their yields, and deduced some consequences from this new form of productive property which generated income without necessitating work. The same was done more extensively by Smith who benefited enormously from these French researches. Hence, insofar as France is concerned, the development of classical political economy is a process which commences with the contributions of Boisguilbert, and it is this which gives him rather than Vauban the enhanced status as one of the founders of classical political economy in the history of economics.

The economic and social order depicted in this gradual development is not the order of Walrasian general equilibrium analysis. The market and competition play a crucial role in the mechanisms through which reproduction is ensured in a classical system, that is, the necessity of prices covering costs to ensure the required inputs in the necessary quantities for reproduction of enlarging it through the appropriate investment of surplus product. This is the *classical* economic problem to which the French economists surveyed by Hébert so richly contributed. Aspects of this analysis, sometimes to a considerable extent, resemble arguments from the much later marginalist period; but marginalist analysis is rarely, if ever, present in these writings. This is as much the case with Cantillon's picture of economic organization with its distinctly eighteenth century orientation, including his discussion of the entrepreneur, as it is with Turgot's exchange models, presentation of the law of diminishing returns, and analysis of capital and interest [see Groenewegen, 1982]. The task of explaining the development of economic theories in the past is difficult enough without introducing irrelevant "anticipations" of contemporary economics by time spans sometimes measured in centuries.

Notes

1. For a detailed discussion of this episode see McLain [1977, pp. 98–99]. Beccaria's lecture appeared in *Ephémérides* [No. 6, 1769, pp. 57–152] with copious notes by Du Pont, and it was their content which caused Melon Junior's annoyance because, among other things, Du Pont had objected to the fact that Beccaria [1769, pp. 375–6] had included Melon among the great French economics pioneers.

2. David Hume and Richard Cantillon, the Anglo-Irish banker whom Hébert includes among the French, presumably because he was first published in French in France. As shown subsequently in this comment, Cantillon is very important in the international transmission of economic ideas, not least because he combined aspects of the founders of the classical tradition in England and France.

3. General equilibrium as an indication of quantitative interdependence of economic variables is inherent in the work of Boisguilbert, Cantillon, Quesnay, and the classical economists in general, but this conception should not be confused with the much later Walrasian model based on quite distinct analytical foundations [see Walsh and Gram, 1980].

4. Smith [1776, p. 679] regarded Mercier's account as the "most distinct and best connected account of this doctrine," as did James Mill's [1824] survey nearly half a century later.

5. Illustrated by Hébert's lack of stress on the quality of Quesnay's "circular flow analysis" and his emphasis on Quesnay's failure "to work out a complete theory of capital accumulation" [p. 203], which neglects Quesnay's theoretical advance of recognizing the role of capital in its various forms in the agricultural production process.

6. No details are provided as to where Cantillon presented his superior "law of price" but the reference is presumably to his important discussion [1755, pp. 117–9] of the relationship between market price and costs or, as Cantillon put it, intrinsic value. This argument more than likely inspired the similar arguments in Quesnay [1757, p. 94], Turgot [1767, p. 120, n. 16], and Smith's celebrated analysis of market and natural prices [1776, Book I, ch. 7]. Vaggi [1983, 1985] has demonstrated the crucial importance of price relations to the physiocratic analysis of distribution and accumulation.

7. The only textual evidence I can find for Hébert's dual model interpretation is Cantillon [1755, p. 59], a model which to me seems to be designed to show that the tremendous importance of landlords' preferences in determining the use of land is independent of whether they cultivate it themselves, the topic of the chapter of which it is the starting point.

References

Baudeau, Nicolas (1771). *Première introduction à la philosophie économique ou analyse des états policés.* In E. Daire, *Physiocrates*, vol. 2. Paris: Guillaumin, 1846, pp. 657–821.

Beccaria, C. (1769). "'Prolusione nell' apertura della nuova cattedra di Scienze Camerali nelle Scuole Palatine de Milano." In *Cesare Beccaria Opere.* Ed. by S. Romagnoli. Florence: Sansoni, 1958.

Cantillon, Richard (1755). *Essai sur la Nature du Commerce en Général.* Ed. by H. Higgs. London: Macmillan, 1931.

Eltis, Walter. *The Classical Theory of Economic Growth.* London: Macmillan, 1984.

Garegnani, P. "Value and Distribution in the Classical Economists and Marx." *Oxford Economic Papers* 36:1984, 291–325.

Groenewegen, P. D. "Turgot: Forerunner of Neo-classical Economics?" *Kenzei Kenkyu* 33:1983, 119–33.

Groenewegen, P. D. "Turgot, Beccaria and Smith." In *Italian Economics Past and Present.* Ed. by Peter Groenewegen and Joseph Halevi. Sydney: Frederick May Foundation, 1983.

Hamilton, Earl J. "The Political Economy of France at the time of John Law." *History of Political Economy* 1:1969, 123–49.

Hicks, J. R. *Capital and Growth.* Oxford: Clarendon Press, 1965.

Keynes, John Maynard (1936). "General Theory of Employment, Interest and Money." In *Collected Writings of John Maynard Keynes.* Vol. 7. London: Macmillan, 1973.

Le Trosne, G. (1777). *De l'Ordre Social.* Munich: Kraus Reprint 1980.

Marx, Karl (1859). *A Contribution to the Critique of Political Economy.* Intro. by Maurice Dobb. London: Lawrence and Wishart, 1971.

McLain, J. J. *The Economic Writings of Du Pont de Nemours.* Newark: University of Delaware Press, 1977.

Meek, R. L. *Social Science and the Ignoble Savage.* Cambridge: Cambridge University Press, 1976.

—————. "Smith, Turgot and the 'Four Stages' Theory." In R. L. Meek, *Smith, Marx and After.* London: Chapman & Hall, 1977. pp. 18–32.

Melon, Jean François (1734). *Essai politique sur le commerce.* In E. Daire, *Economistes financiers du 18ᵉ Siècle.* Paris: Guillaumin, 1843.

Mercier de la Rivière, P. P. (1767). *De l'ordre naturel et essentiel des Sociétés politiques.* In E. Daire, *Physiocrates,* vol. 2. Paris: Guillaumin, 1846, pp. 445–638.

Mill, James. "Economists." *Encyclopaedia Britannica,* Supplement to the Third Edition, Vol. III. Edinburgh: Constable, 1824, pp. 708–24.

Petty, Sir William (1662). *A Treatise of Taxes and Contributions* in *Economic Writings of Sir William Petty.* Ed. by C. H. Hull, re-issued. New York: Kelley, 1965.

Quesnay, François (1757). "Men." In R. L. Meek, *The Economics of Physiocracy.* London: Allen & Unwin, 1962, pp. 88–101.

Schelle, G. *Oeuvres de Turgot et Documents le concernant.* Paris: Félix Arcan, 1913–23.

Smith, Adam (1755). "A Letter to the Authors of the Edinburth Review." In *Essays on Philosophical Subjects.* Ed. by W. P. D. Wrightman, J. C. Bryce, and I. S. Ross. Oxford: Clarendon Press, 1980.

—————. (1776). *An Inquiry into the Nature and Causes of the Wealth of Nations.* Ed. by R. H. Campbell and A. S. Skinner. Oxford: Clarendon Press, 1976.

—————. (1795). "The Principles which Lead and Direct Philosophical Enquiries, illustrated by the History of Astronomy." In *Essays on Philosophical Subjects,* ed. by W. P. D. Wrightman J. C. Bryce, and I. S. Ross. Oxford: Clarendon Press, 1980.

Turgot, A. R. J. (1751). *On Universal History.* Trans. in R. L. Meek, *Turgot On Progress, Sociology and Economics.* Cambridge: Cambridge University Press, 1973.

Turgot, A. R. J. (1767). "Observations on a Paper by Saint Péravy." In *The Economics of A. R. J. Turgot.* Ed. by P. D. Groenewegen. The Hague: Nijhoff, 1977, pp. 109–22.

Vaggi, G. "The Physiocratic Theory of Prices." *Contributions to Political Economy* 2:1983, 1–22.

Vaggi, G. "The Physiocratic Model of Relative Prices and Income Distribution." *Economic Journal* 95:1985, pp. 928–47.

Walsh, V., and Gram H. *Classical and Neo-classical Theories of General Equilibrium.* New York: Oxford University Press, 1980.

8 THE SCOTTISH ENLIGHTENMENT AND POLITICAL ECONOMY

Herbert F. Thomson

Scotland in 1700

As the birthplace of Adam Smith and the land where systematic economic analysis made its first appearance, Scotland holds the pride of place in the annals of economic thought. In Smith's time, a system was regarded as a wide range of phenomena, all causally related by some simple concept or common principle that could provide unity and harmony amidst an apparent chaos of diversity. Political economy had already received recognition in France and England as a subject for investigation, but a certain comprehensive quality was imparted by academic writers in Scotland such as David Hume and Adam Smith.[1] The Scottish writers share with the physiocrats the distinction of pursuing their investigation with a purpose other than that of promoting the welfare of the sovereign or of their own enterprise. And perhaps more important, the writings of the Scottish school had their origin in the universities, whereas early writings on political economy in France and England were generally the work of *ad hoc* pamphleteers. Though we frequently refer to the Scottish political economists as a "school," they did not adhere to any one leader or set of doctrines. Unlike the French

221

physiocrats, they had a mutual interdependence that was quite informal and unintentional.

No thinking person would have predicted, in 1700, that Scotland would be the cradle of the first system of political economy. Scotland was an agricultural nation of around 1 million people, many of whom were subsistence farmers living far from the centers of industry. Edinburgh, the national capital and its cultural center, was a city of 60,000 people, who served in the armed forces and in the clergy of England, France, and The Netherlands, and worked in the factories and commercial establishments of all these countries. There was as yet little sign of industrialization in Scotland, and the four Scottish universities had achieved small academic distinction. England, France, and The Netherlands would all have been nominated as likelier candidates than Scotland to give birth to a new science of political economy.

The underdeveloped condition of Scotland in 1700 may have been a reason, in conjunction with the easily available opportunity to make comparisons with foreign nations, for the heightened interest in political economy. The failure of the Darien Company in 1703 had ruined many of the wealthier people in the nation and discouraged the hopes of others. And a series of catastrophic harvest failures had threatened the livelihood of the poor, producing famine in some regions of the country. Opportunities for domestic employment were few, leading public opinion to the view that Scotland must gain access to wider markets. Public opinion had formed exaggerated expectations of the wealth that might be realized through commerce with distant and exotic colonies, such as Darien, Mississippi, the Indies, or the South Seas. And the British Empire, which included colonies in America, in the West Indies, and in India, seemed to offer precisely the type of market that was required for Scotland's economic growth. These circumstances convinced a reluctant Scottish parliament of the futility of striving for industrial progress while confined to a region that remained small, isolated, and economically self-sufficient.

Yet Scotland was not, in 1700, totally independent of England. Both kingdoms had been ruled for more than a century by a common monarch, and many important decisions affecting Scotland were made in London. Andrew Fletcher of Saltoun has been cited as a leading opponent to a more complete union with England.[2] Most of the arguments advanced by Fletcher touched on the superior virtue of the small and independent state, even when this independence entailed some sacrifice of wealth. Though Fletcher's discussion of these issues was at an ideological level, one may suspect that opposition to union also came from those who stood to lose from the competition the larger English firms were certain to offer to the local Scottish monopolies. The gains from union were to be free access to the English market and to the benefits of the Navigation Acts, at a cost of similar access to markets in Scotland for English firms. The consequences of market integration were not as well understood in 1700 as in 1970, but some of the adverse effects were obvious. The removal of the parliament from Edinburgh to London was universally deplored. Partly because of the intense public discussion and controversy it engendered, Scotland's union with England in 1707 had a greater impact on economic literature than the other important enactments of that era. The slow pace at which the benefits of the union were realized helped to keep the debate alive for several decades after the original decision. Indeed, the discussion has not altogether exhausted itself at this time.

The English Constitution of 1688 was another enactment which had a profound effect on Scottish political and economic thought. Its lagged effects on Scotland, and on England itself, were concurrent with those of the Act of Union. The Constitution marked the end of arbitrary rule from the Throne, and established the supremacy of Parliament and of the civil service. Ironically, it terminated the rule of both countries by the Scottish Stuart dynasty, but it introduced a more moderate and impersonal form of government, and brought greater security for life and property. In England, the Constitution strengthened trial by jury, and in both countries there was an increased professionalism among lawyers and judges. England's credibility was enhanced by a more moderate political atmosphere. It would be an exaggeration to state that a truly popular form of government was instituted in England or Scotland around 1707. The form of government in Adam Smith's time had long been an oligarchy, patterned in many respects on the writings of Harrington and on the practice of Venice. Suffrage was limited to a small group of property owners, whose votes could in many cases be bought. Many parliamentary constituencies were altogether under the control of some feudal lord. Both England and Scotland had experienced large-scale confiscations of property during the seventeenth century; in Ireland the land redistributions, conducted largely by Sir William Petty, were even greater. But property rights in Scotland were generally stabilized after 1745, due process of law was generally observed, and a continuity of succession in government was established. The last large scale internal rebellion in England was in 1688 and in Scotland in 1745. After this time, thrift and industry were encouraged by a new sense of security.

The strengthening of the Bank of England and the founding of the Bank of Scotland were parts of the scene at the end of the seventeenth century. The existence of these banks permitted more individuals to borrow funds at market rates of interest. In 1700 the banking industry had scarcely existed in Scotland. About five-sixths of the money and of the financial transactions in Scotland involved coin, and the Bank of Scotland operated only in Edinburgh. But the growth of banks brought about an extended use of credit in both Scotland and England. By the end of the eighteenth century, bank notes constituted by far the greatest portion of the money supply, and Bank of England notes competed with those of the Bank of Scotland. Adam Smith [p. 281] notes:

> I have heard it asserted, that the trade of the city of Glasgow, doubled after the first erection of the two public banks at Edinburgh, of which the one, called the Bank of Scotland, was established by act of parliament in 1695: the other, called the Royal Bank, by royal charter in 1727. Whether the trade, either of Scotland in general or of the city of Glasgow in particular, has really increased in so great a proportion, I do not pretend to know. If either of them has increased in this proportion, it seems to be an effect too great to be accounted for by the sole operation of this cause.

At this time, securities and paper currency were becoming important forms of property. This new liquidity increased the mobility of the population, and must have enhanced the propensity of the propertied class to live in cities. Adam Smith, John Law, and many others have commented on the power of money and credit expansion to stimulate commerce and industry, but they have seldom noticed its tendency to create a *rentier* leisure class, living from the interest on bonds and transferring their wealth easily through bank notes or bills of exchange. Nor have they taken note of the tendency of such people to move to the cities and to travel abroad. Shortly after 1700, we hear of numerous people of leisure living in or near Edinburgh, giving this city a greater resemblance to London or to Paris or Amsterdam. And we read of increasing numbers of Scotsmen travelling to London for the sessions of Parliament or for the social scene.

Still another event of this era was the establishment of the Presbyterian denomination as the official Church of Scotland, though without the same authority over dissenters that had been customary under previous ecclesiastical regimes in Scotland. Presbyterianism was the popular form of church government, incorporating a considerable degree of democracy. Salaries of Presbyterian ministers were modest, even at the higher levels of authority, and various dissenting Presbyterian sects continued to flourish under minimal restraints. Catholics, Episcopalians, and Methodists also practiced their religious observances without molestation. However, faculty members at the Scottish universities were required to give formal acceptance to the Church of Scotland. By the standards of the twentieth century this arrangement hardly appears liberal, but it was far more so than in previous centuries. In earlier decades, any change in the religious establishment had necessitated an almost complete replacement of university faculties.

Adam Smith [p. 762] remarks on the religious establishment in Scotland:

> The presbyterian clergy, accordingly, have more influence over the minds of the common people than perhaps the clergy of any other established church. It is accordingly in presbyterian countries only that we ever find the common people converted, and almost to a man, to the established church.

This accolade to the presbyterian clergy may be exaggerated and Adam Smith hints that his true preference might be for a regime, such as that of the Quakers in Pennsylvania, with no established religion, provided that such a disestablishment could be made without an utter collapse of the state.

As a result of a more democratic form of church governance in Scotland, the parish schools for the lower class of people were superior to those in England or France. Adam Smith [p. 737] states:

> In Scotland the establishment of such parish schools has taught almost the whole common people to read, and a very great proportion of them to write and account. In England the same establishment of charity schools has had an effect of the same kind, though not so universally.

Literacy and other academic achievements for the lower middle class has remained a high priority in Scotland. A recent issue of the *Economist* [Sept. 7, 1985, p. 16] states that in 1984 the number of students in England remaining in school past the age of 16 was 27%, while in Scotland the number was 45%.

Adam Smith's assessment of the Scottish universities can be summarized in his observation that they were intended for the education of the clergy, but that their curricula had become increasingly inappropriate as more "young gentlemen of fortune" enrolled as students. Though Rae estimates that even in Smith's day the majority of the students at the University of Glasgow were still preparing for ecclesiastical vocations [Mackie, 1854, p. 78; Rae, 1895, p. 50] there were also many students preparing for careers in medicine or law. The curriculum, in 1700, was still largely based on Aristotle and lectures were conducted in Latin. Even in that era, it was difficult to conduct discussions of current problems in political economy through the medium of Latin. The gradual substitution of English for Latin, which began in Glasgow and Edinburgh, was the achievement of professors who placed a higher value on analysis and explanation than on professional prestige. It is somewhat surprising that a clergyman, Francis Hutcheson, was the first to make this substitution at Glasgow.

The difficulties presented by an obsolete curriculum taught through a dead language were aggravated by the extreme youthfulness of the students and by the lack of faculty specialization. David Hume [pp. 13–14] states:

> As our college education in Scotland, extending little further than the languages, ends commonly when we are about 14 or 15 years of age, I was left after that to my own choice in my reading.

In addition to the artificiality of studying an ancient Greek text through its rather mechanical and wooden translation into medieval Latin, certain substantive difficulties were inherent in the ethical works of Aristotle. An aristocratic and agrarian orientation in Aristotle's *Ethics* lent support to a tendency, already prevalent in Scotland and England at that time, to look with disdain on commerce and trade. As in Greece in Aristotle's time, landlords enjoyed higher status than people who had made equal fortunes through commerce. Feudal traditions still survived, at least with regard to social status. Moreover, Aristotle's tolerance or approval for the institution of slavery was in such contrast to the emerging spirit of a new age in Scotland that it became a major consideration in the rejection of the philosophy and text of Aristotle.

Adam Smith contended that in the Moral Philosophy course, the students had been taught sophistry, subtlety, and casuistry, rather than receiving encouragement to examine causal explanations based on natural law [Smith, p. 727]. A refreshing innovation was introduced around 1700 through the study of Greek and Latin texts in the original language. Even the works of Aristotle might have been more rewarding if studied in the original Greek.[3] But the preference in Scotland at this time was for the works of the Stoic writers, especially for Cicero and Seneca.

Three concessions must be made in favor of the Latin and Aristotelian tradition in Scotland. It established a common language with the universities in Europe, and especially in The Netherlands, where university curricula were also in Latin. These studies tended, especially when supplemented with readings from Plato, Cicero, Seneca, and Horace, to facilitate comparisons of customs and attitudes with those of an era about 2,000 years in the past. Moreover, the philosophy of Aristotle, with all the defects that Adam Smith refers to, may have had a greater element of universalism than was found in more recent works on political economy.

Money, Credit, State Economic Planning, and John Law

One diagnosis of Scotland's misfortunes around the year 1700 was that a scarcity of money and an insufficiency of spending had been causing industrial stagnation, or underdevelopment. A name associated with this thesis was John Law of Lauriston (1671–1729), the son of a goldsmith in Edinburgh. In Law's youth, no bank existed in Scotland, though loans were often made by goldsmiths. Though without the advantage of a university education, Law had become familiar in his father's shop with money lending, and this experience may have compensated for some parts of a university education.

While still a minor, Law migrated to London and attempted to make his fortune through gambling. Interest in gambling and in all forms of speculation was rampant at this time, and there was great public excitement about fortunes made in the service of the British East India Company or through trading in securities. Law's expertise in calculating the mathematical odds on each card distribution and his phenomenal recall of the cards in play won him a reputation as a statistician. Calculations of this type also helped him win a reputation, in later years, as an economist. Law's tombstone describes him as "this calculator without a peer." But in London, John Law overplayed his hand, fell deeply into debt, and was forced to flee to the continent to escape a death sentence for a duel that proved fatal to his opponent.

Returning a few years later to Scotland, Law won the support of the Duke of Argyll and of other prominent noblemen who sponsored him in a set of proposals to the Scottish parliament designed to foster economic recovery and growth. A pamphlet published in 1701 was entitled *Proposals and Reasons for Constituting a Council of Trade for Scotland.* His suggestion was mainly to simplify taxation and to abolish the farming of the revenues (that is, the contracting out to private individuals of the authority to collect taxes). Law also proposed subsidies for new industries, the freeing of raw materials from import duties, and an employment program to be funded by the state. These original proposals for economic recovery appear modest and sensible in terms of the strategies undertaken in later centuries, but Law's proposals would have entailed large government deficits.

A second pamphlet, entitled *Money and Trade Considered, with a Proposal for Supplying the Nation with Money,* was published and submitted to the Scottish parliament in 1709. Law here asserts that more money and lower interest rates are the appropriate stimulus for a sluggish economy like that of Scotland. Influenced in his analysis by the quantity theory of money, as outlined by Locke and Montesquieu, Law contended that an influx of the precious metals had in past years brought prosperity to Europe, through a lowering of the interest rate and through an increase in profits. He also held that a contrived expansion of paper money might have a similar effect. To this end, he proposed an expansion of the money supply sufficient to satisfy the demand for it in all branches of industry. His preference was for paper money, both because it was more convenient than specie and because it could be issued in quantities precisely equal to the demand. But he showed deference to the conventional wisdom of his day by insisting that the issue of paper money must represent or be secured by land or other valuable nonmetallic objects.

At this time (1709) Law also submitted to the Scottish parliament a proposal for a state bank which would be empowered to issue currency on the security of land. This proposal was similar to the program of Benjamin Franklin which was adopted in Pennsylvania a few years later with moderate success. But the Scottish parliament resolved that "the forcing of any paper credit by an act of parliament is unfit for this nation."[4] Another observer states that Law's scheme was rejected, not on economic grounds, but because it was so contrived that in the course of time it "would have brought all the estates of the kingdom to depend on the government [Epinasse, 1968, p. 672]. The main objection to Law's schemes in Scotland at the time of their proposal was not their inflationary potential, but the coercion and the centralization of authority that would accompany these schemes.

Programs heavily dependent on monetary measures have since been undertaken in many countries where stagnation prevailed. Since Law's remedies were directed to secular stagnation and not to cyclical recession, he has often been described as an incipient Keynesian [Hyde, n.d., p. 86] Keynes himself preferred to trace his intellectual descent from Malthus. But the adoption of an inconvertible paper standard in peacetime in Scotland or England would have been more difficult in Law's era than in later centuries. A necessary preliminary would be some prohibition on the circulation of full-bodied coin, to be followed by a gradual increase in the quantity of paper outstanding.

Historians have suggested that the rejection of Law's schemes by the Scottish parliament was due to the natural caution and conservatism of the Scottish people. A spectacular sequel to Law's proposals to the Scottish parliament came after Law's migration to France. In 1716, when Law's friend, the Duke of Orleans became regent of France following the death of King Louis XIV, Law presented a similar agenda to the French. Though Law's request to organize a state bank in France was at first refused, he was permitted to form a bank of his own which received increasing public recognition. Law's *Banque Generale*, which was the first bank of any kind yet established in France, was at first successful. Its notes circulated at a premium over coin, due partly to a promise to redeem the notes in coin of the same standard and weight as on the day of issue. This commitment appeared conservative at that time since the redemption of paper money in France had generally been in adulterated metal. A year later, the French government passed an ordinance permitting the notes of Law's bank to be accepted in payment of taxes. With this high credit rating, Law began to lend money at low rates of interest for the expansion of French industry of all kinds. The allocation of funds was not based so much on profitability or on safety as on priorities for national development. At this stage in his career, Law had established his reputation as a national benefactor and as the creator of a successful system of credit expansion.

Law's initial success warped his judgment and also tempted the cupidity of the Regent. Law went beyond the banking industry to set up *The System*, a scheme of colonization that was intended as a French rival to the British East India Company. The official name of this company was *The Bank of the Indies*, but it was generally called the *Mississippi Scheme*, and the stockholders were called *Mississippians*. The Mississippi Scheme was given title to all French territory in the Mississippi basin, and Law proposed the colonization of this territory, naming its capital New Orleans, in honor of the Regent. Other state monopolies were also assigned to The System, including all French trade with Senegal and the rest of Africa and with the French possessions in the East Indies and in China.

The name of the company was at this time changed to *Banque Royale*, and its notes carried the personal guarantee of the King of France. Law's bank was next assigned the liability for the entire French government debt that had been accumulated in the course of the expensive foreign wars of King Louis XIV. This meant a de facto monetization of the national debt. John Law was made director-general of the bank and controller-general of French finances. Shares of the Mississippi Scheme advanced in price from 500 *livres* to 18,000. The sale of additional shares enabled The Company to pay off the vast debt of France. People lined up for many blocks from the Paris office to purchase new shares. Law was momentarily the most popular man in France, and his scheme of monetary expansion appeared to have solved the most pressing problems of government indebtedness and economic stagnation.

Early in 1720, individuals began to sell their shares for bullion, which they subsequently shipped out of the country. The bank was then obliged to suspend payments in bullion, and the selling of stock in The System grew to an avalanche. Great fortunes disappeared within a few weeks as millionaires became destitute. Even the most draconian edicts against holding gold or silver, enforced by a police state and house searches, tended only to reinforce the hoarding or export of the precious metals and to undermine public confidence in the bank and the government. Law was forced to flee from France to save his life, and the Mississippi Scheme took its place with the Tulip Craze in Holland and the future South Sea Bubble in England as one of the great speculative manias of all time. Since the Mississippi Scheme enjoyed a greater degree of government sponsorship than similar schemes in England, Scotland, or The Netherlands, the damage to the French government was greater.

A. V. Anikin, a Russian economist, has described Law's platform as consisting of two planks: an extensive expansion of credit and greater role for the state within the economy [Anikin, 1975, p. 96]. In support of the second proposal, Anikin cites a recent French work: *John Law et Naissance du Dirigisme.* Law himself is quoted as saying: "It is a fortunate country where action can be considered, decided upon, and carried out within twenty-four hours, instead of twenty-four years like England [Anikin, 1975, p. 113]. Law had an exceptional opportunity to test his theories on a national theater, and the theories that he experimented with were widely prevalent at that time. As a result, the programs he sponsored were discredited for many years. Suspicion of high finance was most conspicuous in Scotland, where Adam Smith and others congratulated themselves on their prudence and good fortune in avoiding the fate of France.

Contemporary reactions in France were mixed. Some socialists, including the Duke of Saint-Simon, continued to admire Law and were willing to welcome him into their camp [Hyde, n.d., p. 86]. Even Voltaire, who was living in France at that time, defended Law, stating that "a system altogether chimerical produced a commerce that was genuine.... In short, if many private fortunes were destroyed, the nation became more opulent and more commercial" [Epinasse, 1968, p. 675]. Great increases in liquidity may have been necessary for a nation in the early process of industrializing.

In assessing the reasons for the collapse of The System, one must consider both Law's own arrogant mistakes at the height of his power and the absolute authority of the Regent. Already saddled with more than a century's accumulation of debt, the Duke of Orleans continued to borrow heavily to support his personal and official extravagances. Law was not able to resist the requests of a prince who was his only sponsor. Law's previous proposals to various governments, and especially to the King of Savoy-Piedmont, had stipulated that the state bank would advance no funds to the government. Loans would be made for industrial development only. But there was no responsible government in France at that time which could withstand the importunities of the Regent. In Scotland, on the other hand, it was the entrenched self-interest of a cluster of noble families, working with the natural caution of the populace, that acted as a brake on extravagant financial projects.

The Mississippi Scheme demonstrates the fragility of the great systems of public finance that emerged in Britain, France, and The Netherlands. Such power over the money supply requires accountability, and the government of France at that time had no system of checks and balances. But the Bank of England, which was given status as a national bank in 1696, was managed more cautiously and was never altogether subject to the whims of a monarch. The emergence of Britain as a haven for the world's endangered funds may date from Law's System and from other alarming episodes of monetary expansion in France. Adam Smith concludes that Law's System was "the most extravagant project both of banking and stockjobbing that perhaps the world ever saw" [Smith, 1937, p. 302]. Smith's fiscal and monetary conservatism was in part a reaction to Law's project.

Political Arithmetic

Another strand of economic thought in Scotland arose from the mechanical revolution of Descartes and Newton. This was the school of political arithmetic, the progenitor of modern economic statistics. Its focus was directed only to entities that could be measured numerically or whose changes could be projected. Like the Scottish school of political economy, it began with a repudiation of Aristotle and of high metaphysics, and it waxed enthusiastic over the prospect of investigations that could be carried on through numbers alone. By necessity, it was more materialistic and more empirical than the mainstream of economic thought in Scotland, which retained an attachment to moral and mental philosophy.

The inventor of the name *political arithmetic* and the first contributor to this discipline was Sir William Petty (1623–1687) who lived a century before Adam Smith. Petty held chairs in anatomy and in music at Oxford, and was at times chancellor of two Oxford colleges, yet he was by no means deeply rooted in academic perspectives. His knowledge of Greek and Latin was acquired in France when he was left behind in Normandy at age 13 from a ship on which he was employed as a cabin boy. His familiarity with anatomy was acquired at Utrecht in The Netherlands while he was a refugee from the Stuart rule in England. And he established his credibility as a professor of anatomy by reviving a young women who had been hanged for killing her child. (The woman was later found to be innocent.) Petty also spent much of his time designing a double-bottom ship. Petty's ship was indeed swift, but it capsized in the presence of the king during its test run exhibition. Petty had an inventive turn of mind and resembled Benjamin Franklin more than he did David Hume or Adam Smith.

Petty's creation of political arithmetic came about in 1652 while he was in Ireland as physician to Cromwell's army. This was through his undertaking, the "Down Survey," which was made as part of an arrangement to divide the forfeited estates of Irish rebels among the victorious troops of Cromwell and the merchant adventurers who had contributed by financing the military expedition. Half of the confiscated Irish lands was to be assigned to each of these groups. After conducting the survey, Petty emerged as the only person with sufficient knowledge of the land and of surveying techniques to take charge of the land distribution. Petty was accordingly appointed to the commission which made the allotments, and he emerged as its sole member. He was placed in full charge of dividing millions of acres of Irish land among those sharing in the conquest.

Petty's responsibilities as commissioner involved him in constant political bargaining as well as in the careful performance of his assignment as surveyor. His membership in both the Irish and English parliaments and his friendship with the ruling Cromwell family were Petty's great strengths on this occasion. Many itinerations between Dublin and London were necessary to defend his own reputation and to complete the assignment of Irish lands in a manner satisfactory to all claimants. Petty also emerged from these responsibilities in Ireland with an estate of 50,000 Irish acres of his own. Much of this land was bought from claimants who chose not to take up their claims.

Petty's achievements were both political and intellectual. He was knighted for his endeavors and declined the offer of an earldom because it would involve too much expense. Petty's Irish estates later became the foundation for one of Britain's greatest family fortunes. His step-grandson, William Petty, earl of Shelburne and later marquis of Lansdowne, were prime minister during the lifetime of Adam Smith and was the signer on behalf of Britain of the peace treaty with America. The Petty-

Fitzmaurice family has retained its wealth and a degree of political prominence and intellectual distinction to this day.

Petty's own manifesto or statement of intent was:

> The Method I take to do this, is not very usual; for instead of using only comparative and superlative Words, and intellectual Arguments, I have taken the course (as a specimen of the Political Arithmetick I have long aimed at) to express myself in Terms of *Number, Weight,* and *Measure*: to use only arguments of *Sense*, and to consider only such *Causes* as have foundations in Nature; leaving those that depend upon the mutable Minds, Opinions, Appetites, and Passions of particular Men, to the Considerations of others [Petty, 1963, p. 244].

Petty's materialist and mechanistic perspective in scientific investigations was typical of the seventeenth century, when Bacon and Hobbes had prevailed over scholasticism and when only empirical evidence received general credence. This mechanistic philosophy had not yet been put to a critical test by Berkeley or Hume, or even subjected to the milder criticisms of Locke. This was an era of revolt against metaphysics, and Petty was the one who articulated this revolt most strongly in the field of political economy. Petty's special association with *political arithmetic* comes from his having coined the term, and from his consistent application of quantitative measures to the study of the national income and the population. He was one of the first to use the term *economist*, which was later preempted by the physiocrats. And he is often considered the father of economic statistics [Anikin, 1975, p. 62; Schumpeter, 1954, p. 211].

Petty probably did not intend to offer political arithmetic as a substitute for rational analysis. Schumpeter warns us not to assume that Petty's "methods...consist in replacing reasoning by the assembling of facts. Petty was no victim of the slogan: Let the facts speak for themselves. Petty was first and last a theorist [Schumpeter, 1954, p. 211]. But it is apparent that Petty thought of political economy mainly as an extension of physics, rather than of ethics. On the other hand, the Scottish political economists were undoubtedly more at home with moral and mental philosophy and jurisprudence than with physics and mathematics.

Petty has also been called the "Father of Demography" [Roncaglia, 1985, pp. 59–60; Anikin, 1975, p. 71]. Petty's *Essay on the Growth and Encrease and Multiplication of Mankind* (1686) may establish a claim to be a precursor of Thomas Malthus. Studies of the population and resources of various countries were among Petty's favorite topics, and comparisons were often made of England and France. But where Malthus regarded the increase in population as a threat to the general standard of living, Petty considered population growth as a source of strength to any nation, adding to its industrial and military power. Karl Marx [p. 391] observes: "Our friend Petty has quite a different 'population theory' from Malthus."

Perhaps because Marx was so generous in Petty's praise, a Russian scholar has described Petty as "the Columbus of Political Economy." Or perhaps this comparison with Columbus comes from his earlier fame as the "Columbus of Mortality Bills" [Schumpeter, 1954, p. 212n.]. Petty and his friend John Graunt were accustomed to use mortality bills as a means of estimating populations. Marx credited Petty with discovering the labor theory of value, with recognizing that land, labor, and capital were the three factors of production, and with achieving some understanding of exploitation theory [Schumpeter, 1954, p. 212n.]. These attributions are a reminder that political arithmetic was not Petty's only claim to fame. Anikin concludes that Petty's *Treatise of Taxes and Contributions* (1662) "is perhaps the most important work of the 17th century, just as Adam Smith's book on the wealth of nations was of the 18th century" [Anikin, 1975, p. 62].

Petty could also be described as the creator of *political anatomy*, since anatomical analogies played an important place in his economic discussions, as they did in those of Thomas Hobbes. According to Schumpeter, Plato may deserve the credit for originating such analogies, but Hobbes and Petty restored them to favor. In discussing Bacon, Petty [1963, p. 129] states:

> Sir Francis Bacon, in his *Advancement of Learning*, hath a judicious parallel in many particulars, between the Body Natural, and the Body Politick, and between the Arts of preserving both in Health and Strength; and it is as reasonable, that as Anatomy is the best foundation of one, so also of the other; and that to practice upon the Politick, without knowing the Symmetry, Fabrick, and Proportion of it, is as casual as the practice of Old-Women and Empiricks.

One scholar observes that the terms *symmetry*, *fabric*, and *proportion* as used by Petty in anatomy are altogether analogous to *number, weight*, and *measure* in his political arithmetic. Adam Smith may have had this passage in mind in comparisons between the practice of medicine and the practice of statesmanship.

In his political theorizing, as in his philosophical reasoning, Petty was a Hobbesian. Petty and Hobbes had been acquainted from the time they studied medicine together in Paris in 1645. Petty shared Hobbes' proclivity toward an absolute state, perhaps because of a dread of anarchy. He could easily accommodate himself to a Cromwellian or to a Stuart regime, and presumably would have been comfortable under the House of Orange as well. In religion, Petty favored more rights for the Catholics in England and more power for the Protestants in Ireland. Petty was famous for his skill in mimicking clerics of all denominations but does not seem to have had a deep commitment to any. He was uneasy at the thought that any religious group might acquire absolute political power. Strong governmental power seemed necessary to Petty for the preservation of private property and to provide occasional therapy for sundry political maladies.

Petty avoids the vulgar mercantilist errors with regard to money. He regards the supply of money and its velocity of circulation as important determinants of the level of employment. Like Keynes, Petty is attentive to the short run, and within this time horizon the supply of money is important. Petty was particularly troubled by the loss of money from Ireland, as that country made payments of rent to absentee landlords in England. Petty supports a "favorable balance of trade" because its mildly inflationary impact stimulates production and employment. In one of his medical analogies, Petty compares money to the fat on the human body, which may lubricate the body and fill it out, or may slow it down. In short, Petty understood the need for economic expansion. Fiscal and monetary policy were not acceptable options at that time, so Petty gives his support to an expansionary trade policy when that seems necessary.

It would be difficult to name another economist whose personal achievements were as numerous and varied as Petty's. Perhaps his most famous quotation is: "Labor is the father of wealth...as lands are the mother" [Petty, 1899, p. 68]. Marx applauds Petty for his early comprehension of surplus value and exploitation. Schumpeter smiles at this insight, adding that "Petty's argument was that high wages would only encourage sloth and that if wages were doubled the supply of labor hours would be reduced to half" [Schumpeter, 1954, p. 214].

Adam Smith's remark, "I have no great faith in political arithmetic," is hardly applicable to Petty [1937, p. 501]. Political arithmetic was to Petty, as to Smith himself, just one weapon from the arsenal. But Petty was lacking in the vision of public welfare that was central to the purpose of Smith, Hutcheson, and most of the Scottish School.

The second person in the line of succession in the political arithmetic school was Gregory King (1648–1712), a surveyor, geneaologist, statistician, and herald. King was a more sophisticated statistician than Petty, but his works were published only posthumously, and they lacked relevance to immediate political problems. King's most important contribution was an attempt to measure the elasticity of demand for farm commodities and thus the tendency for their price to fluctuate with changes in their supply. Adam Smith was familiar with the work of King through quotations by Davenant, and Lauderdale and made extensive use of King's paradox. King's best known work was *Natural and Political Observations and Comparisons from the State and Condition of England* (1696).

Belonging to a later era in economic history was Richard Price (1723–1791). Price was a dissenting minister who interested himself in nearly every philosophical and statistical problem. Price's early writings were in support of liberty and of the cause of American independence. His biographer in the *D.N.B.* states that his work, published in 1776, may have been an important reason for the drafting of the American Declaration of Independence. Credit for this action is more often assigned to Price's friend, Thomas Paine. Price was given an honorary doctorate at Yale at the same commencement as George Washington. At least in its early stages, Price also involved himself in the agitation leading to the French Revolution. His other close friends included Benjamin Franklin, Joseph Priestley, and his noble sponsor, Lord Shelburne, the prime minister. Price was frequently consulted and quoted on financial subjects by William Pitt.

Price's significant contribution to political arithmetic was a series of writings on the importance of debt reduction, with the recommendation that it be achieved through the use of a sinking fund. The principle of compound interest was examined by Price, both to demonstrate the danger of a large public debt and to show the merits of a sinking fund as a means to extinguish the debt. Richard Price must be given much of the credit for establishing the credibility of the English financial system, which was soon to become the great repository for the world's financial assets. Ironically, it was England's large increase in its public debt, supported by regularity in making payments of interest and principal and by success in controlling inflation, that made pound-denominated securities so attractive to foreigners.

Political arithmetic was less congenial to Scotland than to England, but one notable Scotsman belongs in this tradition, Sir John Sinclair of Ulbster (1745–1835). Sinclair was the proprietor of vast estates in northern Scotland, and won fame for the improvements he made on his own land. But his lifetime career was as a member of Parliament and as the first president of Britain's Board of Agriculture. He was referred to as "the agricultural Sir John." His first important work, published in 1784, was *The History of the Public Debt of the British Empire*. But his more noteworthy achievement was the *Statistical Account of Scotland* (1791–1799). This 20-volume work was compiled mainly from reports from the parish ministers of Scotland, each of whom submitted an account of the population and improvements within his own parish.

Sir John's enthusiasm for improvements was exceptional. Improved agricultural methods had become the fashion of the time, so there was no difficulty in generating public interest in this subject. The Duke of Bedford and other great agricultural improvers began the custom of scheduling agricultural exhibits as features of weekend gatherings at their country houses where prizes were awarded for the best cattle, sheep, chickens, and farm crops. Sinclair's own exhibits were too far removed from the centers of population to attract attention or attendance but he himself was assiduous in attending exhibits at estates near London. Sinclair was the least inclined of any of the political arithmeticians to engage in abstract or theoretical reasoning.

Despite Adam Smith's professed disdain for political arithmetic, he made frequent use of its methodology in his own reasoning. In his chapters on the rent of land and on the price of silver Smith examines data from distant times and places. But the theory which Smith attempts to explain or prove always comes before the statistical data, and the theories are usually complex and paradoxical.

Francis Hutcheson and the Scottish Universities

The most distinctive feature of the Scottish political economy was its close relationship to the universities. In particular, it had its origin in the universities of Glasgow and Edinburgh. These universities were located in growing cities, and student enrollments of these universities shared in the expansion. The increase in the student enrollment in turn permitted a greater degree of faculty specialization and a larger faculty. The growing complexity of society imposed further demands on the curricula of these universities. The enrollment at the University of Glasgow in Adam Smith's time was about 300, but the spectacular growth of the city in the following years enhanced both the demand for university services and the ability of the universities to meet this demand.

These universities provided little instruction that would be directly useful in business. Such training was far removed from the ideal of a university that prevailed at this time, even in such an industrial city as

Glasgow. The study of chemistry and of logarithms, themselves a great advance over the subject matter of the previous century, was as far as these universities had moved toward injecting a practical emphasis into their curricula. These subjects were considered useful in agriculture and in ordnance. Adam Smith also suggested that courses in dancing, fencing, and horseback riding might be useful to university students, though he did not recommend that they be included in the curriculum at Glasgow [Smith, 1937, p. 721]. The "learned professions" of medicine, law, and the ministry had been given the primary attention in the Scottish universities.

It was from the Moral Philosophy course in these universities that political economy emerged, and particularly from the jurisprudence section of this course. It had long been the custom in the Scottish universities to enroll in only one course each year, and Moral Philosophy was usually assigned to the last year of university studies. It was therefore taken when students were somewhat older than in the other courses. Adam Smith remarks that the threefold division of the university curriculum into logic, natural philosophy, and moral philosophy seemed quite in conformity to the natural order of things [Smith, 1937, p. 725].[5] But James McCosh protested that this division of the material was dictated more by the necessity of studying all the works of Aristotle in three years.

An important innovation that occurred after 1700 was the introduction of natural jurisprudence into the Moral Philosophy course. This occurred first in Edinburgh and then in a more decisive way in Glasgow. Natural jurisprudence included a study of the works of Grotius and Pufendorf, the philosophical jurists who undertook to derive systems of jurisprudence from principles of reason alone. Grotius and Pufendorf were the new scholastics who had been introduced into the curriculum when an era of Protestantism had rendered Thomas Aquinas and Duns Scotus obsolete. Francis Bacon has described natural law as a quest for the "Law of Laws," which should form a pattern for practical legislation. Adam Smith's predecessors at the University of Glasgow accepted this understanding of natural law and used it as a standard for criticism in the field of jurisprudence. But Smith himself differed in his interpretation of natural law and showed less interest in jurisprudence. He preferred to describe what *tends* to happen, rather than what ought to happen. This new approach to nature may have been inspired by Bernard de Mandeville, who went far toward abolishing moral distinctions and placing all behavior in the realm of an amoral nature. Thus, Smith's concept of an "invisible hand" reflects a concept of natural law, but it is more like a law of physics than a law of behavior.

John Locke and Thomas Hobbes are often included among the natural law philosophers. It was through Locke's prestige and influence that a section on mental philosophy was added to the Moral Philosophy course in the Scottish universities. This subject dealt with psychology and epistemology, and was particularly concerned with questions of the passivity or spontaneity of the human mind. Such discussions later became a standard feature of the Scottish philosophy, which described itself as a "realist" philosophy. Though Adam Smith has little to say about mental philosophy in his *Wealth of Nations*, it is the main theme of his *Theory of Moral Sentiments*.

Gershom Carmichael (1672–1729), Hutcheson's predecessor in the chair of Moral Philosophy at Glasgow, was responsible for the widespread dependence on Grotius and Pufendorf and on their version of the natural law philosophy. In his *Introduction to Moral Philosophy*, Hutcheson identifies the sources of his lectures and expresses his particular indebtedness to Carmichael:

> The learned will at once discern how much of this compound is taken from the writings of others; from Cicero and Aristotle; and to name no other moderns, from Pufendorf's smaller work, *De Officio Hominis et Civis Juxta Legem Naturalem* which that worthy and ingenious man the late Professor Gershom Carmichael of Glasgow, by far the best commentator on that book, has so supplied and corrected that the notes are of much more value than the text [Hutcheson, 1753, pp. 111, 118].

Carmichael had translated Pufendorf from German into Latin to make it accessible to students in Scotland, and had written a compendium to accompany this work. Carmichael represents the dominance of the scholastic version of natural law in the Scottish universities. In theology, he was a staunch Calvinist, but he was receptive to new ideas from Germany, France, and Holland. Adam Smith's derogatory remarks about scholasticism and casuistry in the universities may refer to the era which Carmichael represents, but Smith touches more on the language and style of scholasticism than on natural law itself.

An important feature of the economic discussions of Pufendorf, Carmichael, and Hutcheson was their balanced emphasis on supply and demand. The discussion usually appeared in the context of the paradox of value, with an ensuing comparison of value in use and value in exchange. All three of these philosophers were attentive to value in use, avoiding a one-sided emphasis on supply and on cost of production. This approach was also taken by Adam Smith in his Glasgow lectures. But in the *Wealth of Nations* a precedent was set of selecting supply and cost of production as the active determinants of value. This approach to value was to dominate British economic thinking for about a century, and was also to include Karl Marx.

Emphasis on literary style was another of the innovations in Scottish university education which began around 1730. It was Lord Shaftesbury who introduced the cult of style into serious literary compositions in England, explaining that literary compositions should be made more palatable to statesmen and to men of refinement. This awareness of style received support from two other trends that prevailed in Scotland at that time. The one was the cultural trend to be more appreciative of the English language, and the other was a philosophical trend to be attentive to beauty and to the secondary qualities, and not just to mass, motion, and number.

Francis Hutcheson (1694–1746) was responsible for planting these innovative ideas firmly on Scottish soil, and in this undertaking he was assisted by his ordination as a Presbyterian minister. His reforms extended beyond the university and into the Church. Involved in this change were the abandonment of Latin as the primary medium for scholarly writing and for classroom discussions, the replacement of the Scottish brogue with a more correct English diction, the careful study of the best stylists among the Greek and Latin writers, conscious attention to the English and French stylists, and a gradual encroachment of *belles-lettres* upon the traditional academic course in logic. This transition from Latin and logic to English and *belles-lettres* was welcomed as much by Adam Smith during the year he occupied the chair of Logic at Glasgow as by Hutcheson himself.

Dugald Stewart, who was a late contemporary of these "new light" innovations in Scotland, states:

> The old systems of natural jurisprudence had entirely lost their credit among men of taste and enlarged views long before they ceased to form a part of academical instruction [1877, p. 166].

But James McCosh, who also took university work in Scotland at this time, contended:

> He (Hutcheson) is evidently indebted to the wits of Queen Anne, such as Shaftesbury, Bolingbroke, Pope, and Swift, who were Frenchifying the English tongue, polishing away at once its roughness and its vigor, introducing the French clearness of expression, and, we may add, the French morals [McCosh, 1875, p. 84].

Parallel to these changes in the university curricula, we encounter a proliferation of literary journals and of translations of works by foreign authors. Interest in literature became widespread in Scotland, even among women, who were not admitted to the universities. Hutcheson's influence was also felt in the field of theological instruction, as he strove to make the Scottish ministers better read and more style-conscious in their sermons.

Hutcheson's dedication to a cult of style did not prevent him from formulating concepts of public interest and utility that became basic to the thinking of the classical school of political economy. The most distinctive feature of Hutcheson's system was the prominence of *benevolence*, which had been totally absent in previous works on political economy. Bentham, at a later time, placed emphasis on the pleasure that any given action affords to the receiver, but he fell short of recognizing the motive for the action. Hutcheson's formulation of this synthesis of benevolence and utility is presented in the following passage:

> The Moment of Good to any person in any given case, is in a compound Ratio of the quantity of the Good in itself, and the Indigence of the person. Hence it appears that a gift may make a greater addition to the happiness of the Receiver, than the Diminution it occasions in the happiness of the Giver. The most useful and important Gifts are those from the Wealthy to the Indigent. Gifts from Equals are not useless, since they often increase the Happiness of both, as they are strong evidence of mutual love [1753, pp. 111, 118].

This passage shows not only an early attempt to quantify utility but also an understanding of diminishing marginal utility. The value of the Good is less when the recipient is already rich, and its value is greater when the recipient is poor.

Hutcheson also provides a utilitarian analysis of hatred. In Hutcheson's dualist, or neoplatonist, system of thought, we find a constant conflict between the virtues and the vices. Political economy had not sufficiently distinguished itself, in Hutcheson's time, from individual ethics. Hutcheson presents a motivational and behavioral assessment of utility at the same time that he attempts to measure utility in quantitative terms.

Hutcheson's obsession with benevolence was also an expression of his own temperament and a carryover from the ecclesiastical era of the Scottish universities. Though Hutcheson stood adamant against religious dogmatism, he retained some of the characteristics of his clerical calling. Leechman, in his introduction to Hutcheson's *System of Moral Philosophy*, states:

> As he (Hutcheson) had occasion every year in the course of his lectures to explain the origin of government, and compare the different forms of it, he

took particular care, while on that subject, to inculcate the importance of civil and religious liberty, and manly zeal for promoting it...he always insisted upon it at great length, and with the greatest strength of argument and earnestness of persuasion [Hutcheson, 1753, p. xxxi].

Hutcheson's students testify that his classroom presentations were more impressive than his writings, and that his case for benevolence was reinforced by exceptional personal generosity.

Despite his overriding emphasis on benevolence as a subjective quality. Hutcheson was also the coiner of the familiar slogan of utilitarians: "The greatest happiness of the greatest numbers." He was the creator of the Greatest Happiness Principle. Hutcheson states:

In the same manner, the moral evil or vice is as the degree of misery and the number of sufferers; so that that action is best which procures the greatest happiness of the greatest numbers [1753, p. 8].

This expression and the related concept of a public interest was generally accepted by the Scottish political economists, and it has distinguished classical economists from the mercantilists, or from Sir William Petty or John Law. These economists had favored national prosperity, but they did not refer explicitly to the welfare of consumers. Their analysis was directed primarily to the means of strengthening or of stabilizing the state. But the classical economists, following Hutcheson and Smith, gave primacy to the welfare of the consumer.

Though consumer welfare was given first place by Adam Smith as the goal of economic activity, it can hardly be said that Smith gave it first priority as a field for analysis. Recent economists have criticized Smith for his neglect of the entire demand side of price formation, and especially for his failure to do justice to diminishing marginal utility. Emil Kauder points out that in turning aside from a tradition that had continued from the time of Aristotle, Smith gave rise to an unfortunate error which persisted for more than a century [see Spengler and Allen, 1960, pp. 288–304]. Yet a comparison of the treatment of value by Pufendorf, Carmichael, Hutcheson, and Smith in his Glasgow lectures, shows that all these authors made a clear distinction between the "natural" price which is determined by cost factors and the "market" price which fluctuates in the short run around the natural price. The need to construct a complete system of political economy appears to have induced Smith in the *Wealth of Nations* to weaken the full explanation of price formation that he had inherited from Hutcheson. The new tradition, which gave prominence to a labor theory of value, departed even further from demand and diminishing utility in the later works of David Ricardo and Karl Marx.

Hutcheson and Smith were in agreement that the necessities of life should be given more prominence in an economic system than life's luxuries. Indeed, this was a proposition which was perfectly in accord with Hutcheson's preoccupation with benevolence. Transfers from the rich to the poor would tend to maximize utility because they would augment the consumption of necessities and reduce the expenditures for luxuries. This effect would also be enhanced by the voluntary nature of the transaction when the transfer was in the form of a gift. This was a conclusion that Smith could concur in, though he did not look for benevolence or gifts to play a large role in the economy.

Though members of the Scottish school were in general agreement that an economic system should provide benefits for all who were able and willing to spend money for consumption, they were by no means convinced that the pursuit of wealth was the highest goal in life. One might expect misgivings on this subject from a collection of writers who were philosophers, academics, clergymen, landlords, and statesmen, but never entrepreneurial businessmen. There is therefore a paradoxical or playful quality in Hutcheson's construction of a hedonistic calculus in conjunction with an obsessive preoccupation with benevolence.

None of the Scottish economists could have been comfortable with a strictly materialist interpretation of history. A desire for professional achievement, or for recognition by one's peers, had been gaining ground both on tribal leadership and on the search for financial gain, even while the *Wealth of Nations* was in incubation. A biographer of John Law contends that this was true even in Law's case [Hyde, n.d., p. 86]. A wish to test his theories, to serve his friends, and to get a taste of political power were more important even to Law than a desire for wealth. The search for economic gain may therefore have been losing its real-world appeal within the upper levels of Scottish society, and giving way to a meritocracy.

Among the cluster of Scottish political economists, we find no revolutionaries and few dedicated social reformers. John Millar of Glasgow and Lord Lauderdale, who were late in the history of Scottish political economy, were the most revolutionary of this group. The reforming zeal of these men was directed to such abuses as grants of monopoly, protective tariffs, or laws of primogeniture and entail. Though Scotland later provided a home for the social experiments of Robert Owen, this successful community was not sponsored by a Scot. The Scottish political economists were convinced that Britain was better off than France, where government intervention in economic affairs was more pervasive. Their recollection of religious tyranny in Scotland and of oppression under the

Stuart regime in England made them willing to endure the lesser ills they were experiencing under the Hanoverian oligarchy. Hutcheson, Hume and Smith all valued personal liberty and security above perfect justice.

Hutcheson, Hume, and Smith have been known as the "Sentimental Moralists" because they insisted that morals were based on a distinctive moral faculty, and not on reason. Reason could be used as an instrument for analysis, but it could not by itself determine ethical norms. Hutcheson [1753, pp. 125–126] says:

> Unhappy would it be for mankind if a sense of virtue was of as narrow an extent as a capacity for such metaphysics.

The tendency to create multiple human faculties to explain our sentiment of benevolence or our sense of beauty was characteristic of the Scottish school. They were unwilling to accept reason as the final arbiter in ethics or esthetics, and consequently their analysis penetrated beyond those entities measured by statisticians.

The main impetus toward the formulation of political economy in Scotland came through an understanding that natural science is a system, and that moral science might undergo improvements like Newton's system if experiments were carried on in a similar manner. The search for a "moral Newtonism" must be considered the main motive for both Hume and Smith. This required comprehensiveness, coherence among the parts of the system, accountability for all the observed facts, and a persuasive style. The facts could be arranged to illustrate the generalization, and not necessarily to support an inductive proof. Their works might have seemed to Bacon, Hobbes, or Petty to border on metaphysics and deductive rationalism. But the members of the Scottish school were convinced that simplicity, clarity, and literary elegance were necessary features of investigations in the moral sciences.

David Hume

David Hume (1711–1776) is Scotland's best-known philosopher, and was her outstanding man-of-letters during the third quarter of the eighteenth century. Born at Ninewells near Edinburgh, Hume attended the University of Edinburgh, spent several years in the independent study of literature and philosophy, and travelled extensively in France and other European countries as a tutor and a member of diplomatic missions. He passed the later years of his life as librarian of the Advocates Library, the finest in Scotland at that time. In 1737, at the age of 27, he published his

Treatise of Human Nature, which established his reputation as "by far the most illustrious philosopher of his age" [Smith, 1937, p. 742].[6]

The *Treatise* was a conscious attempt to construct a "moral Newtonism" [Willey, 1941, p. 112; Hume, 1898, p. 8]. So great was the influence of Sir Isaac Newton at this time that his method seemed to offer a key for the reconstruction of all other areas of knowledge. Hume's hinge concept or paradigm was that in the principle of the Association of Ideas one might find a moral counterpart to gravitation. Science became, in Hume's philosophy, a product of the mental habit of associating ideas with each other, and of postulating the observed regularity in the appearance of these ideas as a cause-and-effect relationship. Like Hutcheson, Hume divorced ethics from reason, and found the basis for ethical judgments in the autonomous passions or affectations of pleasure, pain, sympathy, or admiration.

Hume attached special significance to the proposition: "Reason is and ought only to be the slave of the passions, and can never pretend to any other office than to serve and obey them [Smith, 1941, pp. 179–186].[7] Though Hume suggested that his skepticism was without practical consequences, this does not appear to have been the case. Such skepticism may have only minor significance for the farmer who has been convinced of the theoretical uncertainty that the sun will rise the next morning, but to the creator of a system of science it could be of vast importance. Hume had emancipated himself not only from the dogmatic moralism of the scholastics but also from the dogmatic rationalism of Descartes and from the mechanical materialism of Hobbes.

Starting his *Inquiry* from empirical principles, Hume shows that no valid proof can be advanced for the existence of a material substance, for the existence of the mind as a substance, or for the existence of causality in any objective sense outside the mind of the thinker. Our only certainties are reduced to immediate impressions, derived from sense experience. Our scientific systems can have only probable truth, as they describe an expectation that the same sequence of impressions experienced in the past will prevail in the future.

For a philosopher whose chief contributions were a denial of any independent existence of mind, matter, or causality, Hume's contributions to a theory of natural causality or equilibrium in the economic world were indeed remarkable. Schumpeter observes that Hume's philosophical views had little impact on his economics [Schumpeter, 1954, pp. 447n.] But he also claims that Hume's *Association Psychology* was significant for sociology, and that the *Psychologism* of Hume is modern in its approach. Whether or not Hume's contributions to philosophy and psychology were directly related to his views on political economy, such expressions of uncertainty regarding his own mental processes brought a reduction in the level of dogmatism in his writings on all subjects.

Hume's *Political Discourses* (1752) contain most of his economic ideas. Four of these twelve — *Of Money, Of Interest, Of Commerce*, and *Of the Balance of Trade* — are by far the most important. These essays were written serially and in a popular style, which was Hume's response to the poor initial reception of his *Treatise of Human Nature*. Most of these essays are written in support of a free market economy, and of the role of *money* as an automatic mechanism to regulate output and prices.

Of Money is a statement of the quantity theory, which had already been explained by John Locke. Monetary theorists were then in general agreement that an influx of precious metals into Europe after the discovery of the Americas had, after a long time lag or interval, raised the general level of prices to three or four times its initial level. This gave empirical support to the thesis that increases in Money give rise to proportionate increases in prices and wages, other things being equal. These other things might include the velocity of monetary turnover or the volume of transactions. One of Hume's contributions was to examine the time lags between the money increase and also the differential effect on various commodities, and to show that, during the interval between the increase in the money supply and the complete response of prices, the increase in money gave some stimulus to the economy. But Hume was more interested in the long-run equilibrium, when the stimulus to productivity would be dissipated. Hume, like Keynes, held that the slower rise in wages would increase profits and encourage new investment until the level of wages reached its long-run equilibrium and drove the new capital out of the country. Hume's analysis was not complicated by fluctuating exchange rates, but he would have been interested in the recent experience of Japan in world markets. Keynes commended Hume for his "transitional mercantilism."

Hume's primary thesis is that most government intervention in the economy is futile. Money can provide a more natural and efficient mechanism (for the allocation of capital) than laws and edicts. Benefits to be received from changes in the money supply or from incurring government debt can be only temporary. The real strength of any nation lies in its commodities and its productive power. These variables are more likely to be increased by specialization in accordance with comparative cost, and the specialization can best be encouraged by a reasonably stable money supply. The main thrust of Hume's doctrines was to support laissez-faire, and to decry government intervention in the economy through tariffs, subsidies, sumptuary laws, or manipulation of the money supply.

It was mainly in the context of the specie flow mechanism between nations that Hume's appeal for natural liberty has most force. Schumpeter [1954, p. 367] maintains that this thesis underwent little change until the 1920s. A favorable balance of trade will bring about an influx of specie, which will raise prices in the exporting nation until its high prices destroy its competitiveness in foreign markets. Or an unfavorable balance of trade will cause a loss of specie until its domestic prices decline sufficiently to correct the unfavorable balance. This reverse specie flow mechanism reinforces the quantity theory of money and demonstrates the futility of most government intervention in foreign trade.

The optimistic conclusion to this natural adjustment mechanism in foreign trade is that trade should stimulate further international specialization and contribute to mutual interdependence among nations. Money and a free movement of commodities can promote prosperity and harmony between trading nations, as well as within each nation. Hume [1955] exclaims:

> As a British subject, I pray for the flourishing commerce of Germany, Spain, and Italy, and even of France itself.

Hume's dedication to free trade and to comparative cost leads him to some disparaging remarks about the effect of high wages. As an economy accumulates capital, its wage scale will rise and capital will begin searching for more profitable havens in foreign lands. Thus, capital accumulation may not enrich a nation or raise its wage scale for any long period of time. Hume visualizes capital as more footloose than it appeared to Ricardo two generations later. Yet, in spite of the burden of a high wage scale, Hume concludes: that this disadvantage weighs lightly as compared with "the happiness of so many millions."

Two curious criticisms of Hume's international equilibrium are raised by the Russian economist, A. Anikin. One is to deny that the influx of precious metals from the Americas tended to raise prices in Europe during the fifteenth and sixteenth centuries. Anikin [1975, p. 134] avers:

> Appearances are deceptive, as the saying goes. For the whole course of this process can and must be explained differently. The discovery of rich deposits caused a drop in the cost of labour to extract precious metals, and consequently, a drop in their value too. Since the value of money in relation to commodities had dropped, the price of commodities rose.

Anikin [1975, p. 134] further denies that increases in the quantity of gold or silver could increase the price level, though changes in the quantity of paper money obviously do.

Hume and Smith share the same outlook regarding the role of generalization in economic reasoning. Hume [1955, p. 286] states:

> General Principles, if sound, must always prevail in the course of things, though they may fail in particular cases; and it is the chief business of philosophers to regard the general course of things.

The search for a few simple and clear principles with which to explain economic phenomena was characteristic of Hume and Smith. This reflects their admiration for Sir Isaac Newton, their fondness for style, and their adherence to a concept of natural equilibrium. This also led to their preoccupation with real variables and with long-run equilibrium. But Hume was less successful than Smith in making political economy an autonomous discipline, distinct from politics, and embracing an entire field of knowledge.

The Scottish Achievement in Political Economy

Adam Smith's *Wealth of Nations* was the crowning achievement of the Scottish inquiry into political economy. But the decade of 1766–1776 witnessed the publication of three memorable works in this area. The first of these was Sir James Steuart's *Inquiry into the Principles of Political Economy*, which was immediately followed by Adam Ferguson's *Essay on Civil Society* [Rae, 1895, pp. 253–254].[8] Smith, Steuart, and Ferguson were approximately the same age, were all associated with the universities of Glasgow or Edinburgh, and were well acquainted with each other.

Sir James Steuart of Coltness (1712–1780) took the part of the Jacobites in the Rebellion of 1745 and was forced to remain in exile in Europe for 18 years, under sentence of death. A substantial part of Steuart's life was thus spent in Germany, France, and Italy. Like other Scottish political economists, he had ample opportunity to make international comparisons. Like Smith's *Wealth of Nations*, his two-volume work, *Inquiry into the Principles of Political Economy*, contained numerous observations from many eras of history and from various parts of the world. Steuart was familiar with Hume's *Political Discourses*, which he was attempting to refute. Steuart, like John Law, was a believer in industrial planning and also held to a large part of the mercantilist outlook. He recommended policies that would enhance the wealth and power of his own country, largely at the expense of foreign nations. It seems somewhat curious that Steuart and Law, the two avowed mercantilists within the Scottish constellation, should both be expatriates who lived much of their lives abroad under sentence of death.

Where Adam Smith was to identify the division of labor as the main engine for increases in industrial productivity, Steuart saw more significance in the use of machinery. From the perspective of the next century, this may have brought Steuart closer to the mainstream of economic thought than Smith. But his policy recommendations include tariffs, bounties, subsidies, and manipulation of the money supply. So great was the public opposition to restraints that Adam Smith easily carried the day against Steuart, and his division of labor shared the popularity of his laissez-faire.

Steuart-Denham, who had added his uncle's name to his own, returned to Scotland about a year before Smith left Glasgow as the companion to the young Duke of Buccleuch. Rae tells of Steuart's attempts to persuade the Glasgow merchants to consider protectionist doctrines, but "he frankly confessed that he grew sick of repeating arguments for protection to these 'Glasgow theorists'" [Rae, 1895, p. 61]. In his discussion with the Glasgow merchants, Sir James was contending both against the self-interest of the merchants and the theories of Adam Smith. These merchants had a lingering resentment over their exclusion from England's overseas markets over recent decades.

Adam Ferguson (1723–1816) competes less directly with Adam Smith. Beyond sharing a common first name, the two Adams were born in the same year, held the two leading chairs of moral philosophy in Scotland, and met each other on numerous occasions. Ferguson was a more convivial type of person than Smith. He was immortalized by Sir Walter Scott for his personal courage at the Battle of Fontenoy, although he participated as a chaplain. One of the main issues espoused by Ferguson was the preservation of the Scottish militia, and one of Ferguson's several diplomatic missions was to serve as secretary to a peace mission to America in 1778. When Ferguson asked to speak to General Washington at the American camp at Valley Forge, he was told that he should negotiate with the Continental Congress, and not with a general in the field.

Ferguson's main interest was in historical change, rather than in the timeless equilibrium analysis which received so much attention from the mainstream of economic thought for more than a century. For this reason, Ferguson is often considered the founder of sociology, as Smith was the founder of systematic political economy. The concept of conjectural, or hypothetical, history is prominent in both these writers, and often it merged with actual, recorded history. This is an approach that has received added emphasis from the work of Karl Marx, whose main interest is in how successive forms of social organization came into being, disintegrated, and were replaced by new societies based on different forms of production. But where the analysis of social change plays only a secondary role in the *Wealth of Nations*, Ferguson makes it the main theme of his *History of Civil Society*. It was also the main theme of John Millar (1725–1801), who taught at the University of Glasgow.

Ferguson's theory states that societies develop through fixed stages or economic structures and that the social organization at any time is determined by its material means of production. Societies commence in a state of nature, without specialization or private ownership of property. The succeeding societal forms are those of hunting and fishing, then a herdsman mode with ownership and domestication of animals, then an economy based on the appropriation and cultivation of the land, then feudalism, which in turn gives way to independent leagues of cities and finally to capitalism. This type of analysis had been popularized on the continent by Rousseau, who was known for his romantic attachment to the state of nature. Rousseau was well known to the Scottish political economists and especially to Hume, who helped him to find refuge in England from the persecution he had experienced in France. But the Scottish political economists postulated a state of nature mainly as a starting point for social and economic development, and not as a utopian ideal. They regarded civilized society as a condition of life that was well worth what it cost in subordination and alientation.

The successors to Smith and Ferguson at Glasgow and Edinburgh were John Millar (1725–1801) and Dugald Stewart (1753–1828). Millar taught law at the University of Glasgow. His familiar publication, *The Origin of the Distinction of Ranks*, places him more within the tradition of Ferguson than of Smith. But Millar had attended Smith's lectures at Glasgow and gave full support to Smith's doctrines of economic liberalism [Rae, 1895, p. 53]. He was also more inclined than the other Scottish political economists to participate in politics, on the Foxite, or liberal, wing of the Whig party. Both Millar and his student, Lord Lauderdale, were lampooned in the London conservative press for their sympathy with the revolutionary movement in France. The following satires from the *True Briton*, February 25, 1793, and June 7, 1793, respectively, testify to the reputation Millar had achieved for educating students for leadership in the cause of social change:

Is it not remarkable that Lords Sempil and Lauderdale, who were long under the tuition of Professor Millar of Glasgow, should so strongly favour the Democratic and Republican French systems, since it is well known that their worthy instructor professes principles *the very reverse!*

Lord Lauderdale protests he never heard of a School for bringing up young men to Politics, except the two Houses of Parliament. Has his Lordship never *heard* of a certain Democratic Professor of Glasgow?

Lauderdale sent a number of prominent English students to take a few semesters of their college studies with Millar at Glasgow or with Stewart at Edinburgh, or with both. These included Lord Henry Petty (later Marquis of Lansdowne), who later held office at cabinet level, and two future prime ministers, Lord Melbourne and Lord John Russell. Lauderdale even arranged for Lord Melbourne (then Henry Lamb) to enter Parliament from his own controlled constituency of Haddington Burghs. The idea of a college for practical politics was probably a real one to Millar, Stewart, and Lauderdale.

Dugald Stewart, whose interests and whose classroom instruction were in the tradition of Smith, taught at the University of Edinburgh. Though not the author of any widely read work,[9] Stewart won distinction for his classroom lectures and for the number and prominence of his students. Stewart made visits to France with Lauderdale at least twice, the second occasion being as secretary to Lauderdale's mission in 1806, when an attempt was made to negotiate peace with Napoleon. At this time, there was no instruction in political economy offered in any of the English universities, and study in Europe was difficult during the hostilities with France. Stewart was probably the only academic lecturer on political economy in the world.

A final member of the Scottish School was James Maitland, eighth earl of Lauderdale (1759–1839). Lauderdale's career was in politics, beginning with membership in the House of Commons at the age of 21. During his career of nearly 60 years, he served in both houses of Parliament, represented both political parties at different stages of his career, and in some years made more parliamentary speeches than any other member of the House of Peers. He was also well acquainted with three kings of Britain and with at least ten prime ministers, and was acquaintanced with Wellington, Napoleon, Talleyrand, and Metternich. The best known of Lauderdale's numerous publications was his *Inquiry into the Nature and Origin of Public Wealth* (1804). His recognition that some form of fiscal policy or of debt management might be necessary in the interest of economic stability places him within the macroeconomic tradition, and he is often listed as a predecessor of Keynes. Lauderdale's purpose in economics was to refute, or to make significant corrections to, the *Wealth of Nations*. Lauderdale accordingly made his main attacks on the doctrines of the division of labor and of natural stability in the economy. However, the doctrine of laissez-faire had become too well entrenched for Lauderdale to make an assault on it.

In 1784 when Edmund Burke was chosen Rector of the University of Glasgow, he came north by way of Edinburgh, stayed with Lauderdale (then Lord Maitland) at his country place at Hatton, and travelled on horseback with Adam Smith, Dugald Stewart, Andrew Dalzel, and Lauderdale to Glasgow, where the party stayed with John Millar. The distinguished group returned to Edinburgh by way of Carron, where they spent a few hours inspecting the new iron works which were considered an industrial wonder of the world. The cannons that were made at Carron became a major factor in the British victories at Trafalgar and Waterloo, and it is noteworthy that this academic group should show equal interest in Burke's brilliant installation address and in the new iron foundry. Adam Smith also made a side trip, along with Burke and Lauderdale, who were not obliged to teach classes the next day, to inspect the scenic wonders of Loch Lomond [Rae, 1895, pp. 388–392].

It is difficult to suggest any one explanation for the constellation of political economists who appeared in Scotland during the eighteenth century. England and Holland were likelier candidates to take the lead in this new science. But the Scottish philosophers showed more excitement at the commercial and industrial advance being made before their eyes. The Universities of Glasgow and Edinburgh were located in industrial cities, and members of their faculties were accustomed to travel occasionally to London. On this seven-day journey by stage coach, they were exposed to new industrial plants being constructed in Yorkshire and along the road to London. Such journeys were made more frequently by members of Parliament, such as Lauderdale and Sir John Sinclair. This group of Scotsmen was also accustomed to travel on the continent and especially in France. Their publications were widely read by statesmen and by the educated public.

Among the many factors that can be cited to explain Scotland's remarkable contribution to economic thought, one must come back to the character of the individual political economists and to the interactions among them. The rivalry among these writers was sometimes intense, yet they were acquainted with each other, discussed each other's manuscripts before publication, and pursued their debates with each other in an urbane and polite manner. But only Lord Lauderdale and Sir John

Sinclair were placed at a level where they might be corrupted by power or affluence.

Notes

1. It must be admitted that the work of Turgot and of the physiocrats was systematic in character, and that it dealt analytically with the same subjects of inquiry that Adam Smith was to investigate. But Smith was far more comprehensive in his treatment.

2. Hont and Ignatieff, 1983. Andrew Fletcher is given considerable attention in this work. Adam Smith likewise expresses alarm that the division of labor might undermine the martial spirit of the people [p. 739]. David Hume also had misgivings about the impact of more commerce and of more division of labor.

3. Schumpeter asserts that the plague of deductive reasoning was in no way the fault of Aristotle. The fault lay in an exaggerated emphasis on Aristotle's logical works, and on the study of these works in medieval Latin, with scholastic interpretations [Schumpeter, 1954, p. 90].

4. Espinasse, p. 672. Smith associates Law with an excessive issuance of currency to stimulate the national economy. "That the industry of Scotland languished for want of money to employ it was the opinion of the famous Mr. Law. By establishing a bank of a particular kind, which he seems to have imagined might issue paper to the amount of the whole value of all the lands in the country, he proposed to remedy this want of money." [Smith, p. 301].

5. "The improvements which, in modern times, have been made in the different branches of philosophy, have not, the greater part of them, been made in the universities; though some no doubt have. The greater part of the universities have not even been very forward to adopt these improvements, after they were made; and several of those learned societies have chosen to remain, for a long time, the sanctuaries in which obsolete prejudices found shelter and protection, after they had been hunted out of every other corner of the world."

6. Smith not only describes Hume as "by far the most illustrious philosopher and historian of the present age," but elsewhere acclaims him as second only to Livy as a historian in all recorded history.

7. Smith contends that Hume's central thesis, that of the primacy of the passions and sentiments, was taken from Francis Hutcheson.

8. Sir James Steuart later adopted the name of "Steuart-Denham," on the receipt of a large inheritance from his uncle.

9. Dugald Stewart's works are published in eight volumes. The best known of his writings was his *Memoir of Adam Smith*, written shortly after Smith's death.

References

Anikin, A. V. *A Science in its Youth.* Moscow: Progress Publishers, 1975.

Bryson, Gladys. *Man and Society, the Scottish Inquiry of the Eighteenth Century.* Princeton: Princeton University Press, 1945.

Campbell, R. S., and Skinner, A. S. *The Origin and Nature of the Scottish Enlightenment.* Edinburgh: John Donald, 1982.

Carlyle, Alexander. *Autobiography of the Rev. Dr. Alexander Carlyle, Minister of Inveresk.* Edinburgh: Blackwood & Sons, 1860.

Cockburn, Henry, *Memorials of his Time.* Ed. by Karl Miller. Chicago: University of Chicago Press, 1974.

Dalzel, Andrew. *A History of the University of Edinburgh from its Foundation.* Edinburgh: C. Innes, 1862.

Espinasse, Francis. "John Law of Lauriston." In *D.N.B.*, XI, 1968, pp. 671–675.

Fay, Charles R. *Adam Smith and the Scotland of his Day.* Cambridge: Cambridge University Press, 1956.

Ferguson, Adam. *An Essay on the History of Civil Society.* Philadelphia: A. Finley, 1819.

Hont, Istvan, and Ignatieff, Michael. *Wealth and Virtue, the Shaping of Political Economy in the Scottish Environment.* Cambridge: Cambridge University Press, 1983.

Hull, Charles. *The Economic Writings of Sir William Petty.* Cambridge: Cambridge University Press, 1899.

Hume, David. *A Treatise of Human Nature, Being an Attempt to the Experimental Method of Reasoning into Moral Subjects.* London: Green & Gross, 1898.

————. *Writings on Economics.* Ed. by Rotwein. Madison: University of Wisconsin Press, 1955.

Hutcheson, Francis. *A Short Introduction to Moral Philosophy in Three Books, Containing the Elements of Ethics and the Law of Nature.* Glasgow; R. & A. Foulis, 1753.

Hyde, J.M. *The Life of John Law.* Amsterdam; Home & Van Thal, n.d. (c. 1938).

Ingram, John. *A History of Political Economy.* New York: Macmillan & Co., 1894.

Johnson, Edgar A.J. *Predecessors of Adam Smith: The Growth of British Economic Thought.* New York; Prentice Hall, 1937.

Lehman, William. *John Millar of Glasgow, 1735–1801; His Life and Thought and His Contributions to Sociological Analysis.* Cambridge: Cambridge University Press, 1960.

Mackie, John C. *The University of Glasgow, 1451–1491, A Short History.* Glasgow: Jackson and Co., 1854.

Maitland, James, Earl of Lauderdale. *An Inquiry into the Nature and Origin of Public Wealth and into the Means and Causes of its Increase.* Ed. by Paglin, 1804. New York: Augustus Kelley (reprint), 1962.

Mandeville, Bernard de. *The Fable of the Bees, or Private Vices, Public Benefits.* London: J. Tonson, 1792.

McCosh, James. *The Scottish Philosophers.* New York: Robert Carter and Brothers, 1875.

Pufendorf, Samuel von. *De Jure Naturae et Gentium libri octo* (Trans. by Oldfather). Oxford: Oxford University Press, 1954.

Rae, John. *Life of Adam Smith.* London: Macmillan & Co., 1895.

Roncaglia, Alessandro. *Petty, The Origins of Political Economy*. M. E. Sharpe, Inc., Armonk, N.T., 1985.

Schneider, Herbert. *Adam Smith's Moral and Political Philosophy*. New York: Hafner Publishing Co., 1948.

Schumpeter, Joseph, A. *History of Economic Analysis*. New York: Oxford University Press, 1954.

Scott, William R. *Adam Smith as Student and Professor*. Glasgow: Jackson & Co., 1937.

Smith, Adam. *An Inquiry into the Nature and Causes of the Wealth of Nations*. (Modern Library Edition) Ed. by Cannan. New York: 1937.

————. *The Theory of Moral Sentiments*. London: Henry Bohn, 1853.

Smith, Norman Kemp. *The Philosophy of David Hume*. London: Macmillan and Company, 1941.

Steuart-Denham, Sir James. *An Inquiry into the Principles of Political Economy, Being an Essay on the Science of Domestic Policy in Free Nations*. London: A. Millar and T. Cadell, 1767.

Stewart, Dugald. *Lectures on Political Economy*. Ed. by Sir William Hamilton. Edinburgh: T. & T. Clark, 1877.

Taylor, Overton H. *Economics and Liberalism*. Cambridge, MA: Harvard University Press, 1955.

Taylor, W. L. *Francis Hutcheson and David Hume, Predecessors of Adam Smith*. Durham: Duke University Press, 1965.

Willey, Basil. *The Eighteenth Century Background*. New York: Columbia University Press, 1941.

Commentary by Salim Rashid
The Scottish Enlightenment: Evaluation of Origins

$[327],$

The Scottish Enlightenment has come to occupy such an exalted place in the history of economic thought that its role is all too frequently seen as a form of discontinuity in intellectual history. As Professor Thomson's article lays inadequate emphasis on the connections of the Scottish Enlightenment, both with contemporaries and with the past, I will focus my thoughts on this issue.[1] In particular, the heterogeneity of the Scots needs more emphasis, as does their dependence on the world-view provided by Christianity.

It is a well-worn cliche to point to Graeco-Roman thought and the Judeo-Christian tradition as the two main sources of Western thought, and the Scottish Enlightenment is no exception in this regard. The aspect of Graeco-Roman thought most relevant for our purposes is the tradition of civic republicanism. The influence of this "ideology" has been well-documented in a number of studies, most notably by J. G. A. Pococke [1975], but the conduit through which it influenced the Scottish Enlightenment has received much less notice. Caroline Robbins [1959] has demonstrated the role of the Common Wealth Men in British intellectual history and the role of Lord Molyneaux in particular. Civic Republicanism and Christianity were so closely linked in the minds of a number of eminent "Irish" thinkers that one can separate the two only for convenience of classification. Francis Hutcheson first rose to prominence in Ireland — his famous refutation of Mandeville is contained in the *Hibernicus Letters* — and the role of the Irish in stimulating the Scots has been largely neglected. If we except the debates over "Private Vices, Public Benefits," incited by Mandeville in the 1720s, it is Ireland that shows the greatest concern for economic discussion between 1720 and 1740. These were years of economic depression, and the poverty of the Irish stimulated them to consider ways out of their misery. Jonathan Swift and George Berkeley are the most famous names associated with this period, but there were also a number of other able economists such as Arthur Dobbs, Thomas Prior, and Samuel Madden. It is also significant that these men organized themselves into a formal society — the Dublin Society — which was committed to the economic development of Ireland. There is a meaningful sense in which it can be said to form a "school" of economics. The pattern of the Dublin Society was later copied by several other societies, and even as late as 1761 a Scotsman could regret that the Scots were not copying the Irish [*Considerations...*, 1762, p. 2].

The *Querist* of Bishop Berkeley [1953] was an enormously successful pamphlet which served to demolish the notion of "money as wealth" while seeking to lay new grounds in considering the welfare of the common man as the foundation for economic policy. Ten editions were printed in Berkeley's own lifetime, and we know that Adam Smith possessed a copy in his library. The economics of the Irish was of necessity focused upon problems of poverty and development, and was far more relevant to the Scots than the contemporary English literature. Robert Wallace, a noted civic republican, picked up Berkeley's ideas and propounded them at some length in his *Characteristics* [1758]. One of the figures he combats is David Hume, whose views on money were quite different from those of Berkeley and Wallace. Hume's phobia regarding the public debt, in particular, is carefully dissected by Wallace. Hume and Wallace had already clashed earlier in a debate over the size of populations in the ancient world [Wallace, 1753; Hume, 1970]. The moderation and good manners that marked this debate have served to hide the sharp differences of opinion between the two men. Wallace was both a civic republican and a Christian; Hume was neither. Indeed, one of the distinguishing features of Hume in this regard is that his outlook is not Scottish at all, but English. The cosmopolitanism, the desire for moderate luxury, the intellectual pleasantry, all take us back to Addison and the *Spectator*. Perhaps this is one reason for the great popularity of the *Essays*: they revived the elegant appreciation of civil life over which Mandeville had cast a shadow.

Berkeley, Wallace, and Hutcheson were all Christians, and the writings of the first two are very clear on this point. Hutcheson is much less explicit about his Christianity, thereby making it more difficult to trace his intellectual thought patterns. Hutcheson's debts to Shaftsbury and his role in formulating the "moral sense" are undoubted, but the influence of his Presbyterian predecessor in the chair of Moral Philosophy, Gershom Carmichael, is more intriguing [Moore and Silver Thorne, 1983, pp. 73–88]. Carmichael is said to have had quite orthodox views and, what is unusual for his age, to have appreciated the merits of the medieval schoolmen. In this connection Hutcheson's remark that Carmichael's notes on Pufendorf's *De Officio* are the more valuable part of the work suggests that the Scottish Enlightenment, as begun by Francis Hutcheson, could have been a channel for conveying scholastic doctrines.

(Two ideas present in Hutcheson — the recognition of subjective value and the importance of competition — should come as no surprise to students of the Middle Ages.) The remark of Professor Thomson that Hutcheson's influence included "the abandonment of Latin as the medium for scholarly writing and for classroom discussion" is misleading. It is true that Hutcheson abandoned lecturing in Latin, but the preface to the translation of his *Moral Philsophy* shows clearly that he still valued Latin as the medium of printed discussion [*collected works...*, 1969, preface]. It was important that the classics (and the scholastics?) remain accessible.

The idea that secularism, or at least "secular Deism" (if one may use the phrase), dominated the Scottish Enlightenment, is but a natural byproduct of the emphasis given to David Hume and Adam Smith while studying the eighteenth century Scots. It is hoped that this bias will diminish with the publication of such works as that of Richard Sher [*Church and University...*, 1985] because a failure to appreciate the active Christian intellectual tradition in driving the Scottish Enlightenment has been fairly widespread. How do we account for the well-ensconced positions of David Hume and Adam Smith after 1755 if the church did in fact *actively* see them as enemies? The fact that church moderates such as Hugh Blair and William Robertson were not quite as orthodox as others is beside the point. What is relevant is that they were never charged with heresy and, more importantly, that they themselves saw a distinct difference between them and David Hume.

What then were the contributions of the Scots-Presbyterian milieu to the economic views of the Scots? Let us take the principal concept discussed by modern libertarians such as Hayek — the idea that beneficence and coherence can be obtained through actions undertaken with no such good intentions. In sermons preached during and after the Jacobite rebellion of 1745, both Adam Ferguson and Hugh Blair emphasize just this point. Ferguson tells his troops in December 1745 of the Jacobites and French that

> they are only made Tools to serve Purposes very different from the Ends they propose to themselves [*Church and University...*, 1985, p. 42].

In May 1746, Hugh Blair reports of the same events that God

> makes the unruly Passions of bad Men work in a secret way, towards Ends, by them altogether unseen [*Church and University...*, 1985, p. 43].

Whether or not Ferguson and Blair believed such things, they clearly expected their congregations to believe them. The tradition of seeing God thus wring good out of evil and produce beneficence where none was intended is no doubt most prominent in Puritan times but it has much earlier origins. St. Thomas Aquinas already considers it an established view when he writes

> even God uses all sins for some good end: for he draws some good out of every evil [Leckachmann, 1977, p. 57].

A historian of economic thought with the widest erudition, Jacob Viner, wrote that laissez-faire was simply the application to economics of concepts long familiar to theologians and moral philosophers. While some work has been done, notably by Milton Myers, in elaborating upon this important statement, it needs emphasis that such thought patterns appear to have been *commonplace* among Scots-Presbyterian congregations [Myers, 1983].

If the main normative proposition of the *Wealth of Nations* has such a close relationship with ideas already commonplace by 1750, what can we say of the originality of other ideas in Smith's *Magnum Opus*? As every student of Smith's life knows, Smith was quite sensitive to asserting his own priorty in expounding the "system of natural liberty." However, if we examine the extracts provided by Dugald Stewart of Smith's rather vehement declaration of 1755, there is no explicit economics to be found! All we find is a blanket assertion that a certain philosophical system also leads to the best economic system. Of the bread and butter of economic analysis, demand and supply, there is no mention. It is known that there was a resurgence of interest in economics in Scotland in the 1750s. One sign of this resurgence was the reprinting, by the Foulis Press, of such economics tracts as John Law's *Money and Trade Considered* and Bishop Berkeley's *Querist*; another sign was the discussion of current economic issues in the meetings of such groups as the Select Society, which Adam Smith is known to have attended ["Lectures...," 1872, vols. 8 and 9]. This suggests the hypothesis that Smith arrived at certain economic beliefs on philosophical grounds and then tried to "fill in the gaps" by turning to the contemporary pamphlet literature.

These suspicions harden when one observes the marked similarities between Smith's views and those of contemporary pamphlets published (or republished) between 1745 and 1766. Here is a list that does not pretend to completeness: John Law and Francis Hutcheson are the only Scotsmen, and neither would really belong to the Smith-Hume version of the Enlightenment.[2]

Topic	Source
Division of Labor	*Encyclopedie* (facts), William Petty and Henry Martyn (analytics).
Diamonds–Water Paradox	John Law
Measure of Value	John Locke and Francis Hutcheson
Wages	Richard Cantillon
Say's Law	Francis Hutcheson and George Blewitt
Functions of Money	Sir Thomas Smith
Corn — Bounty	William Richardson
Internal Corn–Trade	Anonymous author of *Reflections on the Present High Price of Provisions*

Smith's version of these doctrines in the *Wealth of Nations* was sometimes inferior to his sources. In the case of the diamonds–water paradox, Smith omitted the solution; in that of the measure of value, Smith presented inflexibly a set of ideas intended by his predecessors only as approximations. Apart from the specific "borrowings" listed above, it cannot be forgotten that Dugald Stewart and his pupils, such as Francis Horner, clearly accused Smith of having adopted and simplified (for the worse) the economic views of the physiocrats. Indeed a careful study of the evolution of Stewart's views on the history of economics shows that, under the influence of Lord Lauderdale, Stewart gradually came to see little originality in Smith's contribution ["Lectures..., 1872, vols. 8 and 9].

Despite the close affinity of so many of Smith's ideas with those of the extant literature, Smith did not become *the* acknowledged authority on economics for almost two decades after 1776. Sir James Steuart, a distinguished representative of yet another facet of the Scottish Enlightenment, was a more perceptive writer than Adam Smith on such questions as population, monetary theory, and the economic development of backward regions. While the generally favorable disposition of contemporaries toward the market made Smith a much more popular author than Steuart, those seriously concerned with economic issues did not hesitate to disagree with the *Wealth of Nations* on specific policy issues. A careful examination of both the periodical literature as well as the speeches of Parliamentary figures shows that it is not until 1791, at the earliest, or perhaps even 1795, that Adam Smith's views became synonymous with "true" economic theory [Rashid, 1982, pp. 64–85; Willis, 1979, pp. 505–544].

If one had to pinpoint Smith's sharpest divergence from his contemporaries and predecessors, it would be Smith's assumption that full employment was the normal state of a free capitalist economy. Smith never defended this issue with extended arguments, but by never treating unemployment as a policy issue, he succeeded in persuading people to neglect what had been something of a preoccupation to many of his predecessors. Sometimes he used examples to illustrate his view, as in his claim that soldiers disbanded after the Seven Years War readily found new employment (used earlier by Sir James Steuart!). More frequently, however, Smith uses an analytical metaphor that was to have considerable influence in the nineteenth century.

Adam Smith is responsible for introducing the idea of the "wages fund." The wages fund is a collection of consumer goods which are accumulated by the capitalist *prior* to production and is the stock from which the wages of the worker are actually paid.

> When the division of labour has once been thoroughly introduced, the produce of a man's own labour can supply but a very small part of his occasional wants...this purchase cannot be made till such time as the produce of his own labour has not only been completed, but sold. A stock of goods of different kinds, therefore, must be stored up somewhere sufficient to maintain him, and to supply him with the materials and tools of his work till such time, at least, as both these events can be brought about [Smith, pp. 276–277].

There are occasions when such an assumption is very convenient, for example, in showing the irrelevance of the distribution of income to the general happiness of society in the *Theory of Moral Sentiments* [Smith, 1759, Part IV, ch. 1]. It also makes plausible the idea that what is not consumed one way is consumed in another. Funds transferred from consumption to savings only serve to change the nature of the tasks put to the workers and do not in any way diminish employment.

> What is annually saved is as regularly consumed as what is annually spent, and nearly in the same time too; but it is consumed by a different set of people. That portion of his revenue which a rich man annually spends, is in most cases consumed by idle guests, and menial servants, who leave nothing behind them in return for their consumption. That portion which he annually saves, as for the sake of the profit it is immediately employed as a capital, is consumed in the same manner, and nearly in the same time too, but by a different set of people [Smith, p. 338].

In particular, such a picture of the capitalist system makes full employment a convenient corollary.

If the Scottish Enlightenment gained much from the English (and Irish) forgetfulness about its own literature, there is one sense in which the tables were turned. As an examination of the debates in Parliament and the pamphlet literature surrounding the Bills for the Naturalization of

Foreign Protestants (1751) and Jews (1753) will reveal, English population theory in the mid-eighteenth century dwelt on international labor mobility, the transference of skills, and the social norms of reproduction. This is a rather different approach from the Malthusian focus upon subsistence incomes. By contrast to the English tradition, both David Hume and Robert Wallace, during their debate on population, and, a little later, Sir James Steuart, in his *Principles*, focused much more closely on the food-population nexus. The analogy of a loaded spring was effectively used by Sir James to make this point [Steuart, 1966, p. 32]:

> The generative faculty resembles a spring loaded with a weight, which always exerts itself in proportion to the diminution of resistance: when food has remained some time without augmentation or diminution, generation will carry numbers as high as possible; if then food comes to be diminished, the spring is overpowered; the force of it becomes less than nothing.

Some English authors, such as Arthur Young, furthered these ideas, and by 1798 they had gained considerable popularity. Robert Wallace had already used the notion of a geometric growth of population in his debate with Hume and, in a later pamphlet, Wallace even applied this concept to predict disaster for Utopian communities. By some excellent timing and much good luck, Thomas Robert Malthus managed to use the ferment stirred by the writings of William Godwin to appropriate the work of the Scots as his own. In a quaint way, poetic justice was done.

Notes

1. H. F. Thomson, "The Scottish Enlightenment and Political Economy" (in this book).
2. *Encyclopedie*, (1755), tome V. Article "Epingle."
Petty, W., *Political Arithmetik* (London, 1690).
Martyn, H., *Considerations upon the East India Trade* (London, 1701).
Ferguson, A., *An Essay on the History of Civil Society* (Edinburgh, 1767).
Law, J., *Money and Trade Considered* (London, 1710).
Locke, J., *Considerations on the Lowering of Interest* (London, 1698).
Hutcheson, F., *A System of Moral Philosophy.* In *Collected Works, op. cit.*, vols. 5 and 6.
Cantillon, R., *Essai sur la Nature du Commerce en Général* (London, 1755).
Hutcheson, F., *Remarks on the Fable of the Bees.* In *Collected Works, op. cit.*, vol. 7.
Bluett, G., *Enquiry into the Nature of Virtue* (London, 1727).
Smith, T., *A Discourse of the Common Weal* (London, 1581).
Richardson, W., *Essay on the Causes of the Decline of the Foreign Trade* (London, 1744).
Anon, *Reflections* (London, 1766).

References

Church and University in the Scottish Enlightenment. Princeton: Princeton University Press, 1985.

Collected Works of Francis Hutcheson. Vol. IV. Hildsheim: George Olms, 1969.

Considerations on the Present Scarcity of Gold and Silver Coin in Edinburgh. Edinburgh: 1762, p. 2.

Hume, D. "Of the Populousness of Ancient Nations." In *Hume on Economics.* Ed. by E. Rotwein. Madison: U. Wisconsin Press, 1970.

Leckachmann, ed. *The Varieties of Economics,* Vol. I. Peter Smith, Boston: 1977, p. 57.

"Lectures on Political Economy." In *The Collected Works of Dugald Stewart.* Vols. 8 and 9. London: Constable, 1872.

Moore, J. and Silverthorne, M. "Gershom Carmichael and the Natural Jurisprudence Tradition in Eighteenth-Century Scotland." In *Wealth and Virtue.* Ed. by I. Mont and M. Ignatieff. Cambridge: Cambridge University Press, 1983, pp. 73–88.

Myers, M. L. *The Soul of Modern Economic Man.* Chicago: University of Chicago Press, 1983.

Pocock, J. G. A. *The Machiavellian Moment.* Princeton: Princeton University Press, 1975.

The Querist. In *The Collected Works of George Berkeley.* Ed. by A. A. Luce and T. E. Jessop. London: Nelson, 1953.

Rashid, S. "Adam Smith's Rise to Fame: A Re-examination of the Evidence." *The Eighteenth Century* 23(1):1982, 64–85.

Robbins, Caroline. *The Eighteenth-Century Common Wealth Man.* Cambridge, MA: Harvard University Press, 1959.

Smith, A. *An Inquiry into the Nature and Causes of the Wealth of Nations.* Ed. by R. H. Campbell and A. S. Skinner. Oxford: Oxford University Press, 1978.

Smith, A. *The Theory of Moral Sentiments.* Part IV. London: Millar, 1759, ch. 1.

Steuart, Sir James. *An Inquiry into the Principles of Political Oeconomy.* Ed. by A. S. Skinner. London: Oliver & Boyd, 1966, I.

Wallace, R. *Characteristics of the Present Political State of Great Britain.* London: Millar, 1758.

————. *A Dissertation on the Numbers of Mankind.* Edinburgh: Hamilton, 1753.

Willis, Kirk. "The Role in Parliament of the Economic Ideas of Adam Smith 1776–1800." *History of Political Economy* 11:1979, 505–544.

Index